Laughing C

CENTRAL LIBRARY
828 "I" STREET
SACRAMENTO, CA 95814
AUG - 2000

Also by Andrew Horton

Three More Screenplays by Preston Sturges (editor)

Play It Again, Sam: Retakes on Remakes
(coeditor with Stuart McDougal)

Buster Keaton's "Sherlock Jr." (editor)

The Films of Theo Angelopoulos: A Cinema of Contemplation

The Last Modernist: The Films of Angelopoulos (editor)

Bones in the Sea: Time Apart on a Greek Island

Writing the Character-Centered Screenplay

Russian Critics on a Cinema of Glasnost
(coeditor with Michael Brashinsky)

Inside Soviet Film Satire: Laughter with a Lash (editor)

The Zero Hour: Glasnost and Soviet Cinema in Transition
(coeditor with Michael Brashinsky)

Comedy/Cinema/Theory (editor)

The Films of George Roy Hill

Modern European Filmmakers and the Art of Adaptation
(coeditor with Joan Magretta)

Laughing Out
LOUD

Writing the Comedy-Centered Screenplay

ANDREW HORTON

UNIVERSITY OF CALIFORNIA PRESS
BERKELEY   LOS ANGELES   LONDON

University of California Press
Berkeley and Los Angeles, California

University of California Press, Ltd.
London, England

© 2000 by the Regents of the University of California

Library of Congress Cataloging-in-Publication Data

Horton, Andrew.
    Laughing out loud : writing the comedy-centered screenplay /
Andrew Horton.
        p.   cm.
    Includes bibliographical references and index.
    ISBN 0-520-22014-5 (alk. paper). — ISBN 0-520-22015-3 (pbk. :
alk. paper)
    1. Motion picture authorship.   2. Comedy films.   I. Title.
PN1996.H668   2000   99-17669
808.2′3—dc21   CIP

Manufactured in the United States of America
9   8   7   6   5   4   3   2   1

The paper used in this publication meets the minimum requirements
of American National Standard for Information Sciences—Permanence
of Paper for Printed Library Materials, ANSI z39.48-1984.

For Caroline,
my very funny and loving daughter

To the memory of those who made us laugh. The motley mountebanks, the clowns, the buffoons, in all times and in all nations, whose efforts have lightened our burden a little . . .
Preston Sturges, *Sullivan's Travels*

CONTENTS

PART IV
Writing Comedy

ACKNOWLEDGMENTS

To all the great comic writers and filmmakers who have made me laugh so much over the years, from Keaton and Chaplin to Sturges and Lubitsch; Renoir, Buñuel and Wilder; Ernie Kovacs, Lucille Ball, Steve Allen and Sid Caesar; on down to the present. Yes, including but by no means only: Abbott and Costello, Adella Adella the Story Teller of New Orleans, Woody Allen, Pedro Almodovar, Fatty Arbuckle, Aristophanes, Jean Arthur, Rowan Atkinson, Dan Aykroyd, Beavis and Butthead, Samuel Beckett, John Belushi, Robert Benchley, Jack Benny, Milton Berle, Shelley Berman, Boccaccio, Humphrey Bogart, Jorge Luis Borges, James L. Brooks, Mel Brooks, Lenny Bruce, Art Buchwald, Godfrey Cambridge, John Candy, Frank Capra, George Carlin, Bill Cosby, Billy Crystal, Rodney Dangerfield, Geena Davis, Gerard Depardieu, Johnny Depp, Charles Dickens, Phyllis Diller, Doonesbury, Jimmy Durante, Gerald Durrell, Blake Edwards, Chris Farley, William Faulkner (really!), Federico Fellini, Henry Fielding, W. C. Fields, Gabriel García Márquez, Giancarlo Giannini, Mel Gibson, Jackie Gleason, Cary Grant, Hugh Grant, Merv Griffin, Gogol, Alec Guinness, Arsenio Hall, Tom Hanks, Goldie Hawn, Ben Hecht, Jim Henson and his joyful Muppets, Katharine Hepburn, Pee-Wee Herman, Bob Hope, Helen Hunt, Ben Jonson, Franz Kafka, George S. Kaufman, Danny Kaye, Diane Keaton, Michael Keaton, Milan Kundera, Burt Lancaster, Ring Lardner, Gary Larson, Laurel and Hardy, Hannibal the Cannibal Lecter ("I'm having a friend for lunch"), Jerry Lewis, Max Linder, Harold Lloyd, Dusan Makavejev, Juri Mamin, Steve Martin, the Marx Brothers, Bette Midler, Molière, Eddie Murphy, Bill Murray, Mike Nichols and Elaine May, Jack Paar, Michael Palin, S. J. Perelman, Pio, Richard Pryor, Don Rickles, Joan Rivers, Julia Roberts, Will Rogers, Dan Rowan and Dick Martin, Rosalind Russell, Mort Sahl, Gabriele Salvatore, Susan Sarandon, Charles Schultz, Jerry Seinfeld, Mack Sennett, William Shakespeare, Phil Silvers, Red Skelton, Barbara Stanwyck, Laurence Sterne, Jonathan Swift, Alain Tanner, Jacques Tati, the Three Stooges, James Thurber, Lily Tomlin, John Kennedy Toole, François Truffaut, Mark Twain, Thanassios Vengos, Wallace and Gromit, John Wayne, Mae West, E. B. White, Robin Williams, Flip Wilson, Jonathan Winters, and P. G. Wodehouse. To my students in comedy seminars and classes I've taught over the years, especially to those teachers in my 1992 summer seminar for high school teachers sponsored by the Louisiana Endowment for the Humanities on Comedy and Culture, and the summer 1997 comedy-writing seminar on the Greek Islands. And to the many readers of *Writing the Character-Centered Screenplay* who have written, faxed, e-mailed, and called: you really have created a worldwide carnival of screenwriters.

To Ed Dimendberg, Laura Pasquale, and Rachel Berchten at University of California Press, who have, with good humor, supported, defended and nurtured my projects with the Press.

To my wife, Odette, and children Sam and Caroline, who have developed a real sense of humor over the years, as well as my older son, Philip, who as an actor is learning to make 'em laugh . . . and cry.

To all comic writers who have helped me in ways they may not realize, including Herschel Weingrod. And especially to Aristophanes and Lakis Lazopoulos.

I cannot forget the people of the island of Kea, Greece, where the first half of the book was written during a sabbatical from Loyola University of New Orleans. I would particularly like to remember an elderly garbage collector on the island who sings as he loads trash onto the garbage donkeys (most of the streets are too narrow to allow cars, let alone a garbage truck, through). When I asked him why he sings as he works, he simply smiled and said, "It's in my nature," and went back to singing and slinging. The second half of the book was written in Wellington, New Zealand, while I was on an exchange semester of teaching film and screenwriting at Victoria University, January through June of 1998. I am most grateful for the generosity and supportive friendship of colleagues at Vic, including Russell Campbell, Phillip Mann, John Downey, and Bill Manhire, as well as the laughter and insights that arose from my talented group in Screenwriting 322.

Finally, to St. Philip Neri (1515–1595), the patron saint of joy, whose most remembered command was "Rejoice!"

Introduction

I wish to make the most comfortable member of the cinema audience feel that he is not living in the best of all possible worlds.
                                          Luis Buñuel, *My Last Sigh*

PRACTICE RANDOM ACTS OF KINDNESS
                                          bumper sticker

Almost like prophets and shamans, comic writers and comic actors become privileged members of the community.
                                          Dana F. Sutton, *The Catharsis of Comedy*

Unexploded Mimes

Fade in:

Chaplin walking his funny walk down the road, his back to the audience, cane swinging. Rosanne in her blue-collar living room, berating John Goodman for, well, everything. Groucho as a most unconventional university president, spewing a line of insults at the faculty and student body. Katharine Hepburn as a clueless socialite, climbing a ladder leaning against a dinosaur skeleton to talk to Cary Grant, the absent-minded professor.

The Three Stooges eye-gouging and bonking each other while squealing with comic-violent glee. Mickey Mouse doing anything he wants to do with that dopey wide-eyed grin and those huge ears. The whole gang on *M*A*S*H,* the television series, clowning around after a successful operation.

Marilyn Monroe trying to arouse a supposedly frigid Tony Curtis on a yacht at night. Robin Williams as Mork or Garp or Popeye, or even the voice of Aladdin's genie, or as a GI disk jockey in Vietnam. Whoopi Goldberg in a nun's habit, leading a gospel choir.

Seinfeld and Kramer having trouble with the apartment's new low-flow showerheads, and George proving once again he's a loser with women. Buster Keaton's deadpan face, in the midst of the disaster of your choice: hurricanes, hundreds of cops chasing him, trains demolishing his newly built home. Woody Allen dressed as a gigantic sperm, swimming "upstream." Jim Carrey with his distorted face stretching in all kinds of computer-animated directions, or as the hapless hero of a "real life" television show, who finally walks out of his televised paradise with a "Good morning, and in case I don't see you later, good afternoon, good evening, and good night!"

Fade out.

These are just a few American film and television comic moments. But what if we include comic strips, comic books, dirty jokes, the works of Boccaccio, Aristophanes, Molière, Shakespeare, Laurence Sterne, Rabelais, Mark Twain, Gogol, Samuel Beckett and Milan Kundera, to add but a few. And why not mention beloved comic screen images from around the world, created by (for example) Buñuel, Fellini, Truffaut, Alec Guinness and Monty Python, together with individual films such as *Shine, The Discreet Charm of the Bourgeoisie, Swept Away, Cinema Paradiso, The White Balloon, Life Is Beautiful, The Gods Must Be Crazy, My Life as a Dog, Never on Sunday, Eat Drink Man Woman, Closely Watched Trains* and *Time of the Gypsies.*

The images and sounds of comedy are endless.

And as one century ends and another begins, one fact seems guaranteed: Comedy will survive and thrive the world over on film, television, and stage, in print, on the street, and in our lives. Thus a toast to comedy through the centuries. *This book is meant as a celebration and discovery of creating comedy.*

Simple translation: comedy delights—even heals, doctors claim—and it definitely *sells.*

Comedy is a diverse muse, as the quotes above suggest. Some of you, like Luis Buñuel, may have an ironic talent and wish to leave the audience unsettled. (Another Buñuel line: "I'm an atheist, thank God!") Others may wish to surprise viewers with "random" generosity as the bumper stick commands. In either or both cases—and in everything in between—realize as you read on that writers and performers of comedy are, as the classical scholar Dana F. Sutton suggests, "privileged members of the community." I firmly believe that.

How to read these pages? The logic of the book moves from the traditions of comedy to a close look at specific examples and then on to the practical act of writing and selling comedy. But for the restless and curious, you could skip to chapter 2 and check out some ideas about nurturing your comic writing, or to appendix 3 to try the Recipe for Comic Jambalaya, realizing that food and comedy have teamed up throughout history. And then explore other chapters. Or you could begin with part 2 and move on. But whichever order you take in my musings, you would shortchange the book and yourself if you start with chapters 11 and 12.

Enough said. Let's plunge in:

Laughing Out Loud: Writing the Comedy-Centered Screenplay is meant to be a practical and theoretical exploration of writing comedy. Moreover, I wish to offer an overview of the many dimensions, possibilities and approaches to a variety of forms of the comic. In particular I mean this primarily as a study of ways in which the comic intersects with screenwriting for feature film, with attention also to episodic television as well as the whole range of documentary film and video. Practical writing suggestions and exercises cover the comic in concept, character, plot, dialogue, structure and plain old physical scene and stage "comic business." As in my previous book, *Writing the Character-Centered Screenplay,* this book analyzes some films in depth and uses examples from throughout the history of comedy, not only in film but from the stage and literature as well, and from countries with fine comic traditions far beyond the shores of Hollywood. I also offer a strong nod to successful "independent" comic films.

Finally, a note on what is *not* covered. Comedy depends so much on performance. Timing, for instance, is half the fun of watching a great comic actor and actress. And the history of comedy has been shaped just as much by the comedians themselves as personalities and artists as by playwrights, authors and screenwriters. But performance per se is not our territory in these pages. Also, only fleeting attention is given to the great pleasures of the musical comedy or the comic musical tradition.

A personal memory to get us started.

Over a year after the tragic Bosnian war ended, my family and I were on vacation approaching the Yugoslav border as we drove through Slavonia, that part of Croatia under United Nations protection after the war. My then-twelve-year-old son, Sam, was first to notice the UN signs on the side of the pothole-marked highway. In several languages there were warnings to BEWARE OF UNEXPLODED MINES. Sam was confused for just a playful instant. "What is an unexploded MIME?" asked Sam. My wife, Odette, our seven-year-old daughter, Caroline, and I all started laughing out loud.

And what would an exploded mime result in? Laughter and joy being spread everywhere? The destruction of things as they were? The interjection of a carnival spirit into stiff and inflexible routines? Certainly we all agreed that an unexploded mime represented an eager potential for mischief and fun, a healthy and imaginative invitation to live fully.

That is the call of this book too, I realize, with a slight change of the sign:

Embrace and cultivate unexploded mimes . . . in your writing and, indeed, in your life. Yes, keep at least several "unexploded mimes" in your comic soul as you write, for these will be the essence of the carnival of freedom and imagination needed to write comedy well.

More specifically, I offer three invitations to help put you in the mood or state of mind to write comedy:

1. Live the comic, in perspective and observations of the world around you.
2. Allow yourself total freedom in the carnivalesque play of the imagination.
3. Enjoy the pleasures of becoming a clown or holy fool or a simple child again whenever you wish.

One further note: I hope these pages are useful for the experienced writers of the comic as well as the aspiring, and also for those writers of drama who wish to incorporate humor and comic elements in their scripts without necessarily producing a "comedy-centered" work. Case in point: *Northern Exposure* won television awards each year as episodic drama. But I would argue that while serious topics were introduced in that memorable show and many moments had "dramatic" impact, at its core the show was, in concept and execution, *comic* in its celebration of a community of diverse characters who exist in a spirit of tolerant acceptance of each other, whether Indian, WASP, Jewish or other.

This hope for my offerings here is also founded on my experience, for I have met award-winning comic screenwriters who have been excited to learn something of, say, the tradition of Aristophanic humor. And, on the flip side, I often run into young writers who know the comic tradition in literature and drama inside out but who need to learn more about how to set off those unexploded mimes inside themselves through the kind of perspectives and practical habits stand-up comedians or comic actors or vaudeville vets cultivate and perfect. Therefore the twin command of this text: *know the comic traditions you wish to work in,* and *cultivate the habits and liberating spirit of carnival necessary to create the comic.*

It's one thing to have a character in your comedy eat his Nike Air shoe because you were influenced by Chaplin eating his boot in *The Gold Rush,* but this book may help you go even further, to realize that Chaplin's scene builds on a *lazzi* (set comic piece) from the commedia dell'arte, recorded in Rome in 1622, called "lazzi of hunger," in which a clown proves how hungry he is after a shipwreck by eating his shoe. You don't need such historical info to be funny. But part of the plan here is to help provide a frame of reference beyond the immediate world of last season's hit sitcom or last year's Oscar nomination that might inform and help inspire you in your own writing.

Part 1 and part 2 are, in this spirit, written not as another history or literary study of comedy you will be tested on. Rather, I have kept the writer of comedy in mind always and have attempted to highlight what I feel is most useful *today* for you as a writer, no matter what stage you have reached in your career.

The Comic Perspective

> Carnival is the people's second life, organized on the basis of laughter. It is a festive life. Festivity is a peculiar quality of all comic rituals and spectacles.
>
> Mikhail Bakhtin

Realize from the start that any simple definition of comedy is doomed to failure. Even to say that "comedy pleases" is dangerous, for comedy can also deeply annoy or threaten people, particularly if they have no sense of humor. Comedians relax millions daily through the laughter they evoke, and yet comic writers have, over the centuries, often wound up in prison, in exile, or worse. What definition, after all, can embrace a territory that includes Shakespeare's *Much Ado About Nothing;* the farting around the campfire in Mel Brooks's *Blazing Saddles* (1974); the years of dark humor evoked by *M*A*S*H,* one of American television's longest-running shows; Elvis in *Forrest Gump* learning his stage wiggles from Forrest Gump's crippled walk; and Dante's Christian epic *Divine Comedy*? Instead, we take our cue from the scholar of comedy Albert Cook, who sensibly suggests that we not waste time with too much classification; rather, "The point is to probe comedy's depths, not chop it into portions" (81). Put another way, we begin our mission of writing comedy with an awareness that we are following in a long and varied tradition spanning thousands of years. Harvard scholar Harry Levin has written wisely in *Playboys & Killjoys* that comedy represents "a live tradition, richly variegated and culturally interrelated, that extends from the Old Comedy of Athens to the sit com of television" (4). Mikhail Bakhtin's quote above about the importance of carnival will also serve us well as we explore a wider vision of comedy than is normally offered.

Let us warm up and take in the larger picture with ten observations that, hopefully, are useful before we embark on a closer look at the elements and examples of comedy and more practical suggestions for writing comedy.

[1] Comedy is a way of looking at the universe, more than merely a genre of literature, drama, film or television.

That is, comedy is a *perspective.* Another way of stating the same point is to say that nothing is inherently funny or sad, humorous or tragic. It all depends on how you choose to look at it. The story of lovers who face family obstacles in getting together is the formula for romantic comedy, as we shall discuss. But it is also the plot of Shakespeare's tragic *Romeo and Juliet* and many of the sad headlines in our daily newspapers. Jean Renoir, the French filmmaker, used to say that reality depends on who you are with, the time of day, and the quality of the coffee. Similarly, what is funny to one person may be tragic to the next.

Long before comedy developed as a genre onstage with Aristophanes, Aesop was telling not just fables but "fable-jokes," such as the following:

A patient, on being questioned by his doctor about his condition, answered that he had had an unpleasantly heavy sweat. "That's good," said the doctor. The next time he was asked how he was, the patient complained of a shivering-fit that had nearly shaken him to pieces. "That's good too," was the doctor's comment. At a third visit, the doctor inquired once more about the man's symptoms and was told that he had had diarrhea. "Good again," the doctor said and took himself off. When one of the patient's relatives came to see him and asked how he was getting on, "Well, if you want to know," he replied, "I've had so many good symptoms, I'm just about dead."

MORAL: It often happens that our neighbors not knowing where the shoe pinches us, congratulate us on the very things which we ourselves find hardest to bear.

(Fables of Aesop, 195)

Aesop's moral says it all. And what of such a perspective? The fun of Aesop's "joke," of course, is the gap between the patient's and the doctor's perceptions of the same data. Today, there is even mounting scientific evidence that we are *born* happy or sad. Period. In studying twins over a forty-year period, scientists have shown that "happiness" (and we can substitute "comic perspective") is determined genetically (Adler, 78). This does not mean that those without such genes can't laugh or have happy moments. But the study does suggest that, "like fat, happiness tends to accumulate more or less arbitrarily on some people more than on others" (ibid.).

Yet the news doesn't stop there: research shows that those with comic perspectives—read: those who laugh a lot—live longer. Accordingly, "Laughing, researchers said, is hearty medicine that boosts the immune system and triggers a flood of pleasure-inducing neuro-chemicals in the brain" (Ricks, 13).

Considering comedy as a perspective rather than a genre helps us grasp the bigger picture. I am simply suggesting that the comic view is an attitude, an ability to look for that which is funny, incongruous, triumphant, upbeat, positive and, we might add, ironic, sarcastic or even darkly humorous. Thus we start with this overview, from which we can move toward specific areas of the comic, such as jokes, gags, story structure, character and themes.

[2] Comedy is a form of "play" that embraces fantasy and festivity.

If comedy is a perspective, it is a wide one that, for instance, contains laughter but may be much more than this. Ludwig Wittgenstein is helpful in pointing out that comedy is a form of "games" (195). This theory of comedy suggests that key to any definition is the awareness on the part of the players (audience or performers and writers) of a *nonthreatening zone* that has agreed-upon boundaries, so that all involved feel safe, comfortable, receptive. Call this a "comic atmosphere" that a comic work establishes and that we recognize through cues, clues, expectations.

The larger territory, therefore, is that of games; comedy is one division thereof. Thus the kinship between a Jim Carrey film, a pro football game, an *I Love Lucy* episode, girls on the playground jumping rope and Mardi Gras in New Orleans or Carnival in Rio. As theoretician Johan Huizinga has so aptly described in his study *Homo Ludens: A Study of the Play Element in Culture*, this comic playfulness has a lot to say about what it means to be human. After all, people laugh, tell jokes, and act out gags, while fish, buffalo, spiders, and even cats do not. More specifically, comedy involves an expression of the twin dimensions of fantasy (or personal imagination) and festivity (which suggests public celebration). Thus comedy involves a crossroads between the individual and the community.

We have as a root for the word "comedy" the Greek *komos*, suggesting a rather drunken "chorus" of fellows singing or crying out satirical insults to others, often dressed as various animals during the festival of Dionysus, the god of wine, tragedy, and comedy. Inventive fantasy is needed to come up with creative insults, and the whole event is "festive" in its celebration of wine, community, and shared dances and meals.

In other words, comedy has much in common, in origin and in practice, with the spirit of carnival. Key to both is not just festivity and public and personal renewal and reaffirmation of the community, but the sense of total freedom from the normal rules of society and culture—a freedom that was originally sanctioned in European culture by the Catholic and Orthodox churches as part of the year's structure. The Russian linguist and literary theoretician Mikhail Bakhtin has well expressed how carnival laughter creates a world within its own boundaries that is "universal, democratic, and free" (66). Thus his term "carnivalesque."

Beyond the actual practice of carnival in the streets, therefore, Bakhtin's term is useful for writers who wish to internalize the carnivalesque in their own writing. The spirit of game-playing and carnival allows for the freedom to turn the world as we know it upside down and inside out without fear of punishment, pain, or consequence.

[3] Comedy and tragedy are near cousins whose paths often cross.

Merry and tragical? Tedious and brief?
That is, hot ice, and wondrous strange snow.
How shall we find the concord of this discord?
Theseus in William Shakespeare's
A Midsummer Night's Dream

Comedy is pain.
George Roy Hill

James Thurber, in his preface to Groucho Marx's autobiography, *Groucho and Me,* notes that while Groucho was fond of saying, "Even trouble has its funny side," he felt that Groucho also understood "the troublesome side of fun" (10). Consider also *Sling Blade* (1996): every audience I've watched it with has laughed throughout the film at the many moments of surprisingly dark comedy. And yet there is no way to speak of this film as a comedy in any traditional sense. What does this suggest about laughter and the very serious? The same goes for that heartbreaking, laugh-evoking true story from Australia, *Shine* (1996), about a brilliant young pianist's mental breakdown and subsequent partial recovery and final romantic and personal triumph. Tears and laughter mix in this Oscar-winning film.

At the end of Plato's *Symposium,* Socrates and Aristophanes are the only ones at this famous drinking-party discussion who are still awake and sober enough to be speaking. They are considering how similar comedy and tragedy are in origin, and indeed in social function, when Aristophanes finally nods off and Socrates, Plato tells us, showers and goes about his day's work.

Certainly Socrates is correct in a number of respects. Samuel Beckett said it well when he noted, "Nothing is funnier than unhappiness." In actual origin, as we have noted, both comedy and tragedy began as celebrations during the feast of Dionysus. Both make use of a chorus and each is performed for the community, using song and dance as well as performance. And yet we cannot mistake the differences. As one classical scholar notes about ancient Greek comedy and tragedy on the stage in Athens, "to a considerable degree fifth-century tragedy and comedy help to define each other by their opposition and their reluctance to overlap" (Tapin, 11).

We can draw a simple graph of performed (stage, film, television) comedy, with farce at the most lighthearted end of the scale and mixed drama-comedies or comic dramas at the other end of the spectrum:

Jim Carrey and Jeff Daniels in *Dumb and Dumber* (1994) live up to the title; this is a no-brainer farce that asks nothing of our emotions or involvement beyond laughter. Preston Sturges's *Sullivan's Travels* (1941), on the other hand, as we shall explain, wants you to laugh and pause to take in an emotional moment as the protagonist and his girlfriend pass through the camps of the homeless. And an Oscar-winning film such as *Kolya* (1996, Czech Republic) strikes almost in the middle, as we shall discuss, aiming for both tears and laughter in the same story, while Samuel Beckett's "absurdist" humor in *Waiting for Godot* raises clowns and the influence of silent comedy to a metaphysical level.

Furthermore, what are we to make of our opening image: Chaplin walking away, alone, with his back to us? He is, after all, *alone,* and comedy celebrates the *embrace,* the continuity of the community of two or more together. Technically, I think, you could argue that Chaplin's films that end this way are dramas in overall effect, laced generously with comedy. Furthermore, Chaplin's close-ups, with his sad, puppy-dog eyes, are definitely meant to pull on the heart strings rather than evoke our laughter.

One further example of the crossing of the dramatic ("tragic") and comic. Consider the ending of *Forrest Gump* (1994): Gump sits *alone* by the roadside as his son has just left for school. Director Robert Zemeckis knows, of course, exactly the effect he wants: a Chaplin ending with a twist. Like Chaplin, Gump is literally alone at the end; the twist is that he is *not* alone in the larger personal sense, because he has a son whom he will be with again after school and because the mysterious and magical feather that descended on him at the beginning has returned here at the end, hinting at some greater force that appears to bless Forrest's life. At this point where the serious and the comic cross, the exact meaning is felt rather than stated, for as the late great *New York Times* critic Walter Kerr has explained, "Tragedy surprises and then eludes us: comedy, like the poor, can be found at the doorstep every day" (125).

This is also the place to acknowledge how "nervous laughter" is the result of these seemingly opposite paths of the tragic and comic crossing. There was holocaust humor made by the victims themselves, and the recent Bosnian war produced numerous popular jokes as well. The well-deserved popularity of *Life Is Beautiful* is another case in point. Haven't we all laughed first at a "sick" joke and then said, "That's not funny," to be answered with the question "Then why did you laugh out loud?"

But the crossing of the serious and the comic can at times be absolutely thigh-slappingly funny. One of my favorite *Northern Exposure* episodes is "Slow Dance," written by Diane Frolov and Andrew Schneider, in which we learn that another one of Maggie's boyfriends has died suddenly ("tragically") after being hit by a falling satellite. This leads to an absurd discussion as Maurice, Chris and Ed realize that the funeral will be difficult since Rick, the deceased, is literally fused with the satellite. The festive and very comic conclusion is that they hold an open-casket funeral anyway, with the corpse/satellite sticking out of the coffin with its odd spikes visible to all.

Finally, what finer cultural expression of how the tragic and comic or sacred and profane cross paths than a New Orleans jazz funeral? I have lived in New Orleans for twenty years and observed at least that many jazz funerals, and the "game" is always the same: solemn music and a slow march to the burial, and then joyful upbeat celebration music once the body is in the ground and the spirit is released as the funeral party dances home. New Orleans singer Kermit Ruffins captures this duality playfully in his song "The Undertaker Man":

> The undertaker man is waiting for you.
> The undertaker man knows exactly what to do.
> The undertaker man is waiting for you.
> So you beta take it easy or he'll see you real soon.
>
> In New Orleans land they got funeral bands.
> Uncle Ratty blew his whistle and they started to dance.
> The undertaker man just rubbing his hands.
> Then he cut loose the body and we struck up the band.
>
> Life is short, sweet and grand.
> Now think about the life of the undertaker man.
> His life is just the same.
> And he's gonna have you ready for the master man.

Simply to pronounce the word "comedy" creates an expectation of laughing out loud. And yet no comedy ever written or performed consists of nonstop laughter from start to finish. The degree to which you wish to blend the worlds of the comic and the emotional is yours to choose, having to do with your overall concept of what you wish to create for yourself and your audience.

Put the twin visions together once more, and comic scholar Wylie Sypher has some wise words to say about the importance of comedy:

> There is a comic road to wisdom, as well as a tragic road. There is a comic as well as a tragic control of life. And the comic control may be more usable, more relevant to the human condition in all its normalcy and confusion, its many un-reconciled directions. It tells us that man is a giddy thing, yet does not despair of men. The comic perspective comes only when we take a double view: that is, a human view, of ourselves, a perspective of incongruity. Then we take part in the ancient rite that is a Debate and a Carnival, a Sacrifice and a Feast.
>
> (*Comedy*, 21)

[4] Comedy is seldom "pure."

This point follows in part from the previous observation. The main suggestion here, however, is that you must be sure of the concept, tone, and structure of your comedy so that you do not mislead your audience or yourself. Parody, for instance, is one of the most difficult comic acts to maintain, as literary scholar Linda Hutcheon has explored in her study. Cervantes began *Don Quixote* as a comic parody of the romantic tradition, but we know what extreme pathos he created in this aging warrior who could be a knight only in his dreams and who breaks our hearts in the final pages, as he is forced to face the crushing reality of his life.

Put another way, comedy is often quite ambiguous. Look once more at the reaction to *Forrest Gump*, for instance. Many liberals liked it as a satire of a multitude of American values, and yet many middle American conservatives saw it as some kind of reaffirmation of their worldview. That both groups found pleasure and laughter in Forrest's odyssey through sixties America is testimony to the ability of comedy to have its ludic cake and eat it too.

Being more specific, we can agree with Woody Allen that it's very hard to be funny for more than 89 minutes. A three-hour comedy? Can you name one? Thus, in your writing, length is certainly an important factor to keep in mind. Don't let your comic muse break down.

[5] Comedy involves a playful and imaginative tension between the constructed and the discovered, between the "made" and the "found."

Or we could say that comedy walks a tightrope between suspense (the expected) and surprise (the unknown). Wit and gags are carefully set up. On the other hand, much laughter is evoked when we simply see or discover what we did not expect.

Wit and jokes (verbal humor) and gags (visual humor) both work as forms of suspense, as the listener or viewer tries to "figure out" what the punch line or "punch image" will be. Hopefully, the audience is surprised at the results, producing laughter and, in swift retrospect, an awareness of how "clever" the author or actor has been.

We can be even more specific about how most gags and jokes work. Take one of Rosanne's old jokes that suggests her refreshing ability to turn social clichés inside out: "We found a form of birth control that really works. Every night before we go to bed we spend an hour with our kids." And we laugh (or groan!). But how and why? The noted scholar Arthur Koestler has explained that what occurs in this and every joke or gag is the joining of "two or more independent and self-contained logical chains" that create a "flash" (release) of emotional tension when brought together (30). Call the first line "Logic A" and the second "Logic B." Laughter is produced by the *flash* between the two as we bring the two logics together in our minds. This means, of course, that a new logic—Logic C—is created in the mind or eye of the listener or viewer (unless the joke or gag is missed). What is the flash, or Logic C? Simply our awareness that these two logics do not go together in our "everyday" experience, in which birth control suggests condoms, pills and willful abstinence, while being with your children is seen as a positive "family value." The gap between the two throws each into a new perspective in a flash. Put simply, laughter leaps across our awareness of the incongruity produced.

Gags work the same way visually. In the Coen brothers' *Fargo* (1996) we laugh as soon as we see police officer Marge Gunderson (Frances McDormand) in uniform, so pregnant that we feel she may give birth in the patrol car while on duty. In this case, Logic A—a police officer—and Logic B—a very maternal figure— are joined in the same image so that we "get it" immediately. But of course gags are just as often in two or more parts, as in a joke structure. In *Sherlock Jr.,* Buster Keaton is a movie theater projectionist who falls asleep; his dreaming "ghost" tries to walk into the film he is projecting. Keaton generates a lot of out-loud laughter as he becomes a comic victim to cinematic editing. Each frame becomes a visual gag, as Keaton starts to dive into a surging sea only to have it cut to a snow bank; then when he tries to lean against a tree we cut to a field so that he falls over, and so on. The point is that we enjoy Keaton's clever riffing on a basic gag—human being as victim of film editing—without consciously taking in how much work it took to "construct" this humor.

The "found" in comedy works quite differently. Here the incongruity that produces laughter comes from our *discovery* rather than careful construction. Proof? Start with the daily newspaper. Is it possible for any newspaper not to have news that is hilarious? I have one item in front of me about a woman in Zagreb, who looked out of her second-floor window, saw a bull terrier attacking her pet poodle in the garden, jumped from her window, and (though she broke her left ankle in the fall) managed to bite the terrier's throat, thus rescuing her beloved poodle. Yes, real life is stranger than fiction; all the more reason to take the time to read and watch the world around you carefully for the unexploded mimes everywhere.

Another example: *The White Balloon* (1995, Iran) is the simplest of tales: a seven-year-old girl in Teheran sets out to buy a goldfish. That's it. The gentle and sometimes hilarious humor in this comedy comes from her travels through the streets of the city, teeming with life in a carnival of diversity and absurdity. At this point the comic and the real or documentary often cross. Rather than "constructed" humor, what we enjoy is watching the various characters she walks by or comes into contact with on the street, as we sense the gap or incongruity between their lives and this intense little girl on a goldfish mission. Incongruity is again at the heart of our laughter, but it is an incongruity based on our discovery of what is ludicrous before our eyes.

Note that the best comedians and writers of comedy are excellent listeners and very good observers. Most folk are too busy to see how funny daily life really is, but to the happily trained eye and ear of the comic, everyone and everything is potential material. Chaplin, for instance, could play a great comic drunk because he had carefully studied drunks—including, sadly, his father—in real life, as he noted in his autobiography.

[6] Comedy implies a special relationship with and to its audience.

Put simply, comedy, especially anarchistic comedy and stand-up comedy, acknowledges the presence of the audience and makes direct contact with it. Chaplin stared directly into the camera, at *us;* Aristophanes' characters often insulted individuals in the crowd; and Woody Allen begins *Annie Hall* (1977) acknowledging not only us, as he speaks of his failed romance, but also the whole tradition of stand-up Jewish urban New York comedy from which he emerged. Ditto for Mike Myers and his constant asides to the audience (read: the camera) in *Wayne's World* (1992).

We are therefore almost always aware of the "game" of comedy being played out with our knowledge, or, as often happens, *without* our knowledge, as we too become the butt of jokes, of gags and of comic violations of various sorts. Comedy encourages the active involvement of the audience. Tragedy avoids such contact and self-awareness as it strives to involve our emotions. In fact, in a tragedy or serious drama, "the inactivity of the audience is a vital prerequisite of the tragic experience" (Taplin, 26).

[7] Comedy thrives on details, for details reveal the contradictions and celebrate the incongruities that bring on laughter.

Shelley Berman used to do a routine about how swiftly romance can be shot down. What happens when you find Miss Perfect, he used to say, and she smiles at you and right between her shiny white front teeth is a big piece of spaghetti caught and dangling before you, which she, of course, cannot see.

Details and humor.

Woody Allen used to say his parents believed in God and carpeting. Here we really have a joke structure in a single line. "Parents" and "God" flow along as a related Logic A, while we are thrown for an unexpected comic loop with Logic B, "carpeting," that precise detail that appears to have nothing to do with God. And yet the laughter is in combining the cosmic and the daily, the sacred and the profane.

As if to highlight this point, Preston Sturges fires off one of his best lines in *Hail the Conquering Hero* (1944): "Everything is perfect except for a few details."

In fact, this line describes most comedy. And it is that series of "few details" that draws the laughs.

[8] In the world of the truly comic, nothing is sacred and nothing human is rejected.

Aristophanes was not afraid to mock the gods, as we shall see, on the ancient Greek stage, and the gang at *Saturday Night Live* takes on every imaginable topic from President Clinton's latest sex scandal to satire of anti-abortionists and the National Rifle Association. Much of the comedy we see on television and in films plays it relatively safe, hoping not to offend many viewers. But as writers we need to recognize that such a limitation of comedy has to do with the censorship of sponsors and timidity of producers, *not* with the nature of the medium. This relates to the second part of our observation as well: nothing human is rejected in the total vision of comedy. Therefore, the scatological and sexual have their rightful role in comedy even if they have been limited in various cultures in particular ways. Think, for instance, how in the United States and other countries there are strong gender biases in comedy. American comedies often allow breasts to be shown but almost never do we see penises. Film scholar Peter Lehman has written with admirable irony about how, for instance, since Hollywood is still primarily controlled by men, jokes about penises abound in American comedy, but viewing the actual "member" is limited to hardcore pornography (58).

As writers, our call is to go beyond such censorship to explore a fuller range of comedy as it may be useful, effective and appropriate to our vision! As we shall discuss, here is where many of the foreign comedies can help us grow as writers. Spanish filmmaker Luis Buñuel is wickedly ironic, for example, in his questioning of religious (especially Catholic) hypocrisy in almost all of his films, including *The Milky Way* (1969), in which a very drunk Jesus tries to tell traveling salesman jokes at his Last Supper. And Yugoslav filmmaker Dusan Makavejev, in a carnivalesque film such as *Sweet Movie* (1974), includes such narrative elements as a Miss World Clitoris Contest and an orgy in a vat of sugar crosscut with documentary footage of the digging up of graves of hundreds of Polish officers murdered by the Germans in World War II.

Once more the message of comedy is clear: don't be afraid to explore, to let go, and to go beyond convention and the "respectable." Note that this is not the same as saying you must beat the audience over the head with unorthodox comedy. No. As we shall explore, any episode of *The Simpsons* or *Seinfeld* manages to insult any number of social and religious groups and get away with it because of its speed, clever dialogue, and cartoonish world of exaggeration that put its viewers at ease.

[9] It is not that comedy has a "happy ending" so much as a *festive* climax that celebrates a community of two or more individuals.

In a comic ending, two or more individuals are together, thus making a statement: whatever happens, we are not alone. Of course in so many Hollywood films, endings have come to be called "happy" because all major conflicts appear to be resolved with a fairytale-like sense that "they lived happily ever after."

As we shall see, Aristophanes' comedies and most of Shakespeare's end in dance, song, and group feasting, suggestive of either a wedding (and thus a vote for social coherence) or a socially desirable change, such as the ending of war, as in so many of Aristophanes' works.

Comedy reassures. The ending suggests new beginnings, which, once again, is a vote for social coherence and continuity. This is true as well of more sophisticated comedies that play with the very notion of closure by denying us neat resolutions. Stanley Tucci's *Big Night,* for instance, gives us one of the most effective endings in an American comedy in recent years, as the two brothers who have just come to blows about their failed restaurant, blaming each other, end by quietly sharing an omelet.

Of course, our odyssey through comedy will reveal a full range of endings, from the clearly impossibly "happy" and thus fanciful, to the quietly assertive, as mentioned above with *Big Night.* It is up to you to choose to what degree you wish to leave the audience either still in a world of make-believe or with a contemporary and realistic "take" on romance, as at the end of *Tootsie,* where Dustin Hoffman and Jessica Lange wander down a New York street negotiating whether she can borrow the halter top Dustin wore when he was a woman.

[10] Comedy is one of the most important ways a culture talks to itself about itself.

One of the best ways to discover what's going on in any country is to watch the pop comedies of that nation, either on film or in their hit television series. This often brings scorn from local film critics and prize-winning filmmakers, of course. Simply weigh the number of Oscars dished out to "serious" films as opposed to comedies to see what I mean. But the fact is, in every country I know, comedy remains, in all its various forms, a most valued barometer of what is really worrying, exciting or bothering folk. Realize, naturally, that we are saying once more that comedians and comic writers are privileged members of society, for the nonthreatening nature of comedy allows them to say whatever they wish and get away with it.

The flip side of this observation, of course, is that comedy is very strongly culture-bound, and thus there is a lot of humor that is "lost" in translation and in export/import. Even the Marx Brothers fared badly in many countries because Groucho's hundred-mile-an-hour lines are so fast, there is no way to get it all on and off the screen in subtitles fast enough, and who is going to try to do a voice dub in Lithuanian or Bulgarian at that speed?

Silent comedy, on the other hand, could travel into the hearts and laughter of the world without subtitles. Chaplin has reached many more millions than Groucho for that very reason.

Let's close with a focus on women and minorities in comedy. As in other areas of society, there is racism and sexism in humor and comedy as well. Think how many "dirty jokes," for example, defame and exploit women or ethnic minorities. (How did Americans get started on Polish jokes?) This point made, we will, throughout this text, point to sterling examples of female comedians, writers, and film and television creators who have helped us reverse stereotypes and satirize clichés. And the large number of foreign films discussed herein is testimony to the rich vein of humor we all need to pay attention to outside our national borders. For more on women and comedy, I highly recommend Kathleen Rowe's study *The Unruly Woman: Gender and the Genres of Laughter*. Remember that if comedy since Aristophanes' day has primarily been a male-controlled thing, women have one way or another managed to get their laughs too. And in the United States, even as early as 1885 there was Kate Sanborn's anthology of female humor, *The Wit of Women* (Jenkins, 256).

Introduction Summary

Invitations to help you create a comic frame of mind before writing:

1. Embrace and cultivate unexploded mimes . . . in your writing and, indeed, in your life.
2. Live the comic, in perspective and observations of the world around you.
3. Allow yourself total freedom in the carnivalesque play of the imagination.
4. Enjoy the pleasures of becoming a clown or a holy fool or a simple child again whenever you wish.
5. Know the comic traditions you wish to work in and cultivate the habits and liberating spirit of carnival necessary to create the comic.

I

COMIC ELEMENTS AND EXERCISES

There was always laughter in the house.
Jokes and quips, sight gags and pratfalls
were the daily bread of our lives.

Jean Houston,
A Mythic Life

CHAPTER 1

Elements of Comedy
That Writers Should Know

Write the comedy you want to write for the pleasure of it. And, ultimately, don't worry about checklists, guidelines, rules, or formulas. Having said that, however, I do hope these pages can be there for you when you wish to double back and review or think over elements in your own work.

In that spirit, let's break down some of the elements of comedy that writers should know about, realizing this is not an exhaustive coverage of the territory and also that a number of other elements are discussed in the following chapters.

Let us begin with laughter.

Libraries are filled with books on laughter, and most are not very funny. No, we will not lose ourselves in theories of laughter—social and psychological—but let's acknowledge that we can't speak of comedy without thinking of or longing for that sudden eruption inside our throats (and minds)—audible or not—known as laughter. Certainly we know how good it is to be in an audience sharing laughter, and it is clearly tied to the pleasures of a group or community experience. But ultimately laughter is individual and often occurs not only when something is "funny" but, as we have already suggested, at an "inappropriate" time. Jean Houston, a philosopher and the daughter of a Hollywood comedian, is a strong believer in how laughter taps us into the mythic dimensions of life. She notes: "Laughter under social conditions allows the soul to be congregationalized, and instead of meeting in mutual enmity and distrust, we allow our unconscious responses to become socialized, trusting and openly infectious" (19). In such a perspective, as one comic scholar suggests, we can speak of laughter, building on Freud, as a form of "comic catharsis," since "comedy is capable of representing things that in the real world have the capacity to be painful" (Sutton, 4).

Finally, we can see a simple division between *laughter of the ridiculous* and *laughter of the ludicrous*. The ridiculous suggests a form of ridicule, and thus of laughing *at* someone or something, while the ludicrous is more simply a laughter that is purely for its own sake.

Finally, how much and what kind of laughter are you after in your script? John Wayne makes me laugh out loud a lot every time I watch John Ford's *The Quiet Man*, about a retired boxer returning to Ireland and courting Maureen O'Hara in a feisty village setting. But Woody Allen's *Hannah and Her Sisters*, on the other hand, pushes comedy so close to drama that my laughter is a subdued "knowing" chuckle rather than a series of belly laughs. It's up to you. But a lot of how you answer the "laughter issue" depends on our next element.

Comic Climate

Successful comedies manage to convey a sense of a particular climate. I am referring, of course, back to the various possible kinds of comedy, but I do not wish to limit the concept by saying "genre" or "sub-genre" of comedy. For climate has more to do with the atmosphere, tone, or flavor your comedy creates. Thus, you are asking yourself, is there a general "climate" in your comedy that is predominantly (but not exclusively) satiric, as in Hal Ashby's memorable *Being There* (1979); parodic, as in Mel Brooks's *Young Frankenstein;* or purely farcical, as in *Dumb and Dumber.* Then again, your script might be meant to be largely feistily romantic, as in *Tin Cup* (1997); gloriously carnivalesque, as in *Mediterraneo* (1991); or funny with very dark edges, as in those films that bridge several genres, such as *Fargo.* None of these are set "types" that should limit your comedy. Rather, what I am suggesting by comic climate is for you to have a clear idea of what tone and overall core trajectory you wish your comedy to embrace.

In chapter 3 we will trace a division between anarchistic and romantic comedy. But we can be more specific here than in my initial remarks above by mentioning scholar Morton Gurewitch's breakdown of comedy into four components: satire, humor, farce and irony (85). These divisions can help you consider which comic climate you are establishing as you think about how the following handle "folly": "Traditional SATIRE excoriates folly finding it ridiculous but also corrigible. HUMOR seeks not to expunge folly, but to condone and even to bless it, for humor views folly as endearing, humanizing, indispensable. FARCE also accepts folly as indispensable, but only because folly promises delightful annihilations of restraint. Finally IRONY sees folly as an emblem of eternal irrationality to be coolly anatomized and toyed with" (Gurewitch, 85). Simply ask yourself which of these four climates best describes the kind of comedy you are after. Having a clearer understanding of your own vision should make it easier to open up further comic depths within yourself.

Areas of Comedy

Next, consider the three major areas of comedy in film and television: comedian-driven, story-oriented, and character-centered, noting that the boundaries are fluid and overlapping and not established in suggestive rather than rigid terms.

Comedian-Driven Comedy

So much of American film and television comedy is comedian-driven. That is, the comedy centers on and is written for and about a known comic. The writers thus must know the comedian and her or his strengths and weaknesses, capabilities and limitations. Film scholar Wes D. Gehring in *Personality Comedians as Genre* suggests that we should view such comedies as constituting their own "genre" (182). Furthermore, the comedian-clown, Gehring holds, makes us laugh for one of two reasons, or perhaps for both simultaneously: the comedian is what we may *wish to become* or is what we are *afraid we may become* (182). In this sense, "The comic is what we do not want to be but are afraid we have become," notes Gehring (182).

As if to underscore the popularity of comedian-driven comedy, *Entertainment Weekly* in 1997 ran a survey and came up with the fifty funniest people alive (note the limitations of such an exercise: all listed are Americans). The top ten are:

1. Robin Williams
2. Jerry Seinfeld
3. Roseanne
4. Jim Carrey
5. Albert Brooks
6. Eddie Murphy
7. Garry Shandling
8. Rosie O'Donnell
9. Richard Pryor
10. Homer Simpson

("The 50 Funniest People Alive," 23–25)

What immediate observations can we make? Yes, there are eight fellows and two gals. OK, nine humans and one 'toon (the only other 'toon in the top fifty weighs in at number 50, Beavis and Butthead). Two are African American, and all but Jim Carrey and Homer Simpson began as stand-up comedians, thus suggesting that even when these comics are structured into a sitcom formula, their talents lie more in the realm of the "anarchistic" (as we shall discuss in chapter 3) than in the territory of a carefully worked-out plot. (And Homer Simpson cracks one-liners like a stand-up comedian.) As Gehring notes, "The storyline of clown comedy provides a humor hall tree upon which the comedian can 'hang' his comic shtick—specific routines" (*Personality Comedians*, 2).

But consider Robin Williams for our focus on the complexity of a comedian-driven work. Described as "a Shakespearean fool on speed" ("The 50 Funniest," 23), Williams is part fool and clown, part stand-up comedian and part comic actor, who can, as in *Dead Poets' Society* (1989) and *The World according to Garp* (1982), break through into pure pathos and drama.

Now let us examine the next ten "funniest people alive," noting that the survey does not include great comics of the past. Number 11 is Bob Newhart; 12, Monty Python; 13, George Carlin; 14, Bill Cosby; 15, Jack Lemmon & Walter Matthau; 16, Carol Burnett; 17, Woody Allen; 18, David Letterman; 19, Rowan Atkinson; and 20, Mel Brooks. This section of the list brings in an older generation of television (Newhart, Cosby, Burnett) and film (Brooks, Lemmon and Matthau, Allen). But this group also broadens the horizon a bit to include England—Monty Python and Rowan Atkinson—and a night-time television host, David Letterman. The rest of the list: Billy Crystal, Mary Tyler Moore, Bill Murray, Spinal Tap, Tracey Ullman, Steve Martin, Whoopi Goldberg, Howard Stern, Ellen DeGeneres, Tom Hanks, Bette Midler, Dennis Miller, Bill Maher, Kevin Kline, Lily Tomlin, Rodney Dangerfield, Goldie Hawn, Penn and Teller, Janeane Garofalo, Steven Wright, Alan King, Tim Allen, Jackie Mason, Ben Stiller, Conan O'Brien, Dana Carvey, Paul Reiser, Nathan Lane, Joan Rivers, Beavis and Butthead.

Comedian-driven comedy is based on name recognition. We thus come to any of their work with certain memories and therefore a range of expectations. In this sense, these practitioners of comedy are genres unto themselves.

And the message for writers associated with name comedians is very simple: you have to know your man or woman well, both their "comic histories" and their possibilities for growth. Take, for instance, Jim Carrey's move from straight farces such as *Ace Ventura: Pet Detective* (1994) to more character-driven and, by his standards, subdued comedy such as *Liar Liar* (1996) and *The Truman Show* (1998).

Story- or Situation-Oriented Comedy

There are those comedies that make us laugh because the plots or situations themselves are so silly, so much fun, or simply so ludicrous that they pull us along primarily by good comic storytelling. Call to mind John Hughes's *Planes, Trains, and Automobiles* (1987), and we can't really speak of character development or social messages. But we can speak of the frantic fun, comically centered on the clock ticking as Steve Martin tries to get home for Thanksgiving while ending up with a loutish John Candy as a companion.

Similarly, the situation or concept of many comedies, especially dark comedies, overshadows both character and comedian performance, as in Terry Gilliam's *Brazil* (1985), Martin Scorsese's *After Hours* (1985), or Mel Brooks's *Blazing Saddles* (1974). For such works, you as writer might purposely avoid including a known comedian or a strong sense of character development because of the other effects you wish to create, as in Gilliam's dark humor about a sterile and dangerous future. Clearly such a division embraces pure farce, as in *Mars Attacks* (1997) with its Martian invasion of the White House. The hilarity is simply built in such a case on the nutty pleasures of flooding us with comic, special effects–generated creatures.

Character-Centered Comedy

Comedies in which we actually care strongly about a character because we can follow a degree of character growth tend to be, as we shall see in chapter 3, romantic comedies, or, put another way, comedies that employ drama and emotion as well as humor and thus are closer to "real life." These would include the classic American comedies of Frank Capra, such as *Mr. Smith Goes to Washington* and *It Happened One Night,* down to more contemporary comedies such as Woody Allen's *Annie Hall* and *Hannah and Her Sisters* and John Hughes's *The Breakfast Club,* and on to "mixed" comedy-dramas such as Steven Soderberg's *sex, lies and videotape,* Stanley Tucci's *Big Night,* and even Tarantino's *Pulp Fiction* and the Coen brothers' *Fargo.*

In each of these there is a plot too, of course. But what attracts us is the way in which richly formed and multifaceted characters are allowed to act, react, change, and grow before our eyes while also making us laugh.

Comic Characters

Back to our point in the introduction that nothing is inherently funny or sad but becomes so by means of perspective. If we apply this to character, we realize that anything that could be said about developing characters in general also applies to comedy. Is your character meant to be a simple caricature or type, as in the commedia dell'arte or as in farce and silent film comedy? Or if your figures are characters with depth, are they introverts or extroverts, cynics or romantics, vulnerable or hardened?

But comedy calls for a special understanding of what kinds of characters one wishes to populate a script with. Briefly stated, comic characters tend to be one of three types or a combination thereof: *imposters, innocents,* and/or *ironic figures.*

The imposter (*alazon* in Greek) is foolish, for he or she is pretentious and thus ready to be made fun of. The ironic figures (from the Greek *eiron*) are assertive and either actual tricksters—those trying to make things happen on the sly for their own advantage— or leaning in that direction. And there are variations: in American stand-up comedy, both nightclub and as practiced for over forty years on television, the wise guy (or, we can add, the wise gal) has been important. Media critic Steve O'Donnell defines these characters as "the sardonic, uppity common Man. The 'wise' part of his name is a joke and also a tribute, because while he's no Socrates, the Wise guy really does make with the smart remarks" (155). Examples abound, from Groucho Marx and Bob Hope to Jerry Seinfeld and Bette Midler. Roseanne is a wise gal, and all the talk show hosts from Jack Paar and Johnny Carson to Jay Leno and David Letterman are wise guys.

Then there are the simple people, the innocents, who like Forrest Gump or Jim Carrey's Truman, seem to get by quite well simply through being passive or reacting to what is imposed upon them. In the extreme case, of course, as with Gump, the innocent appears foolish or, to borrow a concept from Russia, like a holy fool (Horton, *The Zero Hour,* 25). Holy fools are those who are called "touched by God" rather than simply "crazy" or "stupid": they are outside the normal realm of social and personal interaction, but they seem to "know" things we don't, thus demanding respect. Gump and Chance in *Being There,* for instance, fall into this category, as does the troubled pianist protagonist in *Shine.*

Put another way, we can appropriate Harry Levin's terms and speak of *playboys and killjoys,* meaning active troublemakers and humorless blocking figures. Of course, comic duos usually embrace one of each to evoke belly laughs: thus Laurel is the playboy to Hardy's killjoy (or straight man) and Paul Newman's Butch is the playboy to Robert Redford's poker-faced Sundance Kid in George Roy Hill's classic buddy Western comedy.

Comic elements are often combinations of these character elements. Seinfeld is definitely an ironic figure, and yet at moments his innocence shines through, while Homer Simpson is almost always the *alazon,* putting on and pretending to be what he isn't, as Marge and the kids constantly remind him. And while Robin Williams became famous as the ironic, manic, fast-talking trickster figure, he has in more recent years worked on his vulnerable and innocent side in films ranging from *The World according to Garp* to *Good Morning, Vietnam.*

Note that comedy, in relation to "character," often playfully calls identity and individuality into question. Consider how many comic plots involve pairs, twins, and doubles and the requisite switching and disguising of identities.

In some cases, we are not speaking of main characters at all. *A League of Their Own,* the Monty Python films, *Mediterraneo, M*A*S*H* (both film and television series), *City Slickers, The First Wives Club,* and, from television, *Cheers, Northern Exposure* and *Friends* are all examples of *ensemble comedies* in which the laughter comes from making sure you have a diverse enough group of figures to generate conflicts, contradictions, and plain old comic confusion. But within these groups, we can definitely find the boasters, the ironic figures and the clueless.

Comic Plots

Once more, what works for any sort of storytelling can be adapted for a comic plot. But I wish to propose a simple list, built around one presented by film scholar Gerald Mast's identification of frequently used comic plots.

1. The Journey (picaresque plot). From Don Quixote to Chaplin and on to Preston Sturges's *Palm Beach Story* or the fine Yugoslav road comedy, *Who Is Singing Over There?* (1980), the Journey allows for any number of adventures to

occur, mixing both surprise and suspense, depending on how such a "road comedy" is defined.

2. Reducto ad absurdum involves taking an idea to extreme lengths. We shall discuss this in chapter 3 as the basis of anarchistic comedy from Aristophanes to Monty Python.

3. Parody and burlesque. Playing with a specific text or genre in a clearly exaggerated and distorted comic vein characterizes plots from *Bananas* (a spoof of revolutionary films) to *Space Jam,* a send-up of sports films, as 'toons meet Michael Jordan and the boys.

4. The wedding of young lovers is, as we shall discuss, the basis of romantic comedy from Frank Capra's *It Happened One Night* to *Pretty Woman, Four Weddings and a Funeral,* and beyond.

5. Central character with a difficult task or quest. Add the common twist from action and drama of a "clock ticking" for urgency, and you have a very adaptable plot, from Buster Keaton trying to find a bride by midnight to receive an inheritance (*Seven Chances*) to Robin Williams attempting to be a maid in order to court back his children from his ex-wife (*Mrs. Doubtfire*).

6. The consequences of one magical or surreal element. Jim Carrey can't lie in *Liar Liar*. John Travolta is an angel who both upsets and helps clarify the lives of those he "touches" in *Michael*. Television's *Early Edition* centers on the concept that somehow a major city's daily paper arrives at our protagonist's apartment every day one day early, thus allowing him twenty-four hours to try to change "history."

7. An innocent reacts to situations thrust upon him or her. Forrest Gump is clueless as to what's going on, but his reactions take on worlds of their own. Likewise, Peter Sellers as Chance in *Being There* is forced to cope with life outside the realm of the only two things he knows (television and gardening) with comic and spectacular results. This is the basis of Voltaire's memorable novella *Candide* as well.

8. Fish out of water. This plot—very common in comedy—is one in which a character or characters have to deal with an environment that is not what they are used to. *Trading Places* would be a prime example, as Eddie Murphy and Dan Aykroyd are "switched" and must fend for themselves in social worlds neither ever knew before as part of a mischievous bet between two wealthy old brothers. As seen below, this plot can often be seen as "inversion."

Comic Plot Devices

The great French philosopher Henri Bergson outlines three plot devices that appear frequently in comedy: repetition, inversion, and reciprocal interference of series, which we would call either crosscutting or parallel action (61). Let us take a closer look and add a few devices of our own to the list:

Repetition

If it's funny once, it will be funny again, especially with slight variations. Although it is enough that Oedipus walks out onstage once with his eyes gouged out in Sophocles' tragedy, comedy thrives on repetition. And this goes for verbal or visual repetition. Hugh Grant says "fuck" at least a dozen times in the opening of *Four Weddings and a Funeral* and, never mind whether some audiences might be offended by such Anglo-Saxon speech, with his harried British accent and because each situation for this verbal outburst is slightly different, the laughter builds and builds. Similarly, Preston Sturges's *Sullivan's Travels* follows not just a journey made by a famous Hollywood director of comedy who wants to discover "real life" but four separate journeys, with each one shedding different laughs at and insight into Sullivan's character.

And repetition can mean multiplication too, as seen in Keaton's short *The Play House,* in which he plays every member of an orchestra onstage and every member of the audience. (A title card appears: THIS MAN KEATON SEEMS TO BE THE WHOLE SHOW!) Similarly, Michael Keaton (no relation, apparently!) "repeats" himself wildly in *Multiplicity* (1997).

Inversion

Turn most things or situations upside down or inside out, and through inversion, you have laughs. Think how many memorable comedies are based on this simple device. *City Slickers* allows Billy Crystal and a gang of friends to turn their daily city lives upside down as they become modern dude ranch cowboys, and the Czech film *Kolya* turns a dedicated and aging bachelor's life inside out as he is forced to care for a Russian boy he finally comes to love. Gender-bending stories from *Some Like It Hot* to *Tootsie* and beyond thrive on the laughter generated when men are forced to "become" women.

Reciprocal Interference

Either through crosscutting or a split screen, "reciprocal interference" can often guarantee laughter. *Four Weddings and a Funeral* has us laughing out loud as we follow at least four individuals or groups preparing to attend a wedding in very different manners. This technique emphasizes contrasting actions happening simultaneously. Sturges uses the credit sequence in *The Palm Beach Story* to tickle our funny bones, as we crosscut between a bride and a groom being kidnapped by a seemingly lookalike couple, who then show up at the church to be married themselves. What we learn later is that one set of identical twins kidnapped the other!

To Bergson's list we can add several standards of comic plotting and characterizations.

Disguise and Exaggeration

Consider the importance of disguise first. As we shall see, Shakespeare thrived on disguise scenes and Aristophanes was a master of exaggeration. Who, for instance, could be more "exaggerated" in word and deed than the *Saturday Night Live* gang or Monty Python? And from Peter Sellers's fruity disguises in his *Pink Panther* comedies to Dustin Hoffman in *Tootsie* or Robin Williams trying to put his "face" back on as *Mrs. Doubtfire*, the hiding of identity has always worked for comic mileage.

Exaggeration is yet another comic tool that needs no explanation. In *The Gold Rush*, it's not just that Chaplin is hungry but that he is so starved he winds up eating his boot and shoelaces as if they were spaghetti. Hunger is thus depicted with such exaggeration that we laugh. And Jack Nicholson as a misanthropic recluse in *As Good As It Gets* is not just *worried* about cleanliness, he is OBSESSED with it: we see in the credit sequence that he has a cabinet full of bars of soap and disposes of each one after a single wash. Allow yourself the freedom to exaggerate as much as you wish, realizing you can always tone it down if what you have written is too far over the top.

Interruption

Luis Buñuel understood how funny it is to simply interrupt an action, especially if that interruption becomes a repeated one. As we shall discuss in chapter 7, his *Discreet Charm of the Bourgeoisie* (1972) concerns a group of upper-middle-class folk who are interrupted every time they try to eat, each instance funnier than the one before. Interruption can, of course, be effective in dialogue as well as in action, for interruption clearly expresses the clash of opposing personalities. The humor surrounding interruption comes not just from the action itself but the reaction as well: what effect does an interruption have for each character involved? And that brings up one final device.

The Reaction Shot

Buster Keaton was a master of the slow burn, the stone face, that pause as he considers what has happened or is about to happen. So much of comedy depends on the reaction evoked in the characters. The Broadway musical (if you can call it that) *Stomp* takes noise, rhythm, and percussion sounds as far as they can go, but a lot of what holds the show together, since no words are spoken (or sung!), is the use of reaction "takes" of the characters onstage to each other and to the audience. Yes, this is the simple and ancient art of mime, but it works brilliantly, as one "stomper" faces the audience and mugs a disapproval face to the audience's attempt to clap in rhythm. The audience roars.

As you write your script, add lines to suggest that we see the reactions of the characters to the comic business you have stirred up.

Chapter Summary

Elements of Comedy to Consider in Your Scripts

1. What comic climate do you wish to establish: satirical, humorous, farcical, or ironic?
2. Is your comedy primarily comedian-, story/situation- or character-driven?
3. What kind of comic characters have you created: imposters, innocents, or ironic figures, or combinations of two or more?
4. What comic plots are you employing, knowing that some of the most frequently used in comedy include
   A. The Journey (picaresque plot)
   B. Reducto ad absurdum
   C. Parody and burlesque (often a very loose structure)
   D. The wedding of young lovers (romance)
   E. Central character with a difficult task or quest
   F. The consequences of one magical or surreal element
   G. An innocent reacts to situations thrust upon him or her
   H. Fish out of water
5. Have you employed such comic devices as repetition, inversion, reciprocal interference, exaggeration, disguise, interruption, or reaction shots?

CHAPTER 2

Exercises to Nurture the Comic Muse

Yes, some writers wake up, shower, get dressed, make a cup of coffee, sit down at the computer or go up onstage, and can be funny immediately, on demand, on time, in rare form. But for the rest of us it's part inspiration, part study, part habit. This chapter focuses on exercises and practices aimed at helping you stretch your comic muscles, learn more about tickling your own funny bone (and other people's), and maybe pick up some inspiration for the scripts you want to write as well. There is no need to do all that is offered here, and certainly no one is standing over you saying, "Do these in the order presented." I would imagine that many would find it helpful to refer back to this chapter, and to keep on using some of these exercises and hints.

Four suggestions to put all in gear:

1. Draw up a "comic profile" of yourself.
2. Turn your workplace into a comic environment.
3. Consider having a writing partner for comedy. Even if you write alone, find someone who can be your "comic sounding board."
4. Form a comic story circle that meets regularly, following the set guidelines for story circles.

Your Comic Profile

Keep a comic profile journal of yourself. You may or may not wish to show this to anyone else, but mainly it is for you and you alone. You shouldn't analyze yourself to death. But there are lasting rewards in casting a playful and observant eye over your life and those who have influenced you.

Ready? On the cover—why not a picture that makes you chuckle or laugh out loud? On separate pages, deal with the following:

- Three early funny memories from your childhood.
- Who seemed to have the most humor: your father or mother? How would you describe their humor? Or if your parents had NO humor, what relative or close family friend did?
- List several friends you loved because of their humor, the ones that really made you laugh. How did they do it? Were they aware they were

funny, or, like my wonderful grandmother on my mother's side, were they funny because they didn't know they were funny?

•   Can you get hold of a handful of photos from family albums that capture humorous moments, or those moments we are all familiar with that were not at all funny at the time, but in replay are a stitch! I still have one of myself, for instance, age two, completely covered in green paint that a hired fence painter had left open while he took a lunch break and that I had, with true delight, discovered.

•   Ten comedies that have given you great pleasure (see appendix 1). Don't start to analyze: just list! But once you have your list, you might want to remember what it was that worked so well for you.

•   Five television series or shows that made you laugh the most as you were growing up. Jerry Seinfeld has said that he was well into his show when he realized he was working very close to the style and letter of Abbott and Costello's TV shows he had loved as a kid (Flaherty, 24).

•   A page on the cartoons you used to read and those you read now. You don't have to write out why these connected with you, but look at your list and begin to see some patterns.

•   A list of books that were funny and you couldn't put down.

•   Now a page or more on those teachers and/or authority figures in your childhood and development who made you laugh.

•   Finally, put a spotlight on yourself—not your writing, but you as a person growing up. Some pages on favorite or forgotten memories called to mind in which you were funny or were the butt of someone else's joke (sick or hilarious or both!).

•   Near the back, some pages for comic self-reflections. Were comedy and laughter a defense mechanism for you or a true festive celebration?

•   Now for a finale, *write your own comic tombstone.* I'm serious. Every group I've tried this with has laughed nervously and then gotten into a hilarious mood, using the "few choice words" as a way to give a final take on a lifetime. After all, isn't that what we are all faced with eventually? Here are a few samples from several workshops I've conducted:

Oh me! Oh my!
Oh me! Oh my!
What a lot
Of funny things go by.
> (Dr. Seuss, *One Fish, Two Fish,*
> *Red Fish, Blue Fish*)

A paraphrase of Charlie Brown coming off the pitcher's mound quite dejected: "How can we lose when we're so sincere?"

An arrow pointing to the tombstone alongside mine, and these words: "I'm with Stupid!"

"IT'S A TAKE!"

A Comic Writing Environment

No, I don't mean a laugh track playing in the background twenty-four hours a day, the comic equivalent of New Age tapes of ocean waves, whales mating, or loons looning. But what can you do to and with your workplace to make it a, well, happier and funnier place? As I write this I'm on a Greek island with a number of humorous photos tacked up on the walls, along with quotations of which I am particularly fond. Music counts for me too: there is a stack of CDs that I find get the romantic and the anarchistic in me going, including those of Ella Fitzgerald, Louis Armstrong, Yugoslav gypsy music, and more. And NO TELEPHONE.

That's what works for me. What about you? Note and confession: The happiest work environment that I have come across in my travels, aside from an animation studio for children in Belgrade, Yugoslavia, was the office of President Havel of the Czech Republic. By means I am not free to reveal, I was able to see his office in the "Castle" in Prague one day, and to smile and even laugh at the tasteful but definitely offbeat modern furniture, white walls with playful dashes of color or modern art, all adding up to a statement that matters of state need not be boring or too serious.

Partners and Comic Sounding Boards

Screenwriting is always a group activity even if you are writing individual drafts by yourself: once completed, everyone else is going to have a shot at trying to make it funnier, "punch it up," add their two cents.

But writing comedy particularly lends itself to working with a partner, or at least having those you really trust and enjoy for their humor going over your material, giving feedback, listening with full attention. Comedy is often such a delicate muse that we can profit from a partner's immediate feedback. There is more to it even than the question, Is it funny? Two minds can sharpen humor, push an absurd situation or character, get on a "roll" with a scene, suggest that one detail that will bring the house down for sure.

Herschel Weingrod has written all of his scripts, including *Twins, Trading Places, Kindergarten Cop,* and *Space Jam,* with his partner, Timothy Harris.

According to Weingrod, the reason he has been so pleased to write with a partner for over twenty years is the following:

> There's nothing better than writing a screenplay with a partner . . . if . . . you basically see the world in the same way . . . i.e., you find the same things funny, the same things tragic, the same things ironic . . . and, most importantly . . . that you both agree never to count. By this I mean, I cannot randomly open a screenplay written by Timothy Harris and myself, read a scene, and proclaim, "Ah, that's my line, that's my scene, that's my description." We leave that outside the door. We have what we call the moment of truth—when we've both written our own versions of the same scene—I hand him mine, he hands me his—we read our respective versions—the moment of truth is when we drop our attachment to what we've written individually and decide collectively what works best for the project. It could be all of his scene, all of my scene, some of his, some of mine . . . whatever the outcome, nobody is keeping score.
>
> (Personal interview, November 6, 1997)

Especially in American television, if you do wind up on a show, you will automatically have a lot of "comic sounding boards" from the rest of the team in meeting after meeting.

And while e-mailing your comedy to friends might get you swift replies from all over the globe, even more so than drama, the reading of a comic script out loud is so important. Turn off the phone, open the wine or Snapple and cheese and crackers, and start reading, sharing the remarks, the laughter, the changes. Part of what will happen in such a process is your increased feeling for (and appreciation of) TIMING and PACE.

Comic Story Circles

Story circles take us back to prehistoric times sitting around the fire in villages or caves. But I am being more specific in speaking about story circles used by professional storytellers such as my friend Adella Adella the Story Teller in New Orleans.

The suggestion is that you form a group of kindred souls—writers or nonwriters, it really doesn't matter. What counts is that you all care about the Comic Muse! That stated, the rules are pretty simple:

1. *Choose a topic for that evening or session.* Let's use one I've tried often, for instance: relate an experience that was embarrassing at the time it happened but that became funny or hilarious as it was told and retold.

2. *Actually sit in a circle so everyone can see each other clearly.* No triangles or rectangles or squares allowed.

3. *Have someone designated as the group leader.* The main functions of the leader (who could be a different person each time) are simply to enforce the rules and to lead a discussion of "what happened" afterwards.

4. *Choose who goes first. That person determines which direction the stories will go in.* Then the stories flow *with no commentary or feedback remarks from anyone* until all stories are told. You must go in order in the direction chosen. But you have the right to say "pass" and then, when the circle is completed, you may add your story at that point. Or you can completely bow out and not tell a story, but you must stay a part of the group, listening to the others and joining the discussion afterwards.

5. *Try not to choose one story and stick with it come hell or high water.* That is, let yourself be influenced by what you hear, so that what you finally choose as your tale may be a last-minute inspiration based on the last comic tale told. This point obviously helps keep the circle creative, fresh, and dynamic.

After all stories are told, the leader leads a discussion of the reactions folks have to what they heard. This final part is absolutely critical to putting the whole experience in focus.

The number of humor-related topics is, of course, endless. Besides the topic mentioned above, I've used with happy results the following (yes, there is some overlap with the items listed under Comic Profiles): your favorite comic film and why; your favorite comedian and why; an off-color joke you like; what comic tombstone do you wish; and stories about clashes of sex and love. Or you could start a story and let the next person continue it, and so on till the last person adds the "comic ending." In fact, many of the comic exercises listed in the next section lend themselves well to the story circle.

The key to the circle is the democracy of having no judgmental feedback while the circle is circling. Storytelling is storytelling; discussion of the stories is what comes afterwards. All writers and seminar participants I've tried it with in script workshop environments have listed the story circle as one of the most effective "tools" they've picked up!

A Dozen Comedy-Centered Exercises

[1] Practice random acts of kindness.

That's the bumper sticker I'm sure we've all seen. But think for a moment how you might actually go about initiating such carnivalesque generosity of spirit.

A dozen long-stemmed red roses with a sweet card to your worst enemy? Well, maybe not, since that could easily be taken as some kind of sick joke. But consider an unexpected invitation to dinner for a friend you haven't seen in so long because you've been "too busy." Or what about surprising the kids by taking a day off, taking them out of school and heading for the beach or a movie or a walk in the mountains. Or taking an extra half-hour now and then to pick up the phone rather than e-mail and actually *talk* to friends or relatives you haven't talked to in months or years. I recently decided to just call some old friends in distant locations I had not heard from or talked to in over a year. The payoff was immediate: I smiled all day as happy memories of the past floated in and out of my mind. Or, a very easy one for the freeway or for driving around town: let that guy or gal cut in front of you with a gracious sweep of the hand and a smile (why have we all become such nervous mean-spirited drivers?!). You get the idea!

[2] Surprise yourself from time to time.

A close cousin of #1, but not the same. This exercise is meant not so much for your writing as for the sheer pleasure of life. Are we talking about that vacation you promised yourself but didn't take? Or is this one an invitation to simply lighten up, figure out how to dump a lot of your worries, cut through difficult relationships with some humor, or perhaps just practice being happier in general with yourself. I once entertained a very "serious" woman film director from Kazakhstan at Mardi Gras in New Orleans. It was her first time in the United States. We had a screening of her very moving film, and then carnival began full force. She immediately transformed into a party gal, grabbing beads at parades and guzzling wine with the best of them. "But I thought you were a very serious person," I said between parades. "Oh, no," she said in charming broken English, "I am really very crazy inside!"

[3] Comic observation: Spend an hour from time to time in the neighborhood park or the mall or playground and simply watch and listen.

This all comes under the heading of sharpening your powers of comic observation. Don't take notes. Just be there and soak it all in. In fact, you might want to repeat this with different "target audiences" in mind. Try the playground to see what kids talk about today and how they interact as they play. Or that McDonald's or Wendy's where the old folk gather each morning to chat: what do they talk about? What's going on in their lives?

Or the mall. Catch teen talk, or the upwardly mobile in a rush. How do they dress? What delicious contradictions make you laugh? You choose where and when, but be purposeful and totally focused on catching details, snatches of dialogue, those actions that define character. For instance, I recently got a huge kick out of noticing who rents those four-seater pedal-bike carriages at Santa Barbara beach. There were young, carefree couples being silly and actually trying to ram each other, nervous Japanese trying for speed and not taking in the view, very young kids who just couldn't get the hang of it, and an elderly couple looking as dignified as all get out. And dialogue? In New Orleans, just sitting on my front steps has for years allowed me to tap into a wealth of African American rap, hiphop, street jive and down-home swearing.

Yes, do take notes afterwards. Snatches you remember, points you might use later. But don't worry during this exercise about shaping or organizing these sit-and-listen sessions.

[4] The humor of real life: Keep a file of pieces from your daily paper that might work their way into future comic writings.

In front of me is a 1997 Associated Press piece by Evan Perez about a grandmother in Florida who slowed down at a highway off-ramp. Two brothers with guns who were fleeing the highway patrol jumped into her brand-new BMW convertible. A hundred miles and several hours later, the police caught up with them, and while she ducked under the seat, the brothers shot it out with the law. The results: one brother killed, the other wounded but captured. The grandmother survived scared but fine. How did she put up with her captivity? "She said she used her sense of humor—joking about who'd play their parts in the TV movie—to calm the men, who were wanted on bank robbery and kidnapping charges in South Carolina . . ." (12). Comedy saved the day. As she said, "I was playing mother to them, friend to them, comic to them. I knew the only chance for me to be let go was to keep them happy."

Take it from there. What did she tell them? Write some of the dialogue. Who was she? How did this "accident" change her life? What if it's told from the point of view of the brother who lived? A monologue of his thoughts in prison? And you can think of many other angles or possible rough exercises to riff off for such a piece.

Certainly this single story offers a wealth of possibilities for a whole script. Keeping such a folder of clippings teaches you well that truism that life *is* stranger than fiction, and that often what looks like a sure thing from the papers would only work if tamed or trimmed.

[5] Comic character study:
Make at least a half-hour interview on video with
someone you consider to be humorous—but do not
let the other person know you are recording
for "comic" reasons!

Nothing would kill the comic faster than making your subject aware of your comic purposes. He or she will start to perform, mug, or simply become self-conscious. But the whole idea here is to carry on a conversation or interview—you dream up the reason and the topic—and enjoy it later, to better figure out what that person does that works so well in terms of humor. Not that you would "copy" this person and his or her speech and actions directly, but the influence may be there. Again, such an exercise is not making fun of anyone. Rather, it helps better understand character and how gesture, voice, and speech are related to laughter. While teaching a screenwriting seminar at Cal State Long Beach one summer, I had a most eager group of students who wound up at Venice Beach with a video camera and came back with some hilarious footage of con artists, street (or should I say beach?) musicians, and fire eaters. The tape taught us all a lot about comedy, improv, and showmanship. More enlightening still, however, are interviews with non-entertainers. And it is even better if the subject is someone you do not know well, so the "interview" will be fresh.

[6] Comic foreground/background:
Write a scene in which two people talk seriously
while six motor scooters going by in the background
provide a comic touch when played against
the foreground.

Often comedy can come from something that simple: the difference between foreground and background, as one action "comments" on the other. You decide who the two people are and what they are talking about. A couple breaking up, perhaps? And why not have each scooter driven by someone carrying something different. What if one is a pizza delivery guy, another a priest, a third a babe, a fourth a policewoman, and so on. And push the exercise. Have each person on a scooter carry some object that clashes with our image of them. Finally, do not allow the couple to see these characters at all.

[7] Comedy-documentary: What famous "departed" person could you have an actor or actress friend pretend to be? While you videotape, have them walk around town or campus talking to people about subjects that relate to that person.

Yes, this exercise takes a little work and it is definitely playing off of Z. Zelnik's "comic documentary," *Tito for the Second Time among the Serbs,* which we will discuss in chapter 8.

Here you are working with an actor or actress and, if you are not a video person, a camera-operating friend too. Your job is to help prepare the actor for this half-improv, half-planned exercise. First there is the fun of choosing your famous figure. We in the U.S. really don't have a single individual as well known and central to our culture as Tito was (and perhaps still is!) to the Yugoslavs. In New Orleans, I would love to give this exercise a shot with Louis Armstrong returning. But you decide. Hint: depending on where you live, this one might be grounds for funding from local arts or humanities councils or other groups. Wouldn't a Kentucky arts council be interested in a comic documentary about Daniel Boone showing up on the streets of Lexington again? Or what about Mark Twain strolling through the mall in St. Louis? Why not Elvis making a glorious return to Memphis? Your imagination is the only limit!

[8] Ensemble comedy: Imagine four to eight guys or gals who gather at one café every morning for a good hour and capture some of the comic banter of the group on any particular morning.

This is a scene/dialogue exercise which could well grow out of #3. You might also wish to take a look at Woody Allen's *Broadway Danny Rose* (1984), which is built around old stand-up comedians meeting daily at a New York deli. As I worked on this book in a Greek mountain village on the island of Kea, I would start each morning with dark bitter Greek coffee in the village square, together with anywhere from five to twenty-two local men, including the former mayor, several taxi drivers, Nicos the bus driver, and several young fellows. I was, first of all, impressed with the great sense of humor that exploded each day. But most of all, I enjoyed catching on to the group dynamics and how any one topic that got introduced would be picked up around the group, looked at one way and then another, and "capped" by someone at some magical point as another topic cropped up. Thus it was a good practice for me to write a few pages about how they got from the price of land per acre on the island to Greek-Turkish politics and on to passionate talk about the Greek basketball or soccer teams. Think how such a gathering might work for a television comedy series, with each episode focusing on a different character or a different comic problem, or an ensemble feature comedy à la *Mediterraneo*.

[9] Visual comedy: In one page, write a complete comic scene with no dialogue.

This exercise keeps us focused on our need for visual humor! How easy it is to simply have our characters crack jokes and spout humorous monologues and voiceovers and witty dialogue. But can you tell a comic story with no dialogue? This exercise may well send you back to look at chapter 4 and rerun Keaton, Chaplin, Jacques Tati, and others. Few exercises force you more clearly to think about comedy beyond that immediate crutch, dialogue.

[10] Comedy from the bringing together of three disparate directions: Create a story from three photos.

This one is common to creative writing class exercises: given three random narrative elements, you must combine them into a story. In the same spirit, find three photos and come up with a comic plot, romantic or anarchistic or both! For example, I have these in front of me:

The first is of two old New Orleans jazz musicians, the Humphrey Brothers—both now deceased—who reportedly played music together around the world but who in their last years never spoke to each other and never even would agree to ride together in the same car. The second, also from New Orleans, is of an unusual Mardi Gras costume: four young people in a penis costume, urinating. And the third is an Associated Press photo of a fight breaking out in the Ukrainian parliament during a discussion on violence at a local parade.

What feature comedy can you think of weaving together these three "ideas," realizing you do not have to be literal about combining the Ukraine and New Orleans? The elements to play with are two old musicians, four young folk in a penis costume, and politicians fistfighting in the government hall during a debate on what to do about violence! What can you do?

I actually saw the penis costume and heard the old musicians years ago. I have not done a script exactly on these three shots, but nearly. Mine started with the costume, as a "what if." What if the four people inside were actually two young couples who had been through good times and bad and this costume became a kind of catharsis for them. And what if their paths crossed with some corrupt New South politicians, with the costume and a political rally literally coming together, and what if the subplot was connected to some great old musicians, the last of their generation. Although I've collected many option checks on the script, the "penis costume" finally proved too, well, Aristophanic for American producers!

Try the same exercise with other photos, or with three different pieces from the newspaper of three varying ideas that are floating around in your head.

[11] Adapt the following television miniseries for your own times in your own area or country.

I've worked happily with one of the former Yugoslavia's most interesting directors of television and film, Srdjan Karanovic. In the 1980s he made a ten-part series for Yugoslav television that is still very popular in reruns. The concept was the following: a series about the 1960s with each one-hour episode set in a different year, starting with 1960 and ending with 1969. The series has as its main figure a fellow who at the beginning is just a teen hanging out with friends, listening to music, learning about girls. At the series' end he is twenty-six, recently married, with a steady job and a member of the Communist Party.

But there is more. Each episode has a major theme tied into the main character's life. One show is centered on rock-and-roll, another on girls, and so forth. His gang of four or five best friends is important too, as each of them goes through changes. The young protagonist's voiceover narration holds all together.

Finally, five minutes of documentary montage concludes each episode, as the protagonist says, for instance, "That was the year the Beatles appeared in America, and Tito visited Egypt, and. . . ." The list continued, mixing nostalgia and history with the personal, "fictional" input of the main character.

Think of your own "decade" series. Who would you follow for ten years, and who would his or her friends be? How would you comically show both your protagonist's changes and those of your country? What theme could you give to each episode? And what five-minute "real" nostalgia montage could you add at the end?

[12] The grown-up children's film: Come up with characters and a plot for a children's film in the vein of *Babe* or *The White Balloon*.

The focus here is on realizing what an important part of the comic spectrum comedy for children has become, and yet how many of these films underestimate children's intelligence and thus succeed in losing both adult audiences and many children as well. Of course, this exercise also asks you to become a child again and enjoy yourself in doing so. You might very well head to the public library or the local bookstores and take a look at some of the truly imaginative offerings in the children's section. Then see what you would come up with using either fantasy or a realistic approach.

II

A WRITER'S OVERVIEW
OF THE TRADITIONS
AND GENRES OF COMEDY

CHAPTER 3

From Stage and Page to Screen:
Anarchistic and Romantic Comedy

Well, don't exult at present, for we're all uncertain still,
But when once we hold Peace, then be merry if you will;
    Then will be the time for laughing,
    Shouting out in jovial glee,
    Sailing, sleeping, feasting, quaffing,
    All the public sights to see.
                Trygaeus in Aristophanes' *Peace*

Wherefore was I to this keen mockery born?
When at your hands did I deserve this scorn?
                Helena in Shakespeare's
                A Midsummer Night's Dream

The history of comedy as a genre has traditionally been the history of stage comedy, from Aristophanes to Shakespeare and Molière and through to the twentieth century, including vaudeville, puppet shows, the circus, and our recent additions to performance-based laughter: cinema and television. Of course, there is also the tradition of literary humor and comedy in short stories and, later, in novels, from Boccaccio and Chaucer down to Henry Fielding, Charles Dickens, Mark Twain, Robert Benchley, Joseph Heller, Milan Kundera, and beyond, which we will discuss briefly at the end of the chapter. But in general, comedy in fiction embraces elements of the two traditions we will outline here, with one important difference: because they are not performance based, they are even freer to blur boundaries and include elements of other areas.

Stage and screen comedy can be seen as following two important roads: anarchistic and romantic. The goal of this chapter is to help you as a writer better understand to what degree the comedies you wish to write fall into one or the other of these major divisions or, as is often the case, to what degree your comedies will be a mixture of the two.

All that we will discuss can be seen as leaning more strongly into one camp or the other, though very few comedies are purely or exclusively one form or the other. As we shall see, anarchistic comedy is associated with Aristophanes and continues all the way down to the Marx Brothers, Monty Python, *Saturday Night Live*, and even the Muppet movies. And romantic comedy appears first with Menander in ancient Greece, continues through the Roman playwrights and on to Shakespeare and Molière, and comes down to us as the dominant form of American film comedy since the 1930s.

Anarchistic Comedy: Aristophanes

> Come at once to supper,
> And bring your pitcher, and your supper chest,
> The priest of Bacchus sends to fetch you thither.
> And do be quick: you keep the supper waiting.
> Aristophanes, *Acharnians*

Aristophanes joyfully shouts to writers and actors over two thousand four hundred years of laughter to say, "Try anything and everything. And besides having fun and evoking laughter, make 'em *think* as well."

The world has never seen a more freewheeling and carnivalesque form of comedy than that of Aristophanes. Elements of his accomplishment shine forth hilariously in W. C. Fields, the Marx Brothers, John Belushi's no-holds-barred performances in *National Lampoon's Animal House* (1978) and *The Blues Brothers* (1980), all the Monty Python films, and on down to that off-the-wall, laid-back independent comedy *Slacker* (1991), the loopy *Wayne's World,* and even *Waking Ned Devine* (1998). But no one has worked with as much total freedom and such a broad and varied range of the comic since Aristophanes' works rocked the ancient theaters of Greece.

Let me add that Aristophanes still packs them in on a summer night in the ancient theaters of Greece. I'm talking about up to fourteen thousand spectators at a crack, the kind of audience we Americans equate with sports events and rock concerts. For Aristophanes is a big green light for directors, actors, choreographers, and set designers to set off a number of unexploded mimes! Yale University once performed *The Frogs* in a swimming pool, for instance. One production of *Peace* I attended in Athens, building on the fact that the ancient choruses would have had leather phalluses attached to strings to raise and lower when needed, presented Trygaeus at the "climax" of the play with a six-foot plastic phallus that he strapped on before enjoying Peace. It is very difficult to capture the exhilaration one feels after a well-done production of Aristophanes. All the more reason why, as writers, we can learn much from the master of "old comedy."

His comedy can be called "anarchistic" or anarchic in the sense the term has been used by critics and scholars such as Henry Jenkins, Steve Seidman, Steve Neale and Frank Krutnik, for in these comedies the structure revolves around a single individual, a simple person with whom the audience can thus identify, who comes up with a "crazy" idea and, after a number of obstacles, succeeds in bringing about a glorious change in his or her culture, which is finally celebrated in a festive ending of dance, song, wine, and food. *Lysistrata* (411 B.C.) is perhaps his best-known work, certainly in the United States. It revolves around a woman, Lysistrata, who has the nutty idea to end war by organizing all of the women of Greece to go on a sex strike. She succeeds, and Athens and her warring enemy, Sparta, enjoy a new world of making love, not war, more than two thousand years before the phrase became a slogan for the anti–Vietnam War movement. In *Peace* (421 B.C.) an Athenian farmer, Trygaeus (his name means "reaper of the harvest"), hatches the idea of ending the war with Sparta by conducting an individual peace with Zeus himself. He accomplishes this by flying on a large dung beetle that manages to fart its way to Olympus, where not only is the treaty concluded but Zeus throws in his long-hidden daughter, Peace, as Trygaeus' bride-to-be as well. The ending is pure festivity—and sexuality, as the chorus of farmers enjoy the goddess Peace in the first example of group sex in Western drama.

Aristophanes' brand of comedy is anarchistic because the main protagonist makes absolutely no compromises. He or she not only "gets away with it" but changes the whole order of a culture or society in the process. This is a comedy of total wish fulfillment and of equal doses of personal fantasy (the crazy idea) and festivity (the celebration of the victory of that idea). In Freudian terms, we could say such comedy is delightful because it is pre-Oedipal; that is, it represents the fulfillment of a child before he or she learns that growing up has to do with making compromises and not getting everything we want when we want it. This is the stuff of, for instance, the Marx Brothers' best features: whether their crazy idea is running an imaginary country (*Duck Soup*) or university (*Horse Feathers*) or taking over (*A Night at the Opera*), we know they will get what they want with glorious comic chaos reigning supreme.

The main elements in his work are, more specifically, (1) flights of lyrical poetry, (2) strong political satire and literary parody, and (3) farcical and even slapstick use of physical comedy. Take *The Birds* (414 B.C.), for instance. The main character, Peithetaerus, and his sidekick, Euelpides, act out the fanciful idea of starting a new country in the sky. After much confusion and confrontation with gods and imposters from the world of men, "Cloudcuckooland" is established and celebrated. Burlesque opportunities abound, as a chorus of brightly plumed birds can dance, fly, fight, have sex, fart, and shit, much to the pleasure of the audience. But direct satire of leading politicians of the day is also hurled about, and other passages include some of the best lyrical lines in all of ancient poetry:

> Golden one, beloved!
> O fairest of birds to me,
> > Playmate, mistress of melody,

Late, so late, thou appearest.
Come, my own, my dearest,
Sound thy silvery flute to sing
Songs in tune with the voice of spring.
Music poured from thy heart to bring
Charm to verse anapaestic.

(*The Complete Plays*, 255)

Throughout this book we will use "anarchistic comedy" to describe the work of those comedians and writers who carry out nonromantic, wildly imaginative and often surreal flights of fancy, satire and parody similar to Peithetaerus's efforts to create Cloudcuckooland, actions which show little regard for character development and plot construction.

Taking a closer look, we can notice further characteristics of comic craft that are exhibited in Aristophanes' ageless and still eagerly performed comedies that can be of use to us as writers as well.

1. Aristophanes' plays are organized by theme and central comic metaphor rather than by plot. Let us consider his earliest surviving play, *The Acharnians* (425 B.C.), written when he was barely twenty. The main character is an Athenian citizen, Dicaeopolis (the name means "righteous citizen"), who wants the Peloponnesian War to end. As in *Peace* and *Lysistrata*, the protagonist forms his own plan of action, since the diplomats and leaders are doing nothing. Thus an individual peace is arranged.

Yet while such a turning point would be the climax of a "well-written" Hollywood comedy, this major action occurs very early on, leaving the rest of the play for comic debates and farcical stage business, and finally for grand festivity in celebration of Dicaeopolis' self-concluded peace treaties. In short, there is almost no plot at all. The same can be said for each of Aristophanes' plays. As we shall see in the next chapter, this episodic, almost nonnarrative approach to comedy is partially reflected in the United States and other countries in a popular vaudeville-style tradition of skits, acts, music, and dance. Thus, looking across the Atlantic at the Monty Python group, we see films such as *The Meaning of Life*, *The Life of Brian*, and *Monty Python and the Holy Grail* as comedies owing more to the British stage pantomime tradition than to narrative or dramatic theater. "Anarchistic" has to do with the form as well as the character/ story itself.

2. Aristophanes' characters are types rather than fully rounded or developed figures. In fact, we cannot talk about any real sense of Aristotelian character change from start to finish in these comedies. Dicaeopolis is the same strong-willed Athenian in the end as he was in the beginning. The change is in Athenian society itself, for it has come around to his point of view.

3. Aristophanes' comedies contain a *parabasis*, a section when a chorus member steps forward to speak seriously about Aristophanes' own intentions in

his comedy. As mentioned in the introduction, comedy often acknowledges the audience's presence. And in Aristophanes' plays, the audience is never safe from insults, physical comic attack, finger-pointing, and at times a sharing of confidences. But while television stand-up is like the stand-up tradition in clubs, dependent on a close working of the audience, and in movies we have those moments of direct address to the audience like the asides in *Wayne's World,* we no longer have extended speeches from the author to the audience, as in this segment of the parabasis from *The Acharnians:*

> First since to exhibit his plays he began,
> our chorus instructor has never
> Come forth to confess in this public address
> how tactful he is and how clever.
>
> (The Complete Plays, 33)

4. Structurally, each play contains several *agons*—verbal duals—which the main protagonist wins because of his or her skills with logic and words. We get "agony" from the original term for "contest," *agon.* The number of such verbal confrontations varies, but in lieu of any strong plot, these battles of wit fuel the laughter and further the main protagonist's fight for his or her idea. In *The Birds,* for instance, there are a series of such contests as a variety of freeloaders attempt to break into Cloudcuckooland but are beaten down by Peithetaerus each time, only to be finally accepted in one festive dance at the conclusion. We can see in these comic agons the forerunners of lickety-split crackling dialogue that has characterized so much of vaudeville and American sound comedy. And as in Aristophanes' battles of words, so in any television sitcom or film comedy dialogue, somebody always comes out the winner!

5. Aristophanes was able to fully draw upon surreal comic fantasy and carnivalesque festivity. Simply imagine the sheer pleasure of seeing a chorus of twenty-four frogs onstage in *The Frogs,* or choruses of wasps in *The Wasps* or birds in *The Birds.* Comedy turns the everyday world upside down and inside out, and Aristophanes' plays do so with particular gusto. As noted above, in part Aristophanes can carry this off because he is not worried about character or plot development. We can think of his anarchistic comedy as *a comic spectacle with a thematic punch line*—which was, more often than not, "Peace at any cost is better than war."

6. Aristophanic laughter occurred as Athens was being destroyed by its grinding war with Sparta. These comedies were not just "entertainment." As writers, we should consider the implications. At no time during the Vietnam War, for instance, did we have a strong anarchistic comedy that made fun of U.S. policy in Vietnam directly. Yes, we can say that Arthur Penn's *Little Big Man* with its black humor about Custer's Last Stand dealt metaphorically with Vietnam. But no one in Hollywood attempted comedy and political commentary head-on

in a popular film. Robert Altman's *M*A*S*H* is definitely anarchistic and full of dark comic insight into the Vietnam War, but once more, the commentary is distanced, as the action in this war comedy takes place during the *Korean* War.

Yet Aristophanes' work is also a lesson to us in that the state paid him to create works of strong criticism of its policies. Anarchistic comedy was, therefore, seen as something cathartic and good for all.

All this ended, of course, when Athens went down to defeat in the war and such freedom of speech was curbed. As one scholar notes, "As soon as Athenians were shorn of their liberties, the plays of this type became quite impossible" (Matthews, 89).

The road was then open, as we shall see, for a more conservative form of comedy: romance.

A wrap: what practical influence can Aristophanes have for writers of comedy today?

Simple. Dare to be different, to take chances, to let your imagination come up with its wildest comic pleasures. Animation has proven a fertile ground for the complete realization of fantasy and festivity. Early shorts featuring Popeye, Betty Boop, and others, together with the fine animation traditions of Eastern Europe, especially the Zagreb School from the former Yugoslavia, took up the challenge of breaking boundaries, exploring imaginative realities with zesty and often thoughtful humor. As practiced by Disney and others, however, the feature animated film has almost always been structured under a "romantic" approach to comedy, with farcical and anarchistic elements on the edges.

But Aristophanes' call for total comedy is sometimes headed in fruitful ways: consider Woody Allen's *Mighty Aphrodite,* with its ancient Greek chorus that unexpectedly turns our attention to a New York story and then blurs the borders of ancient drama and New York romantic comedy, as choral figures appear throughout the film.

Aristophanes' lyrical voice also instructs us that we should not be afraid to turn away from laughter to open up spaces in a comedy for lyrical or quieter moments. Comedy is large enough and durable enough to embrace these strands and allow us to return to laughter and farce and festivity afterwards.

Putting it all together, Aristophanes appears to us today as particularly modern. His nose-thumbing at narrative, drama, and character development and his celebration of fantasy and festivity suggest a strong "meta-theatrical" view that characterizes the postmodern world. A closer look at the ancient Greek comic bard can be especially fruitful for television writers, for, as we shall see, so many programs, from *The Simpsons* to the ensemble shows such as *Cheers, Northern Exposure, M*A*S*H* and *Friends* to the comedian-centered sitcoms like *The Cosby Show* and *Seinfeld,* are only loosely concerned with plot and are much more open to zany experimentation than feature film comedies.

Romantic Comedy

Menander, Greece, and Rome

As noted, romantic comedy has since the mid-1930s dominated American film comedy, and indeed has been the major form of European stage comedy since the time of Menander in late classical Athens. The focus of such comedy is on boy-girl relationships, particularly as related to the conflict between personal desire and family and social institutions. Traditionally the goal of young (for the genre celebrates youth!) couples is to reach that most official of all unions, marriage. But whether or not the knot is actually tied on camera or stage, overcoming personal differences within the couple and triumphing over blocking figures—familial or social or both—is the stuff of the tight plotting that romantic comedy requires. *In comparison to Aristophanic comedy, therefore, plot and character development count for a lot more.* Add one more important dimension: romantic comedy concerns the domestic more sharply than does anarchistic comedy, which tends toward a much broader sociopolitical canvas.

Finally, in American screenwriting particularly, it is difficult to find films that do not include romance—comic or dramatic—as either the main plot or the secondary one. Thus romantic comedy becomes the playing field upon which we can explore the contradictions between love and sexuality, honesty and deceit, personal desire and social decorum, private obsessions and public customs. Romantic comedy's spotlight on the seemingly opposite pull between sexual gratification (which is nondiscriminating) and idealized love of one individual can provide all the tension, pathos and comedy you need to devise a story in this popular genre. Romantic comedy calls for laughter, but because of its subject and approach it demands pathos as well. Anarchistic comedy tickles the mind; romantic comedy wants to warm the heart and, yes, in its extreme form, to produce a few tears as well. As Steve Neale and Frank Krutnik point out, the line between comedy and romantic melodrama is often thin (108).

Menander is the acknowledged father of the genre. Born in 342 B.C., he was several generations behind the master of Old Comedy and thus grew up with a diminished realm of possibilities due to the defeat of Athens by Sparta and the subsequent loss of many freedoms.

Until 1959 we had no complete play by the founder of "New Comedy," but the publication that year of the recently discovered manuscript of *The Dyskolos* (*The Grouch*) changed all that. The play makes it possible for us to say with certainty that as the father of romantic comedy, Menander is also the parent of the well-plotted comedy. Furthermore, his comedy allows for a lot more individualization and character-shading than did Aristophanes' brush-stroke cartoon figures. Anyone wanting to write the next popular comic romance will profit from grasping Menander's accomplishments.

The Dyskolos, set in the countryside outside of Athens, revolves around the efforts of a handsome young lad, Sostratos, to wed a striking young lass, Myrrhine, whose father, Knemon, an old farmer, happens to be a dyskolos (a misanthrope or "difficult one"). (Yes, Molière's Misanthrope echoes Menander!) Sostratos enlists the aid of an earthy trickster-friend, Chaireas, to help him reach his love and deal with the obstructing father. Chaireas is pure laughs, interested in only immediate sexual gratification. As he says: "A friend of mine is horny for a whore: my plan's abduction. I get loaded, burn her door down, am totally irrational. I get him laid before they're introduced. Delay can only swell his love: a swift relief cures swift amours" (8).

But warnings are brought by Sostratos' slave that the Grouch is piping mad and very dangerous. We soon are treated to Knemon himself, who bellows about his desire to be left alone. Yet when Sostratos is about to give up, Myrrhine appears and takes away his breath. Many of his lines are asides to himself, including "Can any of the honored gods save me now from love?" (1.205). The plot thickens as we learn the Grouch has a jealous stepson, Gorgias, who learns of Sostratos' interests from his slave, Daos, at the beginning of act 2. When Gorgias tries to push Sostratos away, our young lover says he's wealthy enough to ask for Myrrhine's hand in marriage without a dowry. This impresses Gorgias, who confides that his father will marry Myrrhine to the man most like himself. Some witty dialogue follows:

SOSTRATOS: But tell me, man, have you ever been in love?

GORGIAS: I can't imagine it.

SOSTRATOS: Why not? Who is stopping you?

GORGIAS: A realistic look at hardship, which is all I have in life.

(2.342–44)

Among the elements we shall track that have remained standard in the genre over the centuries are (1) the triumph of love over adversity; (2) the representation of "adversity" in terms of difficult parents or parental figures; (3) the doubling of romance—literally in this case, with two weddings presented in the conclusion; (4) a focus on male friendship, complete with a debate of the various points of view in regard to love and practical life; (5) the location of the drama in a country or nonurban setting; (6) the use of slaves and servants, not just in the courting/romance plots but also as comic relief and thus a kind of self-parody of love from within the story itself; (7) sudden conversions and swift plot reversals (the Grouch falls into the well and subsequently has a change of heart in terms of his estate and daughter's future); (8) the inclusion of the gods or nonhumans, seen here in the prologue delivered by the god Pan, whose shrine and surrounding area mark the location of much of the romance; and (9) in contrast to Aristophanic comedy, a sense of realism that is true to life as we generally know it.

The limitations are also clear, the largest being the lack of development of the female protagonist, Myrrhine. (As critics have pointed out, however, this has more to do with the subservient position of women in classical Greek society than with an individual failing in Menander.) And while the characters are clearly individualized, we are not, with Menander, speaking of complex comic character development.

The same may be said of the great Roman comic playwrights Plautus and Terence, who imitated and appropriated Menander's comic art. They tended to keep the plots and many of the characters but dropped much of the Greek atmosphere and locale, infusing these works with Roman details. Thus, "Latin comic drama is singularly unreal, as unreal as certain English adaptations from the French and the German, in which we feel a blank incongruity between the foreign code of manners on which the story is conditioned and the supposedly Anglo-Saxon characters by which it has to be carried out" (Matthews, 97).

We will soon see how Shakespeare was able to bring a marvelous complexity to these romantic formulas and traditions. But the Latin authors developed in the opposite direction, simplifying everything so that even the thickest member of the audience would catch the comedy and follow the basic plot. Why? For a very realistic reason: Plautus, Terence and the other Roman comic writers had to write for a tough crowd: The audiences they faced were full of foreigners who spoke Latin badly and riffraff who wanted straightforward bawdy and simplistic fare. Plautus especially succeeded in bringing a thorough knowledge of Roman low-life, complete with its slaves, braggart soldiers, and clowns, into his comedies. Under the Romans, "comedy" triumphed much more than any idealized sense of "romance."

Shakespeare and Comedy of the Green World

> Lovers and madmen have such seething brains,
> Such shaping fantasies, that apprehend
> More than cool reason ever comprehends.
> The Lunatic, the Lover, and the Poet,
> Are of imagination all compact.
>> Theseus in Shakespeare's *A Midsummer*
>> *Night's Dream* (5.1)

Our brief close-up on Menander helps us see how far Shakespeare brought romantic comedy in his dramatic and comic consideration of "lovers and madmen" almost two thousand years later.

The scholar of drama C. L. Barber has explored how we can view Shakespeare's romances as comedies of "the green world" (21). Barber and others explain how Shakespeare was creatively playing with both the Menander and Roman traditions of romantic comedy. But he was infusing these sources with a rich British festive tradition of "the green world": country carnivals, folklore, songs, dances, customs, tales, and humor. In short, Shakespeare practiced the theme of this book: know your traditions and then allow yourself the freedom to let your personal fantasies and imagination soar!

Our representative example will be *A Midsummer Night's Dream* (1600). The whole play is cast as a kind of carnival taking place within the framework of a wedding feast as Theseus, Duke of Athens, is to wed Hippolyta, Queen of the Amazons. This "romance" between the Duke and Queen is a given, never really developed or questioned. In this sense Theseus and Hippolyta become the bedrock and thus the center of stability, loving acceptance and good humor around which the comic and romantic chaos is created. Theseus sets both the romantic and comic tone for the whole play as he informs Hippolyta that he plans to wed her "With pomp, with triumph, and with revelling" (1.1).

Shakespeare's comedy is layered both in plots and subplots, and in characters and minor characters. What follows is not just a doubling of lovers, as in Menander, but a true multiplying of them, beginning with the initially at-odds youthful foursome: Lysander loves Hermia, who is also loved by Demetrius, who in turn is loved by Helena. Before Theseus' marriage can take place, he must help negotiate the confusions of desire and parental wishes, as Hermia's father brings his case to the Duke, demanding his daughter marry Demetrius.

As these plots unfold through twists and turns and various scenes, the location switches (as in Menander) to the countryside outside of Athens, where Lysander and Hermia hope to flee the obligations of Athenian law. This "green world" becomes the space where freedom reigns and where fantasy and festivity can be acted out. Of course, Shakespeare's Athenian countryside resembles nothing so much as the forested English countryside he knew so well, having little in common with its Greek namesake. But as we have pointed out, William is simply following the Roman tradition of turning "Athens" into a distant never-never land.

Within this green world, anything goes . . . and does! Shakespeare weaves in hilarious comic relief with the band of country bumpkins who are to perform for the wedding festivities. Thus we have Quince, Bottom, Snout, Starveling, Snug and Flute—the Six Stooges, for sure—providing a farcical visual and verbal parody not just of romance but of theater itself as they ponder the very nature of acting, performance and audience reception. Yet as Norman Sanders so well observes in discussing the clowning figures in *The Two Gentlemen of Verona*, "It can therefore be argued that the comic scenes do not simply satirize and belittle the love and friendship codes subscribed to in the main plot, but reveal them in a new light" (35). This troupe within a troupe performs *Pyramus and Thisbe* (our fourth couple, so far), evoking belly laughs and Hippolyta's memorable line "This is the silliest stuff that ever I heard." But in its green-world simplicity, the troupe further points out the splendor of the kind of all-embracing love the Duke and Queen are celebrating in their marriage.

All of this would seem more than enough for even a talented playwright. But Shakespeare dusts all with the fanciful magic of Puck and the realm of country fairies and woodland spirits. Oberon and Titania, King and Queen of the Fairies, offer us yet another lens through which to enjoy and perceive romance, serving as otherworldly doubles of Theseus and Hippolyta.

There is no need to review all of Shakespeare's clever and well-plotted intrigue of crossed purposes and mixed-up magic (the wrong lovers woo unintended recipients once Puck's love-altering drugs are administered, leading up to the most comic and simultaneously surreal and bizarre union of all—Titania's love for Bottom, whose head has become transformed into that of an ass). But let us simply acknowledge that Shakespeare is a master of comedy in part because he can manage such comic density without missing a beat and with a perfect sense of timing, moving between farce and true romance, anger and forgiveness.

Note that on one level Shakespeare and Aristophanes share a vision of comedy as embracing a full range from the lyrical to the satirical and farcical. The young lovers speak some of the finest lines on love in the English language, while at the same time the Bard from Stratford-on-Avon can delight in the mischief of fairies and country clowns who, in their silly behavior, are given lines that speak clearly about the nature of love. Bottom, for instance, informs us of one of the basic truths of the play:

and yet, to say the truth,
Reason and love keep little company together
now-a-days;

(3.1)

And Shakespeare's conclusion is as festive as anything Aristophanes devised: song, dance and lovers reunited rule the day. We can also suggest that both Aristophanes and Shakespeare understood the importance of a driving pace, though they employed such comic speed through different means: increasingly complex plotting for Shakespeare, sequential agons mixed with choral appearances, all focused on a single theme, for Aristophanes.

The similarities end there, however, for Shakespeare has masterfully explored the human heart, revealing both the complexity of love and its lighter, magical side as well. The sudden transformations, the disguises and "friendship" discussions, the victory of lovers over adversity, and the intrusion of the other world, plus the comic use of servants, all echo Menander and the Roman comic poets. But the end result is both an affirmation of love and a lingering questioning of the seemingly randomness of it all.

Puck's direct address to the audience at the conclusion is absolutely in comedy's tradition of establishing a special relationship with its audience. But Shakespeare has injected much more, as we have suggested. Not only has he included British country festivals, songs and folklore, but in Puck's closing words the romance and comedy are given an edge, a philosophical brush, as he makes us all finally aware not just of the theatricality of the production we have viewed but of life as a stage as well:

> PUCK: If we shadows have offended,
> Think but this (and all is mended)
> That you have but slumber'd here,
> While these visions did appear.
>
> (5.2)

So we leave the theater, not laughing out loud, but with perhaps a wry smile and the beginnings of a tear or two.

What lessons are to be learned by writers of comedy from the Bard of Stratford? Let us list just a few. These points have roots in the tradition that went before him, but they are worth restating and examining, even in Shakespeare's relatively weak comedies, such as *The Two Gentlemen of Verona*.

1. *Don't be afraid to be experimental.* Fairies? Asses' heads? Bumpkin actors? Shakespeare took chances and made them all pay off! Shakespeare isn't afraid to go over the top with an idea. The holiday green world he creates onstage in *A Midsummer Night's Dream* and other comedies appears to spring from the spirit of carnival within himself as he wrote.

2. *Explore the complexity of relationships caught in the jaws of blind passion and idealized love.* Shakespeare never allows his characters to fall into the sentimental or melodramatic. But the comic and "fantastic" (magical) frame of the play allows for a surprising number of sharply etched short scenes in which we come to know each of the four lovers more completely, both as couples and as individuals. In other words, unlike Aristophanic comedy, Shakespearean comedy explores the realm of the psychological.

3. *Go for straight-on zany farce for the fun of it and to highlight the reality of the love stories.* Clearly Shakespeare had fun going over the top with his comic country folk from the green world. And yet he manages to capture even these minor characters so that we do not simply laugh at them as caricatures but sense the character in them as well.

4. *Create female characters as bright or brighter than the male leads.* We noted that the women in Menander are shadows, and women in the Roman comedies are not much better. But Shakespeare creates fully realized women who are as intelligent and articulate as they are sensitive and emotive. Take Hermia's comment to Lysander on his apparent fickleness (he is smitten with Helena once Puck has done his magic mischief):

HERMIA: Hate me, wherefore? O me, what new my Love?
Am not I Hermia? Are not you Lysander?
I am as fair now, as I was erewhile.
Since night you lov'd me; yet since night you left me.
Why then you left me (O the gods forbid)
In earnest, shall I say?

(3.2)

It has always been one of the deep pleasures of reading or viewing Shakespeare that none of the males can rest easy or believe they can get away with outrageous schemes, for the women do see through them and, more often than not, top the males and set them straight.

   5. *Give the surreal or the magical a shot if you wish.* Comedy is rooted in the real, but in romantic comedy the magical can help you illuminate, explore and highlight the center to your script. Puck remains one of Shakespeare's most memorable characters, and certainly the confusion he brings down on the various lovers makes the sudden reversals of the romantic comic genre less "unbelievable," since we understand the game we are privy to. Frank Capra's *It's a Wonderful Life* (1946) plays at Christmas every year in large part because of the magical realism of angels coming down to check on small-town America. And the wings for John Travolta in *Michael* (1997) and for Denzel Washington in *The Preacher's Wife* (1997) add both humor and insight into the worlds into which these "angels" fall.

Comedy and the Tradition of the Novel and Print Fiction

   This section will be brief, for what applies to the stage has had a strong influence on printed comic fiction as well. Thus Charles Dickens, once an actor, moved from the stage to the study to write novels that both make us laugh and go for the tear, especially of social injustice. And while we can think of the hundred tales in Boccaccio's *Decameron* as short stories, they are actually presented as tales told in a group performance situation, as are Chaucer's *Canterbury Tales,* written shortly afterwards.

   Rather than a history of comedy in fiction, therefore, I offer my pick of eight works I personally recommend for writers of comedy. Once more, the list is meant to be provocative rather than exhaustive or traditional. Taken together, this list offers a challenge to you to try anything you want to in writing for the pure pleasure of it beyond all other reasons! Unlike drama and cinema, which are time-defined and budget-controlled, prose fiction has the freedom to go anywhere, to think and do anything it wishes. That spirit is important for screenwriters to stay in touch with.

1. BOCCACCIO, *Decameron.* Writing in the mid-fourteenth century in Italy, Boccaccio cleverly combined one hundred tales within the frame of seven young women and three young men escaping from the plague that struck Florence in 1348. For two weeks in the countryside these genial youths tell one tale each per day for ten days, all reflecting themes of love, chance and intelligence. While some are pastoral or dramatic, most range from satirical and scatological to romantic comedy, sexual farce and picaresque adventures. Always a pleasure to read, and many could trigger ideas for your scripts!

2. FRANÇOIS RABELAIS, *Gargantua and Pantagruel.* Published in several volumes in the mid-sixteenth century in France, Rabelais's freewheeling tales of two giants, Gargantua and his son Pantagruel, were condemned by the authorities at the time as scandalous but have become classics of comic literature. As the Russian literary critic Mikhail Bakhtin has pointed out, Rabelais's work represents perhaps the purest form of carnivalesque literature we have, for Rabelais lived in an area of southern France that still had a very rich tradition of carnival and the spirit of freedom, festivity and fantasy that carnival implies. To read him is to enjoy a master storyteller for whom all appetites are appreciated and celebrated and within whose pages a love of ideas is also reflected. Thus Rabelais ranges from pure farce to serious satire of all phases of French culture, but with the saving virtue of laughter covering and embracing all.

3. LAURENCE STERNE, *The Life and Opinions of Tristram Shandy, Gentleman.* One of the early English novels, Sterne's anarchistic work has fun breaking all the rules. By novel's end, the title character is barely five years old, a fact that reflects Sterne's freewheeling and almost stream of consciousness approach to fiction as well as the fact that the author died before he completed his hilarious tale. A book that has influenced modern writers from James Joyce on, *Tristram Shandy* delights for the pure spontaneity of its nonchronological and nonlogical jumps from topic to topic, character to character, and time period to time period. You can't get any further away from the Well-Made Hollywood Script than this, a fact that makes it worth reading from time to time just to remember that we should take no rules as sacred.

4. JOHN KENNEDY TOOLE, *Confederacy of Dunces.* This is not only the classic New Orleans novel in a fully carnivalesque tone and manner, but a wonderful gallery of minor characters who represent the diversity of that colorful city on the Mississippi. The main character is Ignatius Reilly, a tub of lard who lives at home with his eccentric mother and who believes in geometry and medieval theology. No plot summary can do justice to Toole's mixture of satire and farce, which has some of the funniest dialogue in American fiction. Anarchy, carnival and, finally, romance of sorts mix in this ensemble comedy that makes you laugh out loud, page after page.

5. BOHUMIL HRABAL, *I Served the King of England.* More will be said in chapter 7 about the "Czech touch" in cinema, but that same touch exists in Czech fiction as well: a concern with the simple man and woman in tales that build humor on the absurdity of real life. This short comic picaresque novel follows a simple waiter through his coming of age as man and his loss of innocence in World War II and his sadder but wiser survival in the postwar period. In Hrabal's prose, the horror of the background of war and Communism never destroys the humanizing humor of the characters in the foreground. A valuable lesson for writers of comedy, indeed. It is Hrabal's novel that became the memorable film *Closely Watched Trains,* which we discuss in chapter 7.

6. MILAN KUNDERA, *Immortality.* Kundera has a unique voice in prose, mixing philosophy and politics, sexuality and farce, absurdity and tender nostalgia effortlessly. As a Czech writer who moved to Paris and now writes in French, he is perhaps best known for the novel that became the strongly etched film *The Unbearable Lightness of Being.* Laughter is central to Kundera's feelings about love, life, politics and everything in between, and for Kundera, laughter is a form both of pleasure and of intellectual positioning. *Immortality* is playfully about everything from aging to Beethoven, Elvis, CNN news and loves won and lost.

7. EUDORA WELTY, *The Collected Short Stories of Eudora Welty.* Welty has such keen insight into character and locale. Her beautifully shaped stories transcend the South, but they succeed in large part because she does so strongly evoke a time and a particular place. The humor comes from the characters and their realistic and believable conflicts, struggles, and contradictions. You might also try her award-winning novel, *The Optimist's Daughter.*

8. WITI IHIMAERA, *Bulibasha, King of the Gypsies.* A moving and often joyous and hilarious tale of Maori sheep-shearing families on the east coast of the North Island of New Zealand during the 1950s. Ihimaera's novel is a coming-of-age tale of a young Maori who loves James Dean, Elvis and his Maori culture, especially his earth-mother-like grandmother, who becomes a truly triumphant figure in an often cruelly patriarchal society. Much of the humor is not only that of character but that of the cultural clashes between Maoris, New Zealand whites and American pop culture.

CHAPTER 4

Physical Humor:
From Commedia dell'Arte and Molière to Vaudeville and Silent Screen Comedy

> I traveled with a circus beginning when I was very young so I never went to school. But I learned the three most important things in life from working in the circus: how to put up and take down a tent, how to make people laugh and cry, and how to collect money.
>
> Director George Sidney

Fact: too much of film and television comedy that does not work, or doesn't work as well as it should, is lacking in a solid sense of physical or visual comedy. Paying not only homage but close attention to the techniques and actual accomplishments of the great silent comedians teaches us a lot about writing comedy. Simple translation: let silent comedy help you sharpen your eyes to the nonverbal world of comedy available to you.

Note that I distinguish between physical and visual humor. By physical I mean what an actor is able to do with his or her body and physical objects. Visual comedy is the larger arena, including humor that could, for instance, emerge from the mere framing of a shot.

In *Sherlock Jr.*, we laugh at Keaton's agile gymnastics, balancing on the handlebars of a driverless speeding motorcycle: physical comedy of daring proportions. Yet in the famous cyclone scene in *Steamboat Bill Jr.* (1928), in which Keaton stands still as the whole front wall of a house falls, missing him by inches because he stands exactly where the doorway falls, we have visual comedy, for the laughter is not generated by Keaton the performer but by the camera's capturing of an event.

This chapter is dedicated to what writers of comedy can learn from physical and visual humor. We are especially concerned with Hollywood silent comedy and its roots in the American vaudeville tradition, as well as its much older sources in the Italian commedia dell'arte. We will also cast an eye and ear in the direction of the vaudeville-styled sound comedy as practiced by the Marx Brothers.

Commedia dell'Arte and Molière

Along with Shakespeare, Molière (1622–1673) remains one of the most enduring creators of stage comedy in Europe. And his art and craft owe much to the Italian commedia dell'arte, practiced throughout Europe from roughly 1550 to 1750. During his twelve years of performances around Europe with his wandering troupe of actors, for instance, he at one point shared a theater used by the great Italian actor of the commedia, Fiorelli, who was the creator of one of the most memorable farcical characters, Scaramouche (Molière, ix).

In the commedia tradition, comedy became a series of stock characters or caricatures, and the performances were given on makeshift stages, often in marketplaces, without written texts. Thus, these comedies were half improvisation and half echoes of the set routines, gags and jokes audiences expected. Comic historian Mel Gordon captures the commedia's significance well: "Commedia troupes developed large audiences composed of all social classes. . . . The most popular entertainments of the first part of the twentieth century—motion picture comedy, both silent and sound, and radio comedy—seem closely related to Commedia. Indeed it is hard to conjure images of the Commedia without seeing Chaplin, W. C. Fields, Bert Lahr, the Marx Brothers, Jack Benny, or Laurel and Hardy" (3).

Consider the importance of this enduring comic form. The bottom line, of course, was physical farce, pure and simple. That is, lots of "lower-body" humor, sexual and scatological; lots of set jokes and fast comic exchanges; and only a bare skeleton of a plot on which to hang the humor. Buster Keaton was, knowingly or not, echoing the structure of commedia when he explained that film comedies were "Gags, gags, more gags and a little bit of plot" (Horton, *Buster Keaton's "Sherlock Jr.,"* 12). Commedia audiences gained pleasure from two directions, watching old scenes and familiar stock characters but also laughing and appreciating the improv and variations on a joke or gag or scene the actors were able to pull off.

Lazzi (*lazzo* in the singular) is the term given for the comic routines that were drawn upon during a commedia performance. The exact definition has been given several ways, but Mel Gordon, who has collected many of them, likes the following: "something foolish, witty or metaphorical in word or action" (4). In fact, lazzi collections break down into various categories of jokes and gags, which can be consulted much like "cheat books" in music: there are acrobatic and mimic lazzi, comic violence lazzi, food lazzi, illogical lazzi, props lazzi, sexual and scatological lazzi, social-class lazzi, stupidity lazzi, word play lazzi, stage/life duality lazzi, and transformation lazzi.

Two examples. Call the first "Lazzo of Being Brained": "Scaramouche hits Arlecchino [another clownish figure] so hard on the head that Arlecchino's brains begin to spurt out. Afraid that he will lose his intelligence, Arlecchino sits and feasts on his brains" (Gordon, 23). This is true comic surrealism, embracing the childhood pleasure of playing and joking with food.

Next, a lazzo of comic violence: "Arlecchino disguised as a dentist fools Pantalone into thinking that his rotten teeth are causing his noxious breath. Using oversized or ridiculous tools, the Doctor [Arlecchino] extracts two or more good teeth from Pantalone's mouth" (Gordon, 14). Think how much of comedy is disguise, violence in comic form, trickery, or exaggeration. All are welded humorously in this set routine.

The commedia's (and, as we shall see, Molière's) message to us is that "originality" in humor, satire and plain old farce does not mean that your material is new, but that it is a new variation on some golden comic nuggets, well tried but always ready for recirculation.

Consider Molière's "originality" as an example. Take *The Miser* (*L'Avare*) in particular. Like Menander, Molière centers his comic darts on a "killjoy" old man. Instead of a grouch, he is a skinflint in his sixties. Following all the formulas of Greek and Roman romantic comedy, there is a complex weaving of plots as the Miser, Harpagon, and his son, Cleante, are in love with the same damsel, Marianne. Meanwhile, there is a parallel set of young lovers, scheming servants, go-betweens, additional parents, and a Mae West–like female "playboy," Frosine, described simply as "an adventuress" (Molière, 110).

There is really nothing new at all in this set-up. And in execution we detect Molière's clever use of various lazzi and conventions, including disguises, sudden reversals, tricksters tricked, and more. Molière's genius lies in how well he plays and amplifies these stock figures and patterns.

Frosine well illustrates how masterful Molière was in shaping a comic character. She tries to vamp the Miser out of some money while at the same time trying to fulfill her role as a go-between. Earlier she has confided to another scamp how she works:

> LA FLECHE: Why, Frosine! What are you doing here?
> FROSINE: Following my usual occupation—acting as go-between
> making myself useful to people and picking up what I can from
> such small abilities as I possess. You have to live on your wits in this
> world, you know, and those of us who have no other resources must
> rely on scheming and hard work.
>
> (Molière, 133)

Thus when the Miser walks onstage, we see Frosine ply her trade, trying to convince him that the young woman in question prefers older men—the older the better—over youth.

We have suggested how Shakespeare was able to turn such farce into a form of comedy with emotional resonance. Molière's talent was to celebrate the comic without bitterness, and without trying to change the world through laughter or explore the darker regions of the human heart. John Wood has written that Molière "shows men through their foibles, vain, gullible, self-obsessed, and it is his achievement that under the impact of laughter, by the solvent of comedy, we experience the moment of truth, feel the compulsion of reason, share his compassion for common humanity" (Molière, xv).

Vaudeville and the Marx Brothers

For Americans, the long-popular tradition of vaudeville provides us with the kind of comic experience represented by commedia dell'arte, and indeed by some of the elements of Aristophanes' anarchistic comedy. The same may be said for variety show entertainment as it appeared in many countries, including France and England ("pantomime"), and as it continues today in countries such as Greece ("epitheorisis").

Like the commedia, the vaudeville tradition involved constant travel; appeal to a mass audience; a mixture of farce, music and witty dialogue; and set characters, situations and acts. Most important, vaudeville, like the commedia, was performance-based and thus a comedian-centered comic form. As director George Sidney suggests in the opening quotation, working a live audience in a circus or on a regular vaudeville stage meant learning to make them laugh and cry. That depended on having a wealth of material to draw on and a polished "act" to hang your work on.

As every film history testifies, almost all of the silent film comedy stars, from Keaton and Chaplin to Fatty Arbuckle and beyond, honed their skills through years of performance on the vaudeville circuit. But not just the silent comedians: the early sound comedians including Mae West, Jack Benny, Fred Allen, Bob Hope, Milton Berle, the Marx Brothers and W. C. Fields learned in vaudeville as well. Henry Jenkins has explained how vaudeville came into being towards the end of the nineteenth century, as "saloon" male entertainment was transformed into a milder, less raw form of showmanship aimed at attracting the whole family. Nine hundred theaters were dedicated to vaudeville alone in 1900 (Jenkins, 44). The vaudeville entertainers had to go for the immediate laugh, given that they would have to make the most of the fifteen or twenty minutes allotted them onstage. This led to an anarchistic approach quite different from that of the "regular" stage. As one *Variety* critic wrote in 1906 about vaudeville actors, "It is his business to do and to do quickly everything which an actor on the regular stage is taught and schooled to avoid" (63).

Add up all of these elements and, as in the commedia, we have a form of comedy—both visual and verbal—that falls on the anarchistic side of the scale.

Throw in the fact that cinema itself was more closely tied to vaudeville than to le-gitimate theater in its origins, and we see the importance of the anarchistic to early cinema. In fact, short films were often shown as an "act" in many stage shows, thus beginning a deeply intermingled relationship between the two entertainment media.

The Marx Brothers—Groucho, Harpo and Chico (and Zeppo and Gummo, to a much smaller extent)—spelled joyful comic chaos whenever they hit the screen in a remarkable series of nutty films that still seem as fresh as when they were made, including *Horse Feathers* (1932), *Duck Soup* (1933), *The Cocoanuts* (1929) and *Animal Crackers* (1930), and two made with Irving Thalberg, *A Night at the Opera* (1935) and *A Day at the Races* (1937). We could also discuss W. C. Fields, Mae West and others, but we will concentrate on the Brothers because they were a team, an anarchistic force but with distinct individual identities. I hope this chap-ter, together with the first two chapters, has helped us view them in a very long tra-dition, going all the way back to the commedia and beyond.

Groucho makes it clear in his autobiography that their comedy grew out of their own lives. They grew up in a poor New York family with a beautiful mother from a small town in Germany and a father from France who was a generally un-successful tailor—"He was the only tailor I ever heard of who refused to use a tape measure" (20). Also living with them were his mother's parents, who spoke no English but had been entertainers. The grandmother was a harpist, which explains how Harpo got started even without music lessons. Only Chico was able to finish grammar school, as the others began work at an early age. Add to all of this the need to move frequently to avoid bill collectors, along with the visits of many rel-atives who were themselves characters, and you have the sense of an ongoing car-nival tinged with the tension of poverty.

But with their mother's hard work and drive, they became an act. They played for more than ten years as one of vaudeville's most successful acts, eventu-ally breaking into Broadway and thus "legitimate" laughter in *I'll Say She Is!* in the early 1920s, and moving from there to Hollywood in 1929 after the crash and after Groucho lost much of the money he had earned from Broadway.

Long before the first cameras began to roll on them, then, they were famous for this anarchistic and irreverent humor. Indeed, much of what we have said about Aristophanic comedy is true for the Marx Brothers and other vaudevillians turned film comedians during the early days of sound comedy. *Duck Soup*, with its disrespect for any coherent plot, is like Aristophanes' best works, unified only loosely by its central theme or concept: Rufus T. Firefly (Groucho), the Prime Minister of Freedonia, declares war on Sylvania just for the hell of it. Satire, festiv-ity and pure comic fantasy cross paths with rapid speed, and besides both visual and verbal humor, we have those lyrical moments when Harpo plays the harp and all laughter stops, as in a vaudeville show but also in the same vein as the lyrical moments in Aristophanes' ancient comedies.

The gags and one-liners bubble endlessly out of this freewheeling satire of war (another Aristophanic echo!). But just as memorable is the classic commedia visual work, especially the famous "mirror scene," in which Groucho's every move is exactly duplicated in a doorway. Such timing and craft goes far beyond simplistic slapstick. Besides being really funny, the scene leaves us with a sense of wonder too: how did they do it?!

Add Groucho's frequent asides to the audience (that is, the camera), which he learned from working live audiences, and we have yet another key element of anarchistic comedy since Aristophanes. Groucho put it this way:

> On the stage, I frequently stepped out of character and spoke directly to the audience. After the first day's shooting on *Cocoanuts,* the producer . . . said, "Groucho, you can't step out of character and talk to the audience." Like all people who are glued to tradition, he was wrong. I spoke to them in every picture I appeared in. (Sometimes they answered back. This I found rather disconcerting.) Nevertheless the movie industry went on just the same, turning out its share of good and bad pictures, and nobody seemed to care whether I stepped out of character.
>
> (*Memoirs of a Mangy Lover,* 172)

Groucho is the *eiron,* the ironic wise guy always mouthing off at a rapid pace. Chico is the womanizing braggart *alazon,* always in trouble, while Harpo is both a trickster figure and a poet with a harp—that is, a clown. And, finally, Zeppo, whose presence is not heavily felt in most of the films, is the "killjoy" straight guy.

To replay a Marx Brothers film from time to time is to help recharge our anarchistic batteries as writers.

I personally feel deep regrets that I never got to see American vaudeville on the stage. However, I saw the British equivalent, the pantomime shows, when I was a kid, and for over twenty years now I have thoroughly enjoyed the Greek counterpart, called the "epitheorises." But what about the legacy of such anarchistic comedy today? The echoes are felt in such films as *Wayne's World, Animal House* and *Blues Brothers.* Yet as we shall explain more fully in chapter 6, while these kinds of films are driven by an anarchistic energy and focus, their origin is much more clearly from stand-up comedy and television rather than a living tradition of vaudeville. In spirit, however, such films represent a similar joyful send-up of all authority and rigidity of social positioning, including romance, politics and family values.

CHAPTER 5

Sound Comedy:
American Screwball Romantic Comedy, Then and Now

I never imagined that mere physical activity could be so stimulating.
Katharine Hepburn to Humphrey Bogart
in John Huston's *The African Queen*

To a very large degree, sound comedy has meant romantic comedy, and in the United States romantic comedy can be identified as screwball comedy in one form or another. Let's take a closer look at what writers of comedy should know about this vibrant genre.

"You make me want to be a better man." It's Jack Nicholson playing Melvin Udall, the rich and famous sixty-something New York romance author who happens to be a recluse and a wicked misanthrope in his real life. "That's maybe the best compliment of my life," says Helen Hunt portraying Carol Connelly, a struggling single parent and waitress in her thirties with a sick son. "Well, maybe I overshot a little," rejoins a slyly smirking, slow-eyed Nicholson, "because I was aiming at just enough to keep you from walking out." Together these two are fire and ice, oil and water—seemingly complete opposites. But by the time James L. Brooks's award-winning *As Good As It Gets* (1997) is over, a quirky romance is under way, as the old cliché—opposites attract—is given fresh, memorable and very funny new coinage in a script by Brooks and Mark Andrus.

Silent film comedy leaned heavily to anarchistic and physical humor, as we explored in chapter 4. But once sound appeared, Hollywood imported New York playwrights, and that meant dialogue comedy, more specifically contemporary ironic comedies of manners and the battle of the sexes, especially among the idle rich. As a basis of what has become known as "screwball romantic comedy," we should review the points made about Shakespearean romantic comedy, for the tradition does trace back that far and beyond. We noted that Shakespeare was not afraid to be experimental, that he explored the complexity of relationships caught in the jaws of blind passion and idealized love, that he made use of sparkling dialogue, that he often went for straight-on farce both for the fun of it and to highlight the reality of the love stories, that he created strong female characters who were as bright as or brighter than the male figures, and he was not afraid to use touches of magic or the fantastic.

American screwball comedy embraces all of the above and one more important element: the romantic couple come from very different social backgrounds. More specifically, one is usually of the upper or wealthy class and the other of the middle or lower class. It is no surprise that this American version of romantic comedy developed in the 1930s, not only as sound came to the movies but as America was working its way through the Depression and thus reevaluating its very values. As film scholar Thomas Schatz comments, "By restructuring the fast-paced upper-crust romance, the screwball comedy dominated Depression-era screen comedy and provided that period's most significant and engaging social commentary" (151).

There are, for starters, four characteristics that writers of comedy need to know about screwball romance:

1. The genre is both the most popular form of American screen comedy and the most enduring.
2. The genre builds on the traditions that have gone before but proves itself very adaptable to changes in cultural norms and perceptions.
3. The genre is a fascinating reflection of the state of male-female relationships at the time the film is made.
4. The genre can't help but offer social commentary as well.

These points hold for classics we will mention such as Ernst Lubitsch's *Trouble in Paradise* (1932), Frank Capra's *It Happened One Night* (1934), Howard Hawks's *Bringing Up Baby* (1938), George Cukor's *Dinner at Eight* (1933) and Preston Sturges's script for *The Good Fairy* (1935); for 1950s films such as Billy Wilder's *Some Like It Hot,* John Huston's *African Queen* and John Ford's *The Quiet Man;* for more recent examples such as Woody Allen's *Annie Hall,* Sydney Pollack's *Tootsie,* Garry Marshall's *Pretty Woman,* Susan Seidelman's *Desperately Seeking Susan,* Penny Marshall's *Jumpin' Jack Flash,* Nora Ephron's *Sleepless in Seattle* and *You've Got Mail,* Michael Lehmann's *The Truth about Cats and Dogs* and Australian P. J. Hogan's *My Best Friend's Wedding* and *Muriel's Wedding*); and for more offbeat films such as Steven Soderbergh's *sex, lies and videotape,* Jeremiah Chechik's *Benny and Joon,* Kevin Smith's *Chasing Amy,* and Bobby and Peter Farrelly's *There's Something about Mary.*

Screwballs in the 1930s

The 1930s were the heyday of screwball comedies, and I highly recommend that writers of comedy view and review films by Ernst Lubitsch and George Cukor, "pre-screwball" directors of sophisticated comedies, and by the golden screwball filmmakers, Frank Capra, Howard Hawks and Preston Sturges, for starters.

Frank Capra has deservedly been celebrated for kicking off the genre with Clark Gable and Claudette Colbert in *It Happened One Night*. Colbert is the rich girl running away from home to experience the "real" world who hooks up with newspaper reporter Gable. As they fall in love, he educates her to the ways of the world; she catches on quickly and even surpasses him from time to time. In one scene, after he has explained how to hitchhike, she goes him one better by sticking out her leg and pulling up her dress a notch. Result: an instant ride from the first car passing by. This Academy Award–winning box office hit sends out a clear populist message that became Frank Capra's trademark: good old American middle-class common sense is a whole lot better than all the money and crazy ideas of the rich, powerful and famous.

Howard Hawks's *Bringing Up Baby* pushes the genre further. Katharine Hepburn is the spoiled Connecticut heiress with a pet leopard, "Baby," who turns completely upside down the life of Cary Grant, an absent-minded zoologist whose project is to find the missing bone for a dinosaur skeleton he is assembling in the Museum of Natural History in New York. Scripted by the great Dudley Nichols and Hagar Wilde from one of Wilde's stories, Hawks's film has won the praise of numerous critics, including Leonard Maltin, who calls it "the definitive screwball comedy and one of the fastest, funniest films ever made" (171).

While Capra's film is grounded in realism—a couple on the road in Depression America—Hawks's comedy, embracing leopards and dinosaurs, is much farther "out there" as a nutty, fairy-tale kind of comedy. The dialogue crackles, the situations (including their brief time in jail) are completely absurd, and the mileage of putting a pet leopard (not to mention an escaped leopard from a local circus) in between this bumbling couple simply multiplies the laughter. Both "lovers" are innocents here, though each is an expert in his (dinosaurs) or her (idle rich) own territory. Neither functions well at all in the "real" world, creating a hilarious comedy of cross-purposes.

The final embrace scene is one of my all-time favorites in American comedy. We end where we began, with Cary Grant up on the scaffolding in the museum with his beloved dinosaur. In comes delightful but air-headed Hepburn, climbing up a ladder to speak with Grant. When the ladder starts to fall, Grant literally embraces Hepburn, and the crashing ladder totally destroys his life's work: the huge dinosaur skeleton comes crashing down, leaving, in long shot, Grant holding Hepburn. We laugh and realize that this couple will do fine forever after, since Grant does not express anger, nor does he let go of Hepburn in revenge! This long-shot embrace is love if there ever was love.

Preston Sturges became Hollywood's first screenwriting director, winning an Oscar in 1944 for his anarchistic, half-screwball comedy *Hail the Conquering Hero*. But before he began directing in 1940, he had written some of America's best stage comedies, such as *Strictly Dishonorable*, and a string of sparkling screen comedies for other directors, such as *Easy Living, Diamond Jim, If I Were King* and *Remember the Night*. Watch any Sturges film for the dialogue, the fine line between character and caricature, the completely nutty premise of the film, the bevy of entertaining minor characters and the sheer comic "density" of each scene. His script for *Easy Living* (1937, Mitchell Leisen, director) is a Sturges screwball comedy at its best. Mary (Jean Arthur) is a working gal who, by chance, happens to be in the way when a billionaire Wall Street investor (Edward Arnold) throws a mink coat off his Fifth Avenue apartment balcony. Two unlikely worlds are suddenly joined, as Arthur naively tries to return the coat and winds up being involved in a world she never dreamed of, as this fish-out-of-water tale joins her with the billionaire's son (Ray Milland), who is trying to earn his own way through life as a waiter. Somehow the film manages to be a seamless light romantic comedy and, at the same time, a very funny satirical look at the stock market, the superrich and American capitalism in general.

Screwball Variation:
Comedy of Remarriage

We usually think of romance as the coming together of young lovers, full of innocence and enthusiasm, their futures spread out before them like a fairy tale of "happy forever after." But many of the most memorable screwball comedies are what Stanley Cavell (in *Pursuits of Happiness*) aptly labels the "comedy of remarriage," about couples, married or not, who separate and then rejoin, finally accepting each other for who and what they are.

Howard Hawks's *His Girl Friday* (1940), from a Ben Hecht and Charles Lederer script, is a memorable example of such a comedy. Actually a remake of *The Front Page* (1931), itself based on the highly popular stage comedy that Hecht wrote with Charles MacArthur, with the gender of one character switched, *His Girl Friday* traces the hilarious recourtship and remarriage of a newspaper editor (Cary Grant) and ace reporter (Rosalind Russell). In the opening scene, Russell barges into ex-husband Grant's office to announce she is marrying a man from Albany, New York (Ralph Bellamy). As they share a meal and begin to fight in familiar ways again, we (and then they) realize they cannot live without each other. What Hecht and Lederer do so well in this take on screwball comedy is demonstrate both how the second time around can be even more fun and how two people can be drawn closer to each other by sharing their profession, in this case the newspaper business.

The ending has the perfect ironic wink that comedies of remarriage tend to have. Hildy and Walter have just been remarried and are about to take their honeymoon. (Part of what broke them apart to begin with was that they never had a first honeymoon, because of deadlines they had to meet on big stories.) Just as they are leaving for that long-postponed time together alone, the phone rings. Another big story is breaking: they look at each other, smile, and there is no doubt this time. The honeymoon will have to wait, once more! This time, however, they joyfully go off to cover it *together.* An embrace ending with a wry and knowing "we've been there before" smile.

Stretching the Boundaries of Screwball

The adaptability and flexibility of the genre appears endless. Consider two examples:

John Huston's *The African Queen* (1951), with a script by Huston and James Agee from the E. M. Forster novel, thrusts Humphrey Bogart (who won an Oscar for his performance) and Katharine Hepburn together in World War I Africa. He is the gin-guzzling Canadian adventurer and man of the world; she is the completely innocent sister of a frustrated British missionary (Robert Morley), who dies of a stroke once the Germans burn his church and the African village. Forced to flee with Bogart, Hepburn comes into her own and matches Bogart's world-weary cynicism with her single-minded anarchistic energy and true derring-do. Hepburn is transformed by her circumstances and the challenge of the African river in a small boat, while Bogart is transformed by his contact with Hepburn, who leads him to give up booze and attempt, against his better judgment, to attack with a homemade torpedo the German gunboat patrolling the large lake at the end of the river.

Huston and team push the boundaries of screwball by mixing in action, history and adventure, and by placing the whole unfolding romance in Africa. He also took a chance by making it a romance of a couple over forty! The results are still fresh, and who can forget the look of pure rapture on Hepburn's face as she steers them through battering rapids, the surprise embrace and kiss once they survive the rapids, and the wonderfully ironic ending as they are married by the German officer on the gunboat, who having condemned them to death as spies, ends by saying, "I declare you man and wife, now proceed with the execution." Of course they survive, and they succeed in the torpedoing of the ship. This romance was made, if not in heaven, in the leech-infested waters of the Belgian Congo.

Kevin Smith's *Chasing Amy* (1997) pushes the genre further than it has ever gone in treating bisexuality. We should mention that one hit of 1997, *My Best Friend's Wedding,* was memorable in large part because of Julia Roberts's friendship with her gay editor, George (Rupert Everett), who helps her through the ordeal of her best (male) friend's wedding. But Kevin Smith, who gave us the no-budget surprise independent hit *Clerks* (1994), absolutely follows the premise that in love, war and comedy nothing is sacred, as straight cartoonist Holden McNeil (Ben Affleck) falls for lesbian Alyssa Jones (Joey Lauren Adams). What follows is magnificent dialogue and scenes that are very funny and very real at the same time, as Holden goes through every possible mental and emotional state in dealing with Alyssa as well as his own identity and sexuality. The film reflects the complexity not just of any relationship, but of changing American times as well. Not a perfect film by any measure, but an exciting and daring one, and admirable for that alone.

The ending, in which they finally do *not* get together again but become more caring and wiser individuals because of their encounter, is perfect.

Close-up on Screwball: *As Good As It Gets*

As Good As It Gets is not a pale contemporary imitation of a golden thirties screwball comedy. It is an absolutely vibrant, outrageously timely take on postmodern end-of-the-century romance that thrives in part because it functions knowingly and joyfully within the tradition of screwball comedy. James L. Brooks and Mark Andrus practice what I have urged throughout: they know their comic history and traditions, and they allow themselves the total freedom to explode mimes of any sort that pleases them.

Let us run the film through the basic screwball codes to see how it plays creatively with the tradition:

1. *The "lovers" come from different backgrounds and social classes.* Jack Nicholson plays Melvin, a rich snob living cut off from the "real" world, and Helen Hunt plays Carol, a working woman, simple but very smart.

2. *One of the "lovers" is a screwball.* Look at Melvin's trail of nutty acts and his list of quirky beliefs and habits, beginning when he drops a poodle down a garbage chute and continuing with his obsessive-compulsive behavior about eating, washing and walking along the sidewalk (avoid all cracks!)—and also his acts of generosity, such as providing a top specialist on a house call for Carol's asthmatic son.

3. *The female character is as bright as or brighter than the male lead.* Richard Corliss's description of Helen Hunt is also a summary of Carol in the film:

> She doesn't ratchet her I.Q. down 15 or 20 points to make the boys feel better. She refuses to play the little girl or the doomed diva. Or the perfect woman, either, for she knows that flourishing at the end of this millennium is an art and a craft, and not many are up to it. But she has the grit to try. She attracts men, and appeals to other women, by being her own complicated

self. *Determined woman, staunch friend, strong mate: the sensible siren* [emphasis added].

("Mad about Her")

Carol is the one who finally cuts through Melvin's defensive curmudgeon posture and is clever enough both to handle him and to appreciate his "screwball" humanity inside.

4. *The film captures the complexity of relationships caught between passion and idealized love.* Nothing would seem more unlikely than the coming together of these two. She has been badly wounded in love and has a child to prove it and to provide for. He was damaged long in the past, but it is to Brooks and Andrus's credit that we are never given any simple explanation as to why or how Melvin became such an insult-hurling misanthrope. And yet his fortune has been made writing about idealized love, even if he appears to shun it in his own life. Carol's actions are a winning mess of contradictions as well. One of the best scenes is surely when she runs over to his place in the rain to tell him she will never sleep with him just because he has provided a top specialist for her son. When she finishes her speech at his door, she catches on to what we and Melvin have seen all along: the rain has made her blouse quite transparent. While at first Melvin shows only mild annoyance, he now appears impressed with her vitality and physical beauty.

5. *Zany minor characters and subplots help define the main couple.* Brooks and Andrus have penned a very funny gay couple in Melvin's building, Simon Bishop (Greg Kinnear) and Frank Sachs (Cuba Gooding Jr.), whose lives become intertwined with Melvin's once he tosses Simon's dog down the garbage chute. Subsequently, after a gay bashing, Simon needs help in caring for the dog and then for himself. Not only does Melvin's gradual and at first grudging acceptance of Simon and Frank trace his growing unfolding as a caring figure, but these moments also include many of the best broadly humorous scenes in the film. All of this culminates in this great exchange late in the film:

SIMON: I love you, Melvin.

MELVIN: I tell you, buddy, I'd be the luckiest man alive if that's what did it for me.

6. *Sparkling dialogue.* As witnessed by the above quote, much of the film is memorable for the swift and witty exchanges. Part of the fun of the dialogue is the gap Brooks and Andrus expose between what is being said and what is actually going on between Melvin and Carol. Take the following example:

CAROL: Do you want to dance?

MELVIN: I've been thinking about that for a while.

CAROL: (*Standing up*) Well?

MELVIN: No.

Concise, pithy, to the point and totally in character. Melvin would not be "nice" and say, "Well, I would like to but I'm not a good dancer" or "Maybe later" or "I'd be too self-conscious as an old guy on the floor with such a looker as you!" And yet part of what works so well in this exchange is that we know Melvin cares for Carol. He just has a screwball way of expressing it.

7. *The film comments on the times.* The message of the film is the old one of redemption through love, and redemption involves acceptance and the embracing of values different from your own. The Nicholson figure would be a very unfunny character if viewed outside the confines of comedy: he is a bigot and a racist, and, as Roger Ebert comments, "He hurls racist, sexist, homophobic and physical insults at everyone he meets." But it is part of the appeal of comedy that narratives can be constructed in which new communities of friends and lovers accept each other for who they are.

Furthermore, through the lens of comedy Brooks and Andrus offer glimpses of the difficulties of life for a single bright female parent, for gays who become victims of gay bashers, and for less-than-stereotypical romantic couples. As odd a couple as Melvin and Carol turn out to be, there is beneath it all a lot more realism in *As Good As It Gets* than in a sappier romance built on pure stereotypes, such as *Pretty Woman* with its handsome rich guy (Richard Gere) and whore with a heart of gold (Julia Roberts).

8. *The embrace ending is also ironic.* No wedding bells in *As Good As It Gets.* Instead we have Melvin and Carol standing outside a New York bakery, waiting to get some of the first rolls of the morning (does this qualify as a "half-baked" ending?). It is an embrace in that a romance has been born. And it is ironic in hindsight in that this coming together is nothing either they or we would have predicted. We can add too that it is a quiet ending. After everything from slapstick to flying insults, Brooks fades out, pulling back, watching a man and a woman talking on an early-morning city street.

CHAPTER 6

Comedy and Television:
Stand-up, Sitcom and Everything in Between

Learn from the rich legacy of television comedy in all its forms. Take inspiration from the best of what makes you laugh, add in what you have learned from the non-television comic traditions we have discussed, and then take on chapter 10 (for a close look at *Seinfeld* and *The Simpsons*) and chapter 12, which asks you to come up with your own comedy series.

There is a lot about television per se that lends itself well to comedy. British media scholar Steve Neale has noted, for instance, that "Television itself, with its separate segments, slots, and schedules, and its different genres and types of programs, can be considered a variety form" (179). We begin with the simple observation that television, in one form or genre or another, has an almost endless need of writers of comedy, gags, jokes, episodes, and comic films. Far more writers of comedy are working in television than in feature films. What I propose in this chapter is to survey the landscape so that you have a clearer idea of which part of the comic television spectrum you wish to approach in chapter 12, when you write with television in mind.

Garry Marshall is one of the most successful writers of television comedy ever, having worked on *Laverne & Shirley, I Love Lucy, The Dick Van Dyke Show, The Odd Couple, Happy Days,* and *Mork & Mindy.* He feels that comedy is stronger than ever on American prime-time television and showing no signs of slowing down. He offers ten tips for today's sitcom writers. I include them here because I think they apply to all television comedy writing:

1. Write from your life.
2. Write for the Stars.
3. Use swear words when pitching scripts.
4. Learn to write physical and visual comedy.
5. Demonstrate you can save the producer a dollar.
6. Marry well, or date superbly.
7. Find a good writing partner.
8. Don't blow your own horn.
9. Find out what the other writers hate to write and write about that to establish your own identity.
10. Follow proper cast party protocol. (Marshall, 24–26)

I leave it to you to think about items 6 and 10! But the rest are most useful and sensible for all of your television writing, from network material to local cable.

Let us turn to the two major areas of television comedy, stand-up-oriented comedy and situation comedy, and see what elements each embraces. We will then look into two variations of sitcom writing: the ensemble comedy and animated episodic comedy.

Stand-up: Anarchistic Comedians

"Stand-up" did not come into popular coinage until the 1960s (Bushman, 23), but we should be aware that the practice in the United States of standing up and making a room full of people laugh stretches back to Mark Twain, who toured widely as a professional lecturer, and even earlier. Stand-up roots can also be seen in minstrel shows and later in vaudeville, both for team comedy—a comic talking to a straight man or woman—and for monologists. Will Rogers, for instance, combined his western persona and stage presence as a clown, and as we have outlined in chapter 4, so many comics, from Bob Hope to Milton Berle, got their start in direct vaudeville performance. Stand-up comedians have traditionally done well on television in variety shows, talk shows such as *The Tonight Show*, and the sitcom.

The stand-up's main appeal is as a kind of social mirror reflecting the constant changes in our cultural values and attitudes. Think about the careers of Jackie Gleason, Mort Sahl, Lenny Bruce, George Carlin, Mike Nichols and Elaine May, Bob Newhart, Jonathan Winters, Shelley Berman, Nipsey Russell, the Smothers Brothers, Dick Gregory, Phyllis Diller, Woody Allen, Joan Rivers, Carol Burnett, Whoopi Goldberg, Lily Tomlin, Joey Bishop, Ellen DeGeneres, or Jerry Seinfeld, to mention a few, and you can trace many of the vast shifts in American culture over the past fifty years. There were those who pushed the envelope on social change and injustice, such as Dick Gregory and Lenny Bruce in the late 1950s and the 1960s, and then there are those in the 1990s such as Paul Reiser, Jay Leno and Jerry Seinfeld, who reflect a less politically involved and much more sardonic and narcissistic involvement with what critic Tom Shayles has called "the everyday trivia of modern life" (Bushman, 48).

We can consider the stand-up comedian an anarchist to the degree that his or her task is to be disruptive, to push the envelope of acceptability in language, taste, stories and subject matter. He or she tends to make fun of sex, politics, religion, manners, gender and racial issues, everything. And yet, the rules of stand-up are clear: the person up there has diplomatic immunity to say and do just about anything. We are, once again, defining the same freedom that we have traced the carnivalesque as embodying: the complete freedom of fantasy and festivity, but shared with a group and therefore accepted as a special kind of community that joins comedian and audience.

Back up a moment, however, to acknowledge how much of television comedy—both stand-up and sitcom—derives from radio. In the United States, radio developed a rather straightforward variety-show format early on, often taken almost completely from the vaudeville circuit. Shows such as *The Eveready Hour, Roxy and His Gang* and *The Chase and Sanborn Hour* put forth a mix of "slapstick on the air" with music, routines, jokes and running commentary. But what has come to be called "situation comedy" really started on the radio, as stars realized if they had a comic persona and a set character, the jokes would be more unified and effective. The characters were consistent; it was the show's "situation" that changed. Jack Benny turned out to be an early pioneer in situation (or, more accurately, "character") comedy with his radio show, which lasted until 1955 (Neale & Krutnik, 215). This became true also of *Amos 'n Andy* and shows by Fred Allen and by George Burns and Gracie Allen as they moved from a daily fifteen-minute format to a weekly thirty-minute show (ibid., 219). But television restored the visual element that vaudeville had so depended on, and early television was once more able to showcase anarchistic, vaudeville-like variety shows.

Now let us return to anarchistic, spirited stand-up television comedy: in the past twenty-five years in the United States, *Saturday Night Live* has been a prime example of this tradition.

Skit Comedy

What was and is the essence of *Saturday Night Live,* which has turned twenty-five and suggests no signs of aging? Creator Lorne Michaels puts it best: "The show is working when we're doing exactly what you were hoping we would be doing, in a way that you hadn't thought we'd be doing it. In a way that is truly funny and original" (Cader, 8). *Not* delivering what you expect, therefore—that element of surprise—is definitely what we look forward to from these wildly anarchistic comedians. They are absolutely exploded mimes, and they explode regularly every Saturday evening.

But Michaels goes farther, to suggest what a community of laughter they have created. He says that this approach "is in the best sense, broadcasting—when a lot of people are having the same experience at the same time and talking about it the next day. That will always be the core experience of the show" (ibid.). Furthermore, he emphasizes that what counts most is *writing* and *performance.*

The role of writers? James Downey, a longtime writer and producer on the show, makes it clear that the biggest misconception about the show is that there is a lot of improvisation going on. The opposite is the case: everything is scripted.

Thus the writing is key. The hardest part of the show these days? "It's hard to find fresh, sincere, non-ironic stuff that hasn't already been worked over," notes Downey (Cader, 28).

At the heart of the show is the anarchistic freedom to try just about anything and everything. Furthermore, there is the fun of bringing on so many different kinds of guests, ranging from early guests such as George Carlin, Paul Simon and Buck Henry on down to Ralph Nader, Julian Bond, Steve Martin, O. J. Simpson, Frank Zappa and the Rolling Stones, to mention but a few.

But within the framework of "anything goes," certain themes, formulas and patterns have become, if not standard, certainly familiar. Characters and motifs recur over the years. Think, for instance, of their parodies of commercials ("Green & Fazio Law Offices: Dial 1-500-HARASSS" or the two-seater Love Toilet, for instance). Samurai skits in the early years (Samurai Divorce!), Gumby, Church Lady, the Sweeney Sisters, Hans and Franz, Wayne's World, Pat, the Richmeister. Now consider the sense of total carnival that has been true for each performer on the show.

Because the stand-up tradition of American television represents a coming together of vaudeville influences (particularly in its loose structure), commedia dell'arte (physical farce) and nightclub acts (wit and joke routines), it is worth looking back at two shows from those glory days of live comedy in the 1950s: *The Ernie Kovaks Show* and *The Steve Allen Show.*

Ernie Kovaks was Hungarian by birth and acknowledges that this ethnic background added to his wry take on the universe as he was growing up in New Jersey. He broke into live radio at a time when he was allowed to be quite anarchistic: he did his own gags, sound effects, routines in a wildly surrealistic vein. When he moved to television, he had already developed a wonderfully nutty sense of absurdist humor, using sound and verbal humor. And he took to visual humor, both as a mime and combining visuals and sound, very swiftly. He was, in fact, like all the Marx Brothers in one person. I can remember, for instance, being cracked up as a kid by his Nairobi Trio—three gorillas (Ernie being one) playing one nutty little tune over and over again—which appeared regularly on the show. Some of his shows are available on tape, and it's worth seeing them. He also had the freedom to do his own ads for Dutch Master cigars, which sponsored the show. With his beautiful wife, Edie Allen, playing both the beautiful blonde and the "straight gal" to his outrageous behavior, he would create commercials that were often funnier than many of the routines on the show. In one, for instance, two cowboys face off for a shootout, one of them smoking a Dutch Master cigar. They draw and shoot, and the Dutch Master cowboy is shot full of holes we can see through—with smoke pouring out of each hole! And the ad simply ends with "Smoke Dutch Master Cigars!"

Steve Allen also combined a vaudeville-like mixture of humor, music (he played piano), skits and a carnivalesque sense of playfulness and experimentation, but in an hour-long format. With a set group of cronies to help out, including Don Knotts and others, every Sunday evening was a delight. There was, for instance, the "Man in the Street" segment, where the camera went outside the studio theater for live interviews with bystanders and the show's regulars.

In both cases, there was a more easygoing attitude about putting together live and taped skits, set characters and new comic experiments for that overall feeling we all brought to watching such shows: "What will they do next?" It's worth building new shows from that same spirit of playfulness and daring experimentation.

Sitcom Then and Now

How many millions of people around the world—not just the United States —have been entertained week after week, year after year, and then indefinitely in reruns by shows with names like *I Love Lucy* and *The Phil Silvers Show* in the 1950s, and *Father Knows Best, Leave It to Beaver* and *Ozzie and Harriet* in the 1960s. In the 1970s we laughed with reality-based shows such as *All in the Family, The Mary Tyler Moore Show* and *Maude*. The 1980s delivered *The Cosby Show, M*A*S*H, Roseanne, Cheers, Murphy Brown*. And the 1990s delighted one audience or another with *Seinfeld, The Simpsons, Ellen, Northern Exposure, The Fresh Prince of Bel-Air, Mad about You, Grace under Fire, Everybody Loves Raymond, Buffy the Vampire Slayer, Friends, Frasier,* and *King of the Hill*.

Technically, "sitcom" defines half-hour episodic comedy (thus *Northern Exposure* and other hour-long shows would not qualify if we were being strict about terms). Perhaps the main point to make about any definition of sitcom is that at heart, *the genre depicts set characters and a set location,* which is traditionally the home or the workplace. As James L. Brooks said about working with *The Mary Tyler Moore Show,* "When somebody called *Mary* a sitcom, we'd be furious. We weren't doing sitcom. We were doing character comedy" (Neale, 236).

American Family Values

Many of the shows concern families, which may be upper middle class (*The Cosby Show*) or working class (*All in the Family, Roseanne*), single parent (*Grace under Fire*) or black (*Fresh Prince of Bel-Air*). The reason for such comic focusing over the years on families is well known. Television is in the home, and home means, for millions, a family and family territory. Family sitcoms thus acknowledge the importance as well as the problems of American family life, and by each episode's close must re-assert the value of the family unit as more significant than any individual disagreements.

Recognize also the changing American values represented in family sitcoms. *I Love Lucy* (1951–57) was popular after World War II, as American women were trying to redefine their roles within home and workplace after years of having gained independence outside the home. The early 1960s gave us fantasy white middle-class families such as the one in *Ozzie and Harriet,* with their guitar-strumming son, Ricky Nelson. And the 1970s brought us Norman Lear's more realistic shows such as *All in the Family,* which were not afraid to show a working-class family dealing with prejudice, stereotypes and controversial issues. The 1980s offered a wide spectrum of family values, ranging from *Roseanne*'s overweight, blue-collar popularity to *The Cosby Show*'s fantasy role models for a rising African American, affluent middle class. Finally, the 1990s have given us animated families (*The Simpsons* and *King of the Hill*), brothers as family raising children when the wife of one is dead (*Full House*), young two-career couples trying to balance career and marriage (*Mad about You*), and, as we will mention, families made of chosen friends (*Friends*) or simply roommates and neighbors and ex-girlfriends (*Seinfeld*).

In addition, observe how many sitcoms could be better described as "stand-up sitcoms" in that the stars began in stand-up. Thus I would emphasize the flexibility of the genre, which appears elastic enough to take on elements of anarchistic comedy within a group of set characters.

Variation #1: Ensemble and/or Just Single

From *M*A*S*H* to *Friends,* episodic comedy has also promoted the notion of friends as family, with all the positive and negative implications of such a statement. Such a group of diverse characters is held together by friendship or necessity or both. As Mick Eaton writes, "The necessity for the continuity of character and situation from week to week allows for the possibility of comedy being generated by the fact that the characters are somehow stuck with each other" (37).

We will take a close look at *Seinfeld* in chapter 10, but there is a very simple attraction to the ensemble comedy series: we get to see seemingly endless combinations of people who can get on each other's nerves but who also pull together against Outside Forces that threaten them in some way. That tension propels us from week to week, be it in the battlefield hospital of *M*A*S*H,* the bar crowd in *Cheers,* or the split between office and apartment life in *Friends, Ellen* and other shows focused on singles.

This is definitely not easy comedy to write, for it means you have to develop strong characters, each of whom is interesting enough to hold our attention. Then there is the need to hit that balance between mutual compatibility and mutual antagonism. *Northern Exposure,* for instance, while technically labeled a "drama" series, nevertheless had us laughing each week with its ensemble of eccentrics all living in a never-never land called Alaska. What worked so well in shows such as *Cheers, Northern Exposure* and *M*A*S*H* was that the writers allowed each character his or her space to be an eccentric and for the group to ultimately embrace that eccentricity.

And yet acceptance does not translate as harmony, for that would be too easy. As John Vorhaus rightly says, "The trick to making ensemble comedy work is to layer in sufficient lines of conflict *within* the group to make the story worth watching. It's not enough to have a bunch of scientists battling a Japanese monster—you want them at each other's throats as well" (68).

Variation #2: Animation

Animation has long ruled the children's market, not only in Disney's features but on Saturday-morning television. *The Simpsons,* however, completely rewrote the rules for a crossover sitcom, reaching both children and adults, as we shall examine in chapter 10. And more recently, *King of the Hill* proved that an animated family—Bobby, Hank and Peggy—could draw a wide audience without the over-the-top surrealistic exaggeration of *The Simpsons*. Animation will surely prove to have staying power with other series to come, and the bottom line is this: with animation you can literally do anything you wish to do.

Think how well animation is suited to build both on stand-up comedy and on sitcoms and to shape a show or episode or film to the particular talents of a given comedian. Review just one sequence: in Disney's *Aladdin* (1992), Robin Williams, perfectly cast as the Genie, pulls off a tour de force "routine" once he is liberated from the lamp for the first time, aided by the imaginative visuals of the animators, who are able to give form to Williams's carnival of voices, acts, accents, personas and parodies.

I do have one piece of advice for writers hoping to break into the animation market. Try sitting through a whole Saturday morning's worth of children's shows to see how lame most animation has become. And then check your nearest specialty video shop to watch the experimental animation, claymation and stop-motion object-centered "animations" that have been produced in Eastern and Central Europe over the years. Pay particular attention to Czech, Zagreb (Croatian and Yugoslav) and Polish animators to see how imaginative animation can be.

CHAPTER 7

Comedies from around the World

Above all, be well and cheerful.
Louka to Kolya in *Kolya*

As an American, I am very aware that it is close to ridiculous to speak of "foreign" humor, for Hollywood and even American independent cinema and television are the beneficiaries of so many comic traditions from abroad. Chaplin came from Britain, Frank Capra from Italy; Preston Sturges was raised as much in France as in the States; Billy Wilder emigrated from Austria; and the list goes on. Yet there are distinct traits and talents that each culture offers, and this chapter is dedicated to "viva the difference."

This chapter is a vote for renting a number of other-than-American comedies to expand our horizons beyond the borders we usually inhabit, geographically, spiritually and creatively as writers.

Britain
Eccentric Anarchists: Peter Sellers, Monty Python, The Full Monty, *and Beyond*

The British have their own brand of humor that celebrates and satirizes eccentricity. In its outrageous forms the pattern is clearly anarchistic, and in its milder species, British comedy as seen by those outside the British Isles is, well, simply *odd* or wryly understated in ways American comedy misses. The tradition runs from the early Ealing Studio comedies of the 1950s such as Charles Crichton's *The Lavender Hill Mob* (1950) and *Passport to Pimlico* (1949) down to the Ealing-like nutty humor of Crichton's highly successful *A Fish Called Wanda* (1989) and even the in-your-face dark humor of *Trainspotting* (1996), in which characters swimming inside a toilet bowl make the drug world of Scotland come to terrifying life, and the off-the-wall humor of the claymation television series of *Wallace and Gromit*.

Peter Cattaneo's *The Full Monty*, written by a rookie screenwriter, Simon Beaufoy, was the surprise comedy hit of 1997, winding up as the largest-grossing (and the word is playfully used too!) British film ever, pulling in over $100 million by 1998. Any film that does that well deserves our full attention. We will briefly chart several layers of British humor in this section, but clearly *The Full Monty* represents a strong vein of working-class British humor that has a long history, especially as it also intertwined in the 1960s with the "angry young man" films and dramas of the day.

Described as the "world's first full-frontal fairy tale" (Essex, 16), *The Full Monty* is an anarchistic ensemble comedy with a warm emotional center and sociopolitical echoes. Propelling this comedy is Gaz's (Robert Carlyle) idea to save himself and his unemployed steelworking mates by creating a male strip review, a ludicrous parody of male hunk reviews such as the Chippendales. Beaufoy's script never looks down on these misfits at the bottom of the British social ladder. In fact, a large part of the success of the script is that each character is given his own identity, space and place, walking that very thin line between parody (and thus caricature) and fully rounded character development. Thus we come to enjoy Dave, Lamper, Gerald, Horse and Guy and the women who try to cope with them. At the center of the whole carnivalesque show, however, is a simple father-son tale about Gaz's broken marriage and his growing son, Nathan, who idolizes his dad no matter what.

The emotional resonance of this carnival thus arises as the sum of the personal tales coming together in a glorious finale, but it is also a result of the socioeconomic situation the characters find themselves in. The opening "documentary," which represents Sheffield, England, in the 1960s as a dynamic place and the steel capital of Britain, simply and forcefully sets up the contrast with the present case of almost total unemployment and social decay. Within this context, the film has done what powerful comedies have succeeded in doing since Aristophanes: striking a chord within its audiences worldwide and evoking laughter at a subject that is absolutely not funny. The final dance sequence, as this motley Monty troupe performs to an old Randy Newman tune, is not one of Aristophanes' total fantasy triumphs, but it is a heart-warming case of personal victory for each Monty member. Do we feel cheated by the rear-view final shot instead of a literal "full Monty"? Absolutely not, say all women and men I have interviewed. As one British female friend put it, "A real full Monty at the end would completely destroy the comedy, for they would be, well, so inadequate! Better to keep the illusion of their triumph!"

The second most popular British film ever was Mike Newell's ensemble screwball romantic comedy *Four Weddings and a Funeral* (1994). If traditional romantic comedy suggests a couple should aim for marriage as a fitting conclusion, this comedy, penned by New Zealander Richard Curtis, winks at us, tracking an engaging but hapless Hugh Grant as a kind of holy fool who has no flair for relationships until he meets a restless soul mate in Andie MacDowell, an American who is uneasy about marrying into British society. As in *The Full Monty*, the script creates a variety of finely etched characters, given full life by such talented comic actors as Kristin Scott Thomas, Simon Callow, Rowan Atkinson, James Fleet and John Hannah. Curtis's script manages a wry balance between parody and affirmation, as shots are taken at various levels of British society and all levels of relationships. The ending, in which Grant and MacDowell exchange vows that they have no intention of every marrying, simply caps the fun of turning romantic comedy inside out and yet upholding the basic fabric of the genre. The funeral is aptly placed and even manages to make a beautiful W. H. Auden poem quite moving, thus creating an emotional counterbalance to the rest of the film.

Focus now on two great British comics, Sir Alec Guinness and Peter Sellers, both of whom proved throughout their long careers that they could play a wide range of characters, from the purely farcical to truly dramatic and emotionally moving figures. Guinness got started in Ealing comedies, especially *Kind Hearts and Coronets* (1949), *The Lavender Hill Mob* (1951) and *The Man in the White Suit* (1951), and in more than thirty features played roles as varied as the commander in *The Bridge on the River Kwai* (1957), an officer in *Lawrence of Arabia* (1962) and even the "force is with you" guru in *Star Wars*. But what he did best in his finest comedies was to show us how simple characters could easily take on other lives and completely cut loose, allowing that wilder, fun-loving creature inside to run free, given the opportunity. We are, once more, speaking of an anarchistic streak.

One example worth revisiting? Anthony Kimmin's *The Captain's Paradise* (1953). Guinness is a ship's captain on a run between the conservative, British-dominated port town of Gibraltar, where he lives a boring and regulated life with his British wife (Celia Johnson), and Morocco, where he lives it up each time he's in port with a spicy cabaret gal (Yvonne De Carlo). The structure is absolutely simple, for we know the inevitable will happen—that the two women will meet, compare notes and not believe they are speaking of the same man.

To Americans, Peter Sellers was the irrepressible bumbling Inspector Clouseau in Blake Edwards's hit series, but this well-loved comic made roughly twenty-four comedies before *The Pink Panther* (1964). Also an Ealing studio star, Sellers was much more comfortable with farce and caricature roles than Guinness, as shown in a string of fine British films such as *The Ladykillers* (1955), *The Mouse That Roared* and *I'm Alright, Jack* (both 1959), and *Two Way Stretch* (1960). For writers of comedy, I recommend a close viewing of Jack Arnold's *The Mouse That Roared*, scripted by Roger Macdougall and Stanley Mann from the popular novel by Leonard Wibberly. If the recent American satire *Wag the Dog* (1997) involves America going to war with a small unknown country (Albania), Arnold's comedy is the reverse: a postage-stamp-size nation headed by Peter Sellers declares war on the USA. And wins. Sellers plays three roles, suggesting the full carnival range of his talent. The eccentric anarchist trait is clearly in view: how dare a nowhere country invade America! Finally, from his American films with strong comic streaks, we should not forget George Roy Hill's delightful *The World of Henry Ori-*

ent (1964) and the touching pathos of his role in Hal Ashby's darkly comic parable *Being There* (1979), made as Sellers was close to death from cancer.

Terry Jones, Graham Chapman, John Cleese, Terry Gilliam, Eric Idle, and Michael Palin are the full Monty . . . Python. This over-the-top British ensemble represents anarchy with a capital "A" with a circle drawn around it, à la graffiti seen around the world. In totally farcical comedies such as *Monty Python and the Holy Grail* (1975), *Life of Brian* (1979), and *Monty Python's The Meaning of Life* (1983), they do what few Hollywood comedies dare to do: cast story and character development to the wind in favor of skits, routines, free-ranging farce, satire, parody and outrageous irreverence. In short, they are both Aristophanic and even further out than the Marx Brothers, a group whose roots echo British vaudeville (pantomime).

For the Python, less is definitely not more. The group has made the world laugh by the sheer outlandishness of its concepts and the degree to which each zany idea is followed. The "Every Sperm Is Sacred" sequence in *The Meaning of Life* remains a classic, going so far beyond any coherent satire of Catholic doctrine that it becomes pure farce on a grand scale. Countless children dance and sing, while babies drop from mothers as they sing, all capped by the rigid Church of England couple that recount they too have made babies, each of the two times in their lives they have made love.

In Python we find the carnivalesque taken as far as it appears it can go in feature comedy. The group exercises a joyful sense of total freedom that Hollywood comedy in particular would never tolerate. And as Terry Jones once told me, they have always been aware that they are taking chances: "When we're good, we can be great, but when we're off, look out!" (personal interview, January 1996). Note that Python is also an example of what I would call process comic writing. Such a talented group working together over the years means that the "writing" represents both individual and group effort, pitching, revision, polishing and riffing. Their weakest film? *The Holy Grail.* The problem? They were trying a bit too hard, for Pythons that is, to adhere to a story. Stories, for true anarchists, can spell something worse than death: boredom!

Spain and Mexico
The Surrealist Humor of Luis Buñuel

Take just one moment in one Luis Buñuel film, *Simon of the Desert* (1965). Very loosely based on the life and mythology surrounding Simon, an early saint from Syria who spent over thirty years sitting upon a tall pillar to be closer to his God, this film is full of Buñuel's irreverent anarchistic humor. In this scene, Simon has temporarily stepped down from his pillar and is besieged by the poor, the sick, the afflicted, all looking for miracles from the saint. Simon blesses a peasant who has no hands, and a miracle happens: two perfectly healthy hands appear. There is a problem, however. One of his children is pestering his father, and so in the peasant's first action with his new limbs, he slaps the hell out of his son! Every time I've seen the film the audience, strong churchgoers or not, bursts into immediate hearty laughter.

That's Luis Buñuel. Born into a very Catholic and conservative area of rural Spain in 1900, in what he called a medieval world, he grew to become a filmmaker in France and Mexico. Buñuel studied in Madrid with the likes of the poet Lorca and became best friends with Salvador Dalí. When he moved to Paris as a young man in the 1920s, he naturally became a part of the artistic scenes of the day, mixing with Picasso, poets, writers and, best of all, filmmakers. He and Dalí established themselves as surrealists immediately with their joint first short film, *Andalusian Dog* (1929), full of shockingly witty shots and moments of humorous parody of religious and social norms. Buñuel, who claims he was influenced in part by American silent comedy, especially Keaton, ends the film much like Keaton's *College:* in Buñuel's film the last shot is of the young lovers not united in an embrace, as romantic comedy would suggest, but as two corpses with their heads sticking out of the sand by the seashore.

Every Buñuel film is full of familiar motifs for those who know his work, but unexpected surprises for those who don't. We began this book with a Buñuel quotation taken from his highly readable autobiography, *My Last Sigh,* and we can state strongly here that whenever you are tired of the safe and predictable comedies that surround you, rent a Buñuel! His films are good for your comic soul's good health!

Five Easy Lessons to Learn from Buñuel about Writing Comedy

1. *Tap into your dreams, fantasies and the unconscious in general for all of its humor, sense of liberation and striking energy and originality.* Surrealism as a movement was founded on such a premise, which leads to familiar objects taking on unfamiliar functions. For Buñuel, this often meant narrative structures that suggested dreams within dreams or fantasies within fantasies.

2. *It is great fun to be irreverent and disrespectful.* Buñuel thumbs his playful nose at the Church (and for him that means Catholic!) and the high middle class. Every time you see an old man in a Buñuel film walking down a street with a cane or on crutches, you just know someone will kick the crutch from underneath him. In perhaps his most irreverent shot of all, he parodies the Last Supper in *Viridiana* (1961) with drunken beggars taking over a Spanish farm mansion and posing in mockery of Christ's final meal.

3. *Enjoy the pleasure of turning social expectations upside down.* In *The Phantom of Liberty* (1974), upper-class guests arrive at a mansion for a dinner party. As they sit around the empty table, we realize the seats are actually toilets, and they lift their gowns and pull down their tuxes as they sit facing each other, chatting, only to leave from time to time to go to a small room in order to eat in privacy.

4. *Go for a loose picaresque plot that allows you to take any side trip you wish.* In *The Discreet Charm of the Bourgeoisie* (1972) each episode stands on its own, but they are loosely connected as a story of a group of upper-middle-class folk trying to have a dinner that never happens. The dominant visual image becomes a shot that recurs from time to time of the group simply walking down a highway. The picaresque, as for Aristophanes, is particularly useful to anarchistic humor, for it allows one the complete freedom to combine the most unlikely of stories and characters within your tale.

5. *Do not preach; keep your spirit of carnival as pure a form of anarchy as possible.* After brief flirtations Buñuel dropped out of the Communist Party, for he realized that in his humor and filmmaking he was not putting forth agendas for social change. He was, rather, making fun of value systems and institutions he did not wish to destroy but merely parody and satirize.

Italy
Love and Anarchy Italian Style in Boccaccio, Dante, Fellini, and Cinema Paradiso

We have covered early Italian romantic comedy (chapter 3) and the long and hilarious tradition of Italian farce, commedia dell'arte (chapter 4). While Italian filmmakers also echo other influences, in the main this double base in farce and romantic comedy holds true for most Italian film comedy. But to mention Italian film comedy is also to look back to the great Italian spinner of prose (as opposed to verse) tales, Boccaccio and his *Decameron* (1349–53), which we discussed in chapter 3.

We see much of this spirit in the work of Federico Fellini, whose films mix passion, sex, innocent love and the decadence and ego of artists attempting to create or find their identities in an Italy that appears to have lost most of its traditional values. *La Dolce Vita* (1960), with a script by Fellini, Ennino Flaiano and Tullio Pinelli, echoes the whole Italian tradition and Boccaccio in particular. Marcello Mastroianni is the pop journalist who comes to realize the emptiness of his life. The times Fellini inhabits are definitely modern, even postmodern, but the texture and conclusion are clearly in a tradition of Boccaccio and even Dante, as Fellini ends his film on a beach at dawn. As the all-night revelers from Rome are wandering down a beach, Mastroianni wanders off by himself and suddenly views a sweet girl of about fourteen smiling and gesturing to him from a distance. They exchange gestures, Mastroianni looking very much like a sad clown. The moment is touching, amusing and sad, but it is finally, as in Dante and Boccaccio, triumphant. Fellini's images suggest that Mastroianni is not completely lost if, at dawn, he can make contact with such innocence, smile, and go on about his life as the camera lingers on the girl's clear, happy face. Her face not only appears in contrast to the shallowness of the noise and confusion of the trendy party lovers we have followed through the film but transforms the meaninglessness of what has gone before, leaving us with an image of hope rather than confusion, despair, triviality.

Fellini's films abound in images that consciously evoke commedia dell'arte, his love of circuses and circus people, his fascination with faces and body types of all sizes and conditions, male and female, and a strong attraction to American silent film comedy, especially Chaplin, Keaton, and Laurel and Hardy. To watch *8½* or *La Strada* or even his later films such as *City of Women* or *Orchestra Rehearsal* is to see how, as an Italian filmmaker, he could absorb and recast foreign comic traditions in his own unique vision.

Giuseppe Tornatore's Oscar-winning *Cinema Paradiso* (1988), from his own script, succeeds in a similar vein. As in Dante and Boccaccio, *amore* is the cornerstone of the narrative of a young boy, Salvatore, growing up without a father in a small Sicilian town after World War II. And as suggested by the whole tradition of Italian comedy, love appears in many forms: our young protagonist falls in love with cinema, with the old projectionist, Alfredo (Philippe Noiret), who becomes something of a father/grandfather figure, and with a young woman his age, and he is in turn surrounded by his widowed mother's love all his life. While the film embraces many stories, high and low, including some very funny scenes of movie audiences enjoying one another as much as the films on the screen, the ending is bittersweet. The film is structured with a contemporary frame, as our young boy has become a middle-aged businessman and husband who returns to his hometown for the funeral of the old projectionist.

We end with the protagonist discovering a special reel of film the old man left him. All of the censored "kissing" scenes the Church had ordered cut from the films are on one reel. Tears and laughter mix as the main character relives his whole life and his life in films, as we see one kiss after another, Hollywood and Italian, French and British. "Paradiso," the name of the cinema, suggests not only a bygone age of movie palaces—and in the end the cinema is pulled down to build a parking lot—but an echo of Dante's *Divine Comedy,* or simply a spiritual level to these loves reel and real.

Gabriele Salvatore's Oscar-winning *Mediterraneo* (1991) ends with a similar nostalgic, distancing scene, as several old friends who had been isolated on a Greek island during World War II return and prepare a simple meal together, talking about the past. This bond of friendship that closes what unfolded as an anarchistic ensemble romance during the body of the film caps an otherwise joyous and hilarious but also sweet mosaic of comic stories. More so than even *Cinema Paradiso,* in fact, Salvatore's film appears as a clear relative to Boccaccio's brand of comedy and humor laced with seriousness.

Italy gave us the Renaissance. And in comedic terms we as writers can learn from the Italian tradition how to mix farce and fantasy, pure emotion and sexuality, all wrapped up in the embrace of Love. This goes even for Italian films more clearly labeled as dramas, such as Michael Radford's very moving *The Postman* (*Il Postino,* 1994), starring the late Massimo Troisi and Philippe Noiret in yet another Oscar winner.

Finally, among the multitude of fine Italian comedies, I would recommend the now unfortunately neglected films of Lina Wertmuller. *Swept Away . . . by an Unusual Destiny in the Blue Sea of August* (1975) and *Love and Anarchy* (1973) both star the affable Giancarlo Giannini in works of imaginative energy and comic vision.

The Czech Republic
Wry Humor and Pathos, from
Closely Watched Trains *to* Kolya

The Czech people have long used humor and wry laughter as a form of national as well as personal survival. Deep in Central Europe, they have often been invaded by the larger countries that surround them, from the Germans to the Russians. In fact, if you ask most Czechs what is the novel that best sums up the Czech character, most would point to *The Good Soldier Švejk* by Jaroslav Hasek, a very funny antiwar tale of a simple "holy fool" who is drafted into the Austro-Hungarian army during World War I and almost single-handedly incapacitates the whole war machine by his bumbling inability to fight, march or kill.

The Czech cinema has proved particularly adept at mixing wry humor and pathos in simple tales about antiheroes like Švejk who "win" not through plan and design but through happenstance and, finally, a good heart. Jiri Menzel's *Closely Watched Trains,* based on the novel of the same name by Bohumil Hrabal, won the 1966 Oscar for Best Foreign Film. Milos, a young and innocent fellow, begins his first job as a railroad employee at a small train station in the countryside during the German occupation. We have an early comic foreshadowing of his fate when he tells us in voiceover that his grandfather was a magician-hypnotist who died trying to hypnotize an army tank that was bearing down on him. The humor grows not out of slapstick or car crashes or giant schemes gone wrong, but rather from the careful attention to detail in the small world of a rural train station as a double plot unfolds: our protagonist tries to learn his job while a war is going on, and a wise-guy playboy who also works at the station takes it upon himself to help Milos lose his virginity.

The ending is a double climax, so to speak, as Milos makes love with an older and very sexually experienced resistance freedom fighter and then becomes an accidental anti-Nazi hero as he drops a bomb on a German munitions train passing by. The ending evokes both tears and laughter simultaneously, for he is such a bumbling klutz that he falls onto the train along with the bomb. In a long shot we see the train blow up, and we know that Milos is dead as well: a hero and a fool in one simple action.

This so-called "Czech touch" has reached Hollywood in the hands of Milos Forman, who walked off with Oscars for *One Flew Over the Cuckoo's Nest* (1975), turning Ken Kesey's anarchistic satirical comedy of the 1960s into a more universal work through what I would call Czech micro-comic details. Forman's early Czech films, including *Loves of a Blonde* (1965), *Black Peter* (1964) and *Firemen's Ball* (1967), are definitely worth watching as well for his ability to wring maximum laughter out of the simplest of situations. Take the premise of *Firemen's Ball,* for instance: a small fire station is having its annual ball. This is ensemble anarchistic comedy, for the firemen as a group are as bumbling as Mack Sennett's Keystone Kops but given the personality and humanity that the Czech touch manages so well. The firemen's new attraction for the ball about to take place is a beauty contest, an event that not only brings out all the inadequacies of the members but leads to the fire station catching fire—and the firemen are too drunk and ill-prepared to put it out. The closing shot is of the freezing firemen and their guests standing in the snow, looking at the rubble of what used to be their station. It is a fine testimony to the power of satire and comedy that the film was banned in Czechoslovakia for years since everyone (rightly!) took the film as a spoof on Communist officials.

It says much for the universality of Czech humor that Milos Forman went on to become one of Hollywood's most esteemed directors, applying the Czech touch not just in *Cuckoo's Nest,* an anarchistic ensemble comedy if there ever was one, but in *Ragtime* (1981), among others, with James Cagney's last performance and a fine Randy Newman score, and the Oscar-winning *Amadeus* (1984), which uses anarchistic humor bright and dark to bring Peter Shaffer's play and screenplay to full potential on the screen. It is helpful to understand that part of Forman's success has been a sharply tuned sense of humor and comedy which he has developed from his national background.

Jan Sverak's *Kolya,* based on a script by the director's actor-writer father, Zdenek Sverak, won the 1997 Oscar for Best Foreign Film. As a comedy that embodies the Czech touch for humor and pathos, it's worth watching on a number of levels. But one immediate reason to study it with pleasure is because it has done very respectably at the box office. In one week in April of 1997, for instance, it was simultaneously playing in twenty-two Los Angeles cinemas and twenty-six New York City area theaters. My point, for American writers particularly, is that I'm not discussing "overseas" comedies just for the sake of being different. Rather, this chapter can be a valuable expansion of comic horizons for English-speaking writers, for it suggests that comedies with subtitles and cultures quite different from our own can find enthusiastic audiences around the world.

That said, let's look briefly at *Kolya*. Again, I emphasize simplicity. This is primarily a two-character film: a womanizing fiftysomething bachelor cellist hard up for cash enters a green card marriage with a Russian woman and soon discovers she has taken off and left him with her five-year-old son, Kolya. Act One ends as the two of them are alone together, the most mismatched pair imaginable. They don't even speak each other's language.

What propels Act Two, of course, is how these opposites comically attract. Each conflict and confrontation actually becomes a means by which Louka, the Czech cellist (played with wonderful verve by the screenwriter, Zdenek Sverak), and Kolya (Andrej Chalimon) come closer together. Once more, no fancy sets, no special effects, no cast of thousands. Simply attention to comic detail, witty but realistic dialogue and fine acting. Humor and pathos abound as Louka becomes a father and Kolya begins to feel he belongs. We laugh as Louka attempts to carry out a seduction in his Prague apartment while Kolya is around, but near the end of Act Two many cry through their laughter as Kolya shows he misses his mother by using the flexible shower nozzle as a telephone, sitting in the tub and carrying out an imaginary conversation with her in Russian.

In many ways this cross-cultural story would be enough for a modest comedy. But *Kolya* offers a much richer texture and series of implications, given that the two cultures are Russian and Czech just before the fall of communist regimes in 1989. The film works fine without the audience knowing Czech history. But for those who do have even a little background, the film is even more impressive. The Russians were deeply resented and hated in Czechoslovakia, for in 1968 the Russian army was sent in to squash what was called the Prague Spring, a time of amazing artistic and political liberalism when the Czech people felt they were creating a new form of "socialism with a human face."

Kolya thus pushes the envelope of Central European comedy by making Kolya, the Russian boy, the cutest kid around and by suggesting a happy family formed by these two seemingly opposite cultures who come to love and understand one another for who they are. Such a theme and story could easily fall prey to sentimentality. But Jan Sverak as director and his father as actor-scriptwriter have managed that delicate balance that only the best comic writers and filmmakers can achieve.

The conclusion ties the personal and social stories together. Communism falls, and both Kolya and the Russian troops must depart. Thus the kind of mixed ending we often find in European films. But does this qualify as a comedy if Kolya is gone? In fact it does, for we have several triumphs. On the larger level, the Czech people are now free to live their own lives. But on Louka's part, he is ready to do what he has never done before: commit to his old girlfriend, Klara, who, though still married to another man, is now pregnant with Louka's child. And there is more: Louka has been banned from the symphony orchestra for years for political reasons never explained, but he is now reinstated and playing with his old comrades once more.

And Kolya? He is returning with his mother to Germany, her new home and Kolya's too. The closing image is the same as the first, but now we understand it: the clouds floating by are seen from a plane, and the voice is that of Kolya humming a tune he has learned from Louka. Though they are apart, this "father and son" have embraced each other, forever.

France
Warm Romantic Farce,
from Renoir to Tati and Truffaut

Take note: Hollywood in the past dozen years has discovered there is quite a pile of money in remaking French comedies. French filmmakers, producers and comedians are not thrilled with this fact, but a fact it remains. Edouard Molinaro's *La Cage aux Folles* (1978) was for years the highest-grossing French film ever, a memorable stage farce turned into a film about a gay couple trying to act straight for the sake of a son returning home with his fiancee. As remade in Hollywood by Mike Nichols with an Elaine May script, *The Birdcage* made beaucoup more millions, with Robin Williams, Gene Hackman and Nathan Lane breathing English-language laughter into this farce. Similarly, Coline Serreau's *Three Men and a Cradle* (1985), whose popular plot concept is captured in the title, went on to be an even bigger moneymaker in English in Leonard Nimoy's remake, *Three Men and a Baby* (1987), with Tom Selleck, Steve Guttenberg and Ted Danson. My point to you as a comic writer is not to rush into the local art cinema to figure out which French comedy to rip off, for Hollywood will continue to do so with predictable results. But I do wish to suggest the strength of the long French comic tradition and the need for a writer of comedy to be familiar with it.

Chaplin, for instance, always said his primary mentor in screen comedy was the French silent comedian Max Linder, who worked in France and the States from 1909 till his death in 1925 (Thomson, 27). Thus France has contributed to screen comedy at least as far back as American comics began making ten-minute comedies.

Since sound films became the norm in the early 1930s, however, a major trend in French comedy has been warm romantic farce. First, we mention Jean Renoir (the son of the Impressionist painter Pierre-Auguste Renoir), who is important to film history as a champion of "poetic realism," a blending of lyricism with a realistic approach to photography and acting. Renoir's best-known work is *Rules of the Game* (1939), which combines farce, tenderness and satire on the eve of World War II as Renoir, playing a major part in the cast as well, sharply etches a portrait of the decaying upper classes of France endlessly playing "games" in a country estate. At one point an aristocrat yells out to his butler, "Stop the farce!" The butler replies, "Which one?" Renoir's approach includes a strong hint of a long theatrical tradition of comedy and satire stretching back to Molière and on through the bedroom farces of Pierre Marivaux and Pierre de Beaumarchais, as well as deep focus and camera movement that emphasizes the reality of the moment, the scene, the characters.

Boudu Saved from Drowning (1932) is Renoir and French romantic farce at their very best. Starring the wonderful French character actor Michel Simon, Renoir's affable social satire traces the story of a French tramp, Boudu (Simon), who is saved from drowning by a middle-class book dealer who feels he is doing a good deed by also offering Boudu a room in his home. Boudu, on the other hand, is not only not grateful ("what right did you have to save my life?") but proceeds to cause complete chaos in the book dealer's home, proving to be both a bull in a china shop and a carnivalesque seducer of the wife and the maid.

The comic writing lesson is clear: use a simple story (a literal fish-out-of-water set-up), mixing social classes, and adding a satire of middle-class values without becoming preachy or overdone, wrapping all in a joyous sense of healthy physical and emotional pleasure.

Renoir also handles the balance of sex and emotion well. Boudu is a rogue tramp but he is totally unpretentious, unlike the bourgeois society he has fallen into. His seductions are, in fact, no seductions at all. The wife and maid are willing partners who enjoy his humor, stories, energy, joy of life. Let's not call this love, but what they share is open and honest affection, and Renoir and Simon bring this to glorious life on the screen.

The ending could not be more perfect. Renoir closes the circle with a boating scene on a river that looks very much like a cinematic version of one of his father's Impressionist paintings. But Boudu's boat overturns. As the family is caught up in the confusion of saving themselves, Boudu floats happily downriver and thus out of their lives. He picks up a jacket from a scarecrow in a nearby field and, like Chaplin's tramp, goes down the road of life again. Being Boudu, however, he is not the unhappy outsider; rather, he is quite clearly thrilled to be on his own once more. Yes, Chaplin was influenced by French farce, and here the wink and influence come full circle as Renoir and Boudu echo Chaplin. Note also that *Boudu* can be seen as referencing an earlier happy French production that borrows from Chaplin: René Clair's *A Nous, la Liberté!* (*For Us, Liberty!*, 1931).

Jacques Tati stands alone among modern comic filmmakers as someone who successfully mastered the art of silent American comedy, especially Buster

Keaton, in post–World War II cinema. There is much to be learned about the power of physical comedy from watching Tati's *Mr. Hulot's Holiday* (1953), *Mon Oncle* (1958) and *Play Time* (1967). Tati was, in terms of my introduction to this study, an exploded mime! As a comic actor/performer, he wrote, produced and directed himself in his comedies, developing the bumbling but affable Mr. Hulot, a tall angular fellow, part holy fool, part scarecrow, part gentleman, part outsider to the goings-on of everyday life, much in the Chaplin tramp mode.

Tati is an anarchist, not a romantic, but an anarchist with a warm heart and gentle laughter rather than belly laughs and guffaws. Like a good mime, he can make any event from playing tennis (*Mr. Hulot's Holiday*) to walking into a modern office, restaurant, airport or hotel (*Play Time*) seem fascinating, drawn out and ridiculous. As Kristin Thomson and David Bordwell note, "Tati blurs the boundary between performance and the comedy of everyday life" (511).

François Truffaut's comic touch is very much in the same tradition. There is a warmth and wry acceptance of the joys and shortcomings of male-female relationships in which, as in Shakespeare and the American screwball tradition, the men usually seem more foolish and hopelessly romantic, while the women appear more rooted to reality and more able to cope with life's frustrations. Add to this Truffaut's status as one of the most important members of the so-called French New Wave and you have a filmmaker who is able to gain a lot of laughs out of jokes built around references either to previous films or to film language itself. In *Shoot the Piano Player* (1960), a criminal swears to another character, "If I am telling a lie, may my dear old mother drop dead," and we cut to an insert shot of an old woman clutching her heart, standing up, and keeling over.

Truffaut's *Day for Night* (1973) remains not only one of his best films but one of the most enjoyable of the many self-reflective film-within-a-film movies that have been made. An Oscar winner for Best Foreign Film, this romantic farce features Truffaut as a French director trying to direct a hopelessly flawed love story with an international cast. Truffaut captures the insanity, the humor and the passion both behind the scenes and on camera, as real and temporary romances are played out among the cast, all under the umbrella of making a movie. The warmth of feeling that is a trademark of Truffaut is clearly evident here in many scenes, as Truffaut the character emerges as an understanding and at times lonely "director" who must play lover, father, best friend, psychiatrist and dictator in order to get his film made. The ultimate romance in the film, of course, is that between Truffaut and his cast, no matter how badly they have let him down: if it weren't love, they wouldn't be there. *Day for Night* does become a carnival of mixed motives, characters, farces, but it is a carnival held together by mutual affection and, finally, acceptance.

The Former Yugoslavia
Balkan Black Humor and Magic Realism

Certainly the former Yugoslavia would seem the last place for a writer of comedy to search for fresh approaches to the Muse. But filmmakers from this troubled part of the world have been highly successful in tapping into rich comic sources as both a form of survival and a celebration of life beyond the absurdity of wars, ethnic and religious conflicts, and poverty. Similarly, the filmmakers from the former Yugoslavia also have drawn from a long tradition of what we can call Balkan magic realism or surrealism that is not unlike the magic realism practiced by South American authors such as Gabriel García Márquez. Dusan Makavejev, for instance, remains perhaps the world's foremost "cine-surrealist" after Luis Buñuel for his hilarious and bizarre collage features such as *Innocence Unprotected* (1966), *Loves of a Switchboard Operator* (1964) and *W.R.: Mysteries of the Organism* (1971). In *Innocence Unprotected* documentary footage of the Nazi occupation of Belgrade during the war is crosscut with one of Serbia's first sound films—a ludicrous melodrama starring an acrobatic strong man of that time—and with contemporary documentary footage of the old actor/acrobat in the 1960s, all interwoven with a musical soundtrack that counterpoints the images on the screen with either Hawaiian music or highly nationalistic folk songs. The result is a true carnival of images that are at times both very funny and also provocative in their juxtapositions, so that the film also serves as a critique of the past as well.

Screenwriters wishing to broaden their comic perspectives can learn much from many of the Yugoslav films of the 1960s up through the present. Let us mention two examples briefly.

Slobodan Sijan's *Who Is Singing over There?* (1980) won awards around the world for its fresh and festive dark comedy of a country bus winding its way to Belgrade on the day that the Germans bombed and destroyed the city in 1941. This ensemble road film tracks a wide cross-section of Yugoslav society, including an old peasant, a sick schoolteacher, a would-be pop singer, village newlyweds and others, all under the tyrannical scrutiny of a walrus-sized bus owner and his half-demented bus-driving son (who at one point drives several kilometers blindfolded!).

What is particularly innovative about Sijan's war comedy, written by Dusan Kovacevic, is the use of two gypsies who open the film, facing the camera and singing what is about to happen, punctuated with a chorus of "I'm miserable, I was born that way. Oh, Mother, but to have dreamed it all." This opening does signal us comically and engagingly that the film is, in a sense, a song, a structuring device that becomes all the more clear as the journey progresses and the gypsies punctuate the film by stepping forward, looking at us, and singing the events unfolding.

A blend of elements of the comic with an exaggerated form of reality close to that of magic realism takes place in the final scene. After a number of raucous, satirical and at times warmly amusing moments, the bus reaches Belgrade. At that moment the gypsies are wrongly accused of stealing a wallet, and as the passengers beat up the gypsies, we hear the German planes approaching overhead. There is a raid, and we end the film with the whole bus destroyed and everyone killed—except the gypsies, who climb out of the ruins and face us one last time, singing their by-now-familiar song.

At such a point comedy and irony cross paths, as we realize the filmmaker has shown us those on the margins of society—the gypsies—as the only survivors. Sijan and his screenwriter have, we realized, pulled off a rare feat: they've made us laugh for over an hour and a half and then managed to make us care emotionally and think about the implications of both the sudden-death ending and the triumphant survival of the gypsies through it all.

Bosnia-born filmmaker Emir Kusturica takes an even more surrealistic approach in his 1996 film *Underground,* which won the Cannes Film Festival's Palme d'Or award as best film. With a script once more written by Dusan Kovacevic, Kusturica fashions a darkly comic tale of a group of Yugoslavs who are held under the streets of Belgrade by a Mafia-like figure, Blackie (Miki Manoljovic), supposedly to protect them from the Nazis. What he neglects to tell them, however, is that at a certain point World War II ended. Thus begins a surrealistic nightmare, at times funny and always bizarre, as weddings, funerals, births and celebrations all take place "underground," until they finally break out during the Bosnian war. The ending moves even further into the realm of magic realism, as the whole segment of land that the main characters are assembled on near the Danube River breaks off and begins to float away as some kind of boat-like island.

Both films therefore suggest the power of employing a wide comic canvas that stretches beyond the confines of everyday logic and experience.

Japan
Ceremony and Carnival
in Akira Kurosawa's Dreams

Akira Kurosawa gave the world some of the most memorable dramatic Japanese films, including *Rashomon* (1951), *Seven Samurai* (1955), *Yojimbo* (1962) and *Dersu Uzala* (1980). In *Akira Kurosawa's Dreams* (1991), however, the aging master allowed himself the freedom to put together a film made up of six distinct dream narratives, separated by fade-outs so that each stands as a story within its own right but related to the others in thematic concerns if not by tone, style or narrative.

Several of the episodes in fact might best be described as nightmares of war, hunger, death and destruction, vividly but darkly etched on the screen. The final episode, which we are concerned with here, in which a young male traveler pauses by a water mill to talk to a very old man about his life by the river, thus becomes particularly important given its concluding position. How to end a series of dreams bright and dark?

The focus in the beginning on the beauty of the river is our strongest cue and clue that Kurosawa is aiming for a triumphant conclusion.

As the old man talks about his simple life of few possessions, we suddenly hear festive but stately music. Then we see a long funeral procession come into view, led by dancing children, all brightly costumed.

The old man explains it is a funeral for a woman he once loved. As they talk, the soothing river in all its beauty flows on around them. As the young man asks more questions, the old villager begins to dress in costume. We and the young man sense that the funeral is not an occasion for wailing and tragic expression. Rather, we see the participants are joyous, not dejected or sad. And when the young man asks the old man's age, he replies, "103," tagging this with a smile and "It's good to be alive. It's exciting!" The old man, now with the costume on, grabs some bells and dances off into the procession. The young man watches quietly, leaves a flower on a stone by the river where someone else died years ago, and walks off down a wooden bridge. We close on the beauty of the sound and image of flowing water, much like a Japanese painting or a haiku.

After the dark sadness of the preceding sections, Kurosawa, like the 103-year-old man, leaves us with joy, with triumph of the individual and group spirit over death, with music, dance and community sharing, in nature. It is "exciting" but it is more: Kurosawa's final section weds us to the comedy of life itself and that is the last laugh, the best laugh, the deepest smile.

CHAPTER 8

Comedy and the Documentary Impulse

A challenge to all writers of comedy: even if you think of yourself as a writer of feature narrative comedy or episodic television comedy, consider the carnival of possibilities that await you in the field of documentary film, television and video work. We will emphasize this point in chapters 11 and 12. But it is worth making here as well, for documentary can allow you as a lover of the comic a more immediate medium that is even more open to experimentation, and at a much lower cost.

Upon its Warner Brothers release, Michael Moore's *Roger and Me* (1989) became the most popular feature documentary ever to play in American cinemas. In part its popularity had to do with its exposure of General Motors' callous closing of a plant in Flint, Michigan, in favor of a new one in Mexico, where labor is cheaper. Moore, a resident of Flint, is the "me" in the title, and Roger is Roger Smith, then the president of General Motors, whom Moore wishes to show what the loss of 40,000 jobs has meant to a once prosperous but now deeply depressed "motor city."

Advocacy filmmaking alone, however, would not have attracted so many paying viewers. What was particularly brilliant about Moore's approach was his use of humor, irony and comedy in pursuit of his goal. What he ended up with is what I have come to call *performance documentary*: a documentary in which one of the characters is "playing" in order to bring out unrehearsed reactions from others. In the case of *Roger and Me,* Moore becomes, on camera, a kind of good-hearted goofball innocent carrying out a simple "anarchistic" idea, as he tells us in voiceover: if Roger Smith really knew the suffering he was creating by closing the plant, he wouldn't have done it, so if Roger can be shown what has happened, he will somehow reverse his actions.

Audiences laughed throughout the screenings, realizing, of course, what a comic set-up the film has. As Moore attempts to enter GM's corporate headquarters in Detroit to meet Smith, without an appointment, dressed in baggy blue jeans and wearing a wrinkled, soiled lumber jacket and an odd cap, of course we laugh as security guards swiftly elbow him out, glancing menacingly at the handheld video camera capturing it all.

Humor, comedy and documentary. Three words that we don't see coming together often enough, for we have all sat through dry and boring documentaries as schoolchildren, and even after graduation most of us came to think that documentaries had to have either Walter Cronkite's fatherly voice or CNN-style jerky, in-your-face shots of disasters, murders and demonstrations. But the theme of this chapter is that Roger Moore and others are on to something important that anyone working in documentary should "seriously" consider: the power of comedy to make documentaries even more effective.

Documentaries with Humor

It is one thing to set out to make a funny documentary, in the old *Candid Camera* style, say, setting up a silly situation and then capturing people's reactions. This section, on the other hand, concerns serious documentaries made more memorable through humor in either conception or execution.

Let us now salute the irrepressible Les Blank (see Horton, "A Well Spent Life: The Films of Les Blank"). Les has made some of the most feisty American documentaries of the past twenty-five years, including his New Orleans Mardi Gras film, *Always for Pleasure* (1978); his Polish-American polka film, *In Heaven There Is No Beer?* (1984); a study of *Gap-Toothed Women;* his record of what American twenty-one-day tours of Europe are like in *Innocents Abroad;* and a look at Louisiana Cajun music and culture in *Spend It All,* to name but a few.

Les's humor is both in his subjects and in his relaxed shooting style, which puts those he is filming at ease. Humor strikes us immediately in the title of one of his best documentaries, *Garlic Is As Good As Ten Mothers.* Les loves food and music, especially regional American and ethnic, and thus it was inevitable that he would make a film dedicated to garlic, affectionately known by millions as "the stinking rose." We could label this anarchistic documentary comedy, as the title provides the very loose thematic structure that allows Les to investigate any and all aspects of garlic lore, from its growth, cultivation and harvesting to its use in foods Hispanic, American, Cajun and more, as well as its powers to cure illness and as an aphrodisiac. I have described Les's approach to filmmaking, in which he eats and drinks with the best of them and shoots miles of film, as *cinema vitalité,* a truly carnivalesque approach to the medium. He participates fully and thus becomes part of the scene he is documenting. Editing becomes the key factor, both to focus his documentaries and to bring out the humor. And he reaches the audience in direct ways as well. I attended one New York screening at the Film Forum during which garlic was cooked onstage and passed down the rows of the theater by scantily clad young women, so that we breathed and ate garlic while watching garlic on the screen. This is participatory cinema at its finest, and such an "embrace" of film, filmmaker, subject matter and audience is comedy in the largest sense of creating and nourishing a community. (Catalogue and tapes are available from Flower Films, 10341 San Pablo Ave., El Cerrito, CA 94530. Phone: [510] 525-0942; Fax: [510] 525-1204. E-mail: *Blankfilm@aol.com.* Website: *www.lesblank.com.*)

Louis Alvarez and Andy Kolker, documentary filmmakers based in New York, are also adept at making humor work for them. In *Yeah, You Rite!* (30 min., 1986), they capture much of what is unique about the various speech patterns and dialects of New Orleans. The subject matter, regional language and culture, is quite serious, and because this is an "educational" film, they were able to obtain various humanities grants and media organization funds to make it. But beginning with their title, humor is a central character.

They begin in New York's Times Square, asking people in the street if they understand the following sentence: "If someone said they would give you a muffalata for laigniappe what would they mean?" Of course New Yorkers come up with hilarious answers, none of them correct. The film then cuts to New Orleans, Dr. John singing on the soundtrack, as it is explained that everyone in New Orleans understands that a muffalata is a spicy Italian submarine sandwich with cheese, cold meats and a special olive sauce, while laigniappe means "something extra," such as a baker's dozen.

Alvarez and Kolker do have experts in language and cultural anthropology speaking in this half-hour documentary, but we are continually entertained by signs misspelled because of dialect rather than lack of spelling ability, by heavily accented locals in Mardi Gras costumes using a carnival vocabulary peculiar to New Orleans, and by the pure variety of individuals interviewed, old and young, black and white, poor and wealthy. It is humorous to cut from a snooty Uptown gentleman who claims his family is new to the city because they have only been there a hundred and fifty years, to a black teenage girl having her hair fixed doing a hilarious imitation of Tulane University East Coast coeds.

This dynamic duo has gone on to make highly successful documentaries shown on PBS and other venues, including a feature documentary on American dialects called *American Tongues* that follows in the footsteps of the New Orleans film, as well as a similar treatment of American politics and of American pop culture influences on Japan, *The Japanese Version.* In this latter film, the concept itself is funny: how do the Japanese adapt and adopt our culture? In one scene in a Japanese "cowboy" bar, business executives after work dress as cowboys and drink bourbon on the rocks. When interviewed as to why they like to dress as cowboys, one fellow says that they admire cowboys for their ability to work together as a team and get the cattle to market so they will succeed in their line of work—the exact opposite of what Americans see as the cowboy image: the lone individual surviving in a harsh but beautiful landscape. (These videos and a catalogue are available through The Center for New American Media, 589 Eighth Ave., 21st Floor, New York, NY 10018-3005).

Performance Documentary

We have mentioned that *Roger and Me* blurs the boundaries between strict documentary and fiction film by creating the "me" character and using him as a "performance" mechanism to bring out the subject matter—General Motors and its negative effect on Flint, Michigan—in a way that is much more dramatic and comic than a Voice of God narration with an unidentified narrator would be.

Such use of comic characters inside a documentary is clearly an example of *performance documentary.* I suggest that this "comic" approach is a very fruitful one indeed. One other example immediately comes to mind. In 1994, while the Bosnian war was being waged, a well-respected Yugoslav feature filmmaker, Z. Zilnik, torn by these events but having almost no money, shot *Tito for the Second Time among the Serbs* on video. What did he do? He dressed an actor up like Tito, complete with sunglasses and uniform and a thick military jacket worn in a kind of Napoleonic pose, and had the actor walk around the central part of Belgrade, talking to "the people" as if he had come back from the dead for a visit.

The anarchistic impulse is clear. And in carrying out this crazy "performance," Zilnik succeeded far more than any CNN or TV news documentary could ever hope to do in catching the feeling of the Serbian people at that very confusing and desperate period. Marshall Tito was a particularly heroic figure in the history of Yugoslavia, for unlike the leaders of many of the Soviet puppet states established in Central and Eastern Europe after World War II, Tito and his Communist partisans did actually defeat the Nazis and thus bring in a popular Communist government in 1945. And, despite all odds, he managed to hold together all the disparate sections of what became Yugoslavia until his death in 1980, with amazing accomplishments in literacy and medical care and a general rise in the standard of living, while (after 1948) standing up to Stalin and the Soviets to establish an independent socialist vision.

The crazy idea of this performance anarchistic documentary, therefore, is that Tito has returned to Yugoslavia after being dead for fourteen years, knowing nothing of what has happened since his death. No preparation or warning is given to the public; from their point of view, someone who looks very much like their departed leader has returned, and the video camera crew following him simply reinforces this "documentary game."

At this point humor, improvisation, pathos and history meet. The actor skillfully asks questions of those he meets and tries to answer questions they have for him, in what becomes a carnival or instant community of "Tito's Return." Half the people say, "We need you back again. You were the best." And the other half shout, "You bastard, it's because of you that we got into this mess." Many moments are touching, as some are moved to tears, but humorous scenes rule, as Tito examines old partisan uniforms and hats for sale at the flea market and talks to hip teens about their culture. There are also numerous laughs as Tito tries to understand: "Why is there a war?" "Who are our friends?" "But I took out international loans, why is there a blockade and sanctions now?"

In chapter 10 I suggest an exercise based on Zilnik's clever and entertaining film. The very concept should, for writers of comedy, open up our imaginations to all kinds of possibilities that do not need major studio or network funding but that could be very effective and hilarious "homemade" films, with social or even political implications as well. (For information and requests for copies of the film, contact The Yugoslav Film Institute, Belgrade. Fax: [38111] 63 42 53. E-mail: *ifilm@Eunet.yu.*)

The Comedy of Improv within Narrative

Tito for the Second Time among the Serbs is, for all its "performance," clearly a documentary. But consider how much laughter can be generated when a narrative film includes significant improvisation, or unscripted documentary moments. Alan Parker deserves a lot of credit for breaking away from his usual commercial fare, including *Midnight Express, Angel Heart* and *Mississippi Burning,* to make *The Commitments* (1991), about an unlikely bunch of Irish working-class guys and gals who get together to form an American-style blues band. With a very funny script by Dick Clement, Ian La Frenais and Roddy Doyle (who went on to do the related "Barrytown" scripts for *The Snapper* and *The Van*), Parker had the good sense and courage to use a cast of Irish unknowns for this ensemble anarchistic comedy.

Yes, there is a script, but much in the spirit of Srdjan Karanovic's *Social Games* (see chapter 10), a large part of our pleasure in *The Commitments* is in enjoying these fresh faces interacting, singing and "acting" as only "real" characters can. Thus, while the script sets the boundaries and may even provide many of the lines, you can be sure that with nonactors, so much of what Parker finally captured depended on the music and the energy level of the performances. Parker had, after all, mixed documentary, improv and humor when he shot *Fame* (1980) using real dance students at the New York High School for Performing Arts. The fragmented nature of that film was tightened up by the time he got to *The Commitments* ten years later. The film is worth studying to see how you can script a film with a lot of humor for what could be a very low budget and a lot of fun in the making, if you accept the spirit of wishing to script a tale that takes advantage of such improvisational documentary moments.

The Humor of Fake Documentaries

Documentaries that are faked can, of course, be yet another source of humor. We could mention the insertion of Gump in historical footage of President Kennedy as one example. And a highly original candidate in this category is Peter Jackson and Costa Botes's *Forgotten Silver* (New Zealand, 1996). Jackson, the director best known for *Heavenly Creatures* and *Bad Taste,* managed to make a fake documentary so convincing that many in New Zealand were at first taken in when it aired on national television.

This forty-minute film has to do with an investigation of a certain Colin Mackenzie, who singlehandedly invented, the documentary claims, such cinematic techniques as the first talking film, the first tracking shot and the first biblical spectacular and shot a series of highly successful silent comedies with a Kiwi comedian named Stan the Man.

To help make his hoax legitimate, Jackson himself appears on camera explaining his discovery, based on old reels of film recovered from the trunk of one of his aunts. But there is more to this hilarious cinematic joke. Botes and Jackson got Harvey Weinstein of Miramax Films, Leonard Maltin and a host of New Zealand experts on camera, testifying to how impressive these old films of Colin Mackenzie are.

Botes and Jackson clearly had fun faking the old films; they are very professionally done to appear authentic. As we see a "clip," Jackson explains in voiceover narration that the first sound film was Mackenzie's movie about Chinese workers in New Zealand, but the film was a financial failure because no one could understand Chinese, "so audiences left the theater in droves."

Of course we can point to another effect of such a fake documentary, especially since many initially believed this one: the fact that documentaries can be falsified can be a frightening realization as well as a comic one, as the history of totalitarian filmmaking and the altering of a nation's history have often proved. *Forgotten Silver* will, however, be long remembered for its ability to make us laugh through the manipulation of the medium, done with a droll poker face and a razor-sharp sense of comic irony.

III

CLOSE-UPS ON COMEDIES

*If anyone among you think that
he is wise, let him become a fool
that he may be wise.*

Saint Paul

CHAPTER 9

Feature Film Comedies

We can now cast an eye more closely over how the various comic elements actually work in seven very different comedies: *Sullivan's Travels, Big Night, A League of Their Own, Get on the Bus, The White Balloon, Clueless,* and *Fargo*.

Space does not allow for a complete breakdown of each film, but for each we will cover the following questions, based on what we have learned so far:

- Does this comedy lean more toward anarchistic or romantic comedy?
- How would we describe the comic climate or type of comedy in this film?
- Which audience is it aimed at, and what special acknowledgement of that audience is made?
- What kinds of characters are established?
- What comic plot elements are involved?
- What of the balance of visual and verbal humor?
- And the ending: how much of an "embrace" is this comedy leaving us with?

Finally, we will list a few comic highlights that make each film special.

Romantic Anarchistic Comedy: Preston Sturges's *Sullivan's Travels*

We introduced Sturges in chapter 5. Let us briefly take a closer look at one of his most celebrated films, *Sullivan's Travels* (1941), which is an absolute must-see for anyone writing comedy. What Sturges pulls off is a rare comedy that seamlessly blends anarchistic and romantic comedy in one glorious film that both critiques Hollywood and American comedy and celebrates them at the same time. Thus the comic climate moves between irony, farce and affectionate, embracing humor.

The plot is a picaresque journey film and a fish-out-of-water tale, ever so loosely inspired by Jonathan Swift's *Gulliver's Travels* in that our main protagonist, Sullivan (Joel McCrea, in the performance of a lifetime), who is a popular Hollywood director of comedy, sets out like Gulliver on four different journeys. But the plot is also Aristophanic in that Sullivan has a Big Idea that he wishes to carry out: to go beyond Hollywood and discover Real Life. And in the tradition of anarchistic comedy, he meets his goal.

Yet, truth be told, he only half succeeds. The other half brings in the romantic tradition. For not only does Sullivan wish to discover Life, he also wishes to make a "serious" film about the dark sides of life called *Oh! Brother, Where Art Thou?* This he does not do. His encounter with real life on the road—and the love of "the girl," never named but engagingly played by a sultry Veronica Lake, who shares his travels—has taught him that ultimately he wishes to continue to make comedies. For as he says at the very end, "Laughter is all some people have in this cockeyed caravan."

The ending: A total and glorious festive embrace. Sullivan has his arm around Veronica Lake, he is surrounded by his eager producers, and he is back in Hollywood, his voyages finished and his career as a comic filmmaker about to continue.

Clearly there is a lot of Sturges's own soul-searching and satire of Hollywood wrapped up in this film, but Sturges keeps it all light and bright, except for a Chaplinesque scene among the homeless. In fact, Sturges delights in shooting (and scripting, of course) each journey in a different film style. Journey #1 is a mad silent comedy chase sequence, as a caravan of reporters tries to follow Sullivan as he sets out on foot as a hobo in search of life beyond Beverly Hills. Journey #2 starts with a farcical sequence, as an old widow tries to entrap Sullivan in her late husband's bedroom, but quickly turns into romantic comedy, as Sullivan and the Girl meet up in a Los Angeles diner. Journey #3 is Sturges's playful and moving tribute to Chaplin, as the Girl and Sullivan hit the road—or rather the boxcar—together and wind up handing out free money to the homeless in a misguided effort to help them out. This brings on Journey #4, as Sullivan is robbed and beaten, loses his memory and becomes a prisoner on a country chain gang.

Characters: Sullivan is really something of a purposeful holy fool, and thus a fish out of water or a total innocent outside of Hollywood. Does he change? Yes: he learns that there is nothing wrong with making comedies.

And he learns this through one of the great scenes in American comedy: Still suffering from amnesia, Sullivan joins his fellow prisoners in a poor black church, where they are invited for a gospel service and a screening of some silent cartoons. As the Pluto cartoon unrolls in the church, the men and the congregation burst into uproarious laughter. And Sullivan, in spite of himself, starts laughing too. Sturges's point is thus simply and powerfully made. Comedy is a kind of healing and communal catharsis.

Veronica Lake is the romantic interest, and she is very much in the romantic tradition of being as sharp as or sharper than Sullivan, and like Shakespeare's women she is able to trade joke for joke, pun for pun, soothing line for soothing line.

Audience: Broad. I've shown the film dozens of times to various audiences, and they all "get it." Once again, proof of Sturges's message of comedy's wide appeal, reaching prisoners and African American parishioners within the film.

Special highlights: too many to elaborate, but here are a few.

- The playful send-up of narrative structure. As in *The Palm Beach Story,* he begins with an ending: what we see is actually the ending of the serious social drama Sullivan is trying to release, *Oh! Brother, Where Art Thou?* It ends with two men killing each other as THE END appears on-screen and we learn we are in a Hollywood screening room.
- Romantic screwball dialogue at its best: the diner scene, in which Sullivan and the Girl meet as she buys him breakfast, includes some of the most memorable of Sturges's fast-paced lines.
- The wonderful understatement of the scene in which the Girl and Sullivan try to catch a boxcar train, as two real hobos watch the new couple's clumsy efforts to jump aboard and one says to the other, "Amateurs."
- The handling of the "silent" Chaplinesque sequence, as a rich musical score adds emotion to their efforts to hand out money, thus dropping the laughter for a few minutes to touch a deeper nerve.
- Finally, the church sequence with the projected cartoon—inspired writing and directing all around.

Add to this that Sturges manages to make this both a "couple" film and an ensemble comedy with his usual gang of wonderful characters—William Demarest, Franklin Pangborn, Jimmy Conlin, Robert Warwick and others—and you have an added treat that makes this timeless viewing.

Fresh Variations on the Buddy Comedy: *Big Night*, a Culinary Comedy

Big Night (1996) is that small, unusual independent comedy that you are impressed got made at all and that manages, seemingly against all odds, to find a "cross-over" audience and make some money. The script, written over five years by actor and co-director Stanley Tucci and his author cousin, Joseph Tropiano, is absolutely an act of love that celebrates the comic spirit of taking chances. A familiar face from secondary roles in such films as *The Pelican Brief* and *Kiss of Death* as well as a lot of television, including *Murder One, thirtysomething* and *Wiseguy,* Tucci originally teamed up with Tropiano with a vague idea based on the mammoth Italian American lunches their grandmother used to prepare every Sunday when they were kids. What they finally ended up with, I think, is the best American script and film ever about food, but also a very touching and funny buddy film about two brothers who, despite all, remain family and friends. And it breaks through the stereotypes of Italian American men as gangsters to present, as Tucci has said, "Italian-Americans with frying pans rather than machine guns" (NPR interview, October, 1996).

The plot is clear and simple. Two Italian immigrant brothers, appropriately named Primo (Tony Shalhoub) and Secundo (Stanley Tucci), in a small New Jersey town in the 1950s are trying to save the Paradise, their gourmet restaurant, before it goes under financially. The main narrative thrust is thus a difficult task to be performed, with a strong anarchistic bent to it: they are refusing to "give the customers what they want." This is a character-driven comedy in which the main humor comes from our delight in getting to know these two brothers and the fine ensemble of characters around them. As critics such as Bob Greene have noted, "This is very much an actors' movie" (13).

More specifically, the story gains comic tension as the clock ticks, for the brothers have one night to prepare the feast of a lifetime in hopes that their special guest will be the popular singer Louis Prima and members of his band, as arranged by rival restaurant owner Pascal (Ian Holm). Naturally they discover by feast's end that Pascal has double-crossed them, and after a fight between the brothers on the nearby beach, we are left with one of the finest endings I can remember in an American comedy.

The romantic element is worked in as a double subplot. Secundo is caught between his affair with Pascal's fiery forty-something Italian American mistress, Gabriella (Isabella Rosselini), and an attractive, no-nonsense younger American girlfriend, Phyllis (Minnie Driver), while Primo, bashful and inept when it comes to women, is attracted to Ann (Allison Janney), the local florist who supplies the restaurant with flowers.

But Big Night is much more than a "save the farm" film with a restaurant in the role of the farm. It is, as Terrence Rafferty notes in his New Yorker review, very much "a fable of art versus commerce" (100), with commerce winning for the immediate future but brotherhood and art being the moral winners in the end. Primo is established as a master chef, and thus as a character he is an artist of the highest order, unwilling to compromise. This fact alone makes him something of an anarchistic holy fool. He is not just unwilling to compromise, but he seems truly clueless as to how America and capitalism function. Secundo, on the other hand, is in every sense the immigrant attempting to adjust to the New World, as seen in the wonderful sequence in Pascal's office and in his joy ride in a Cadillac with the salesman (played by co-director Campbell Scott). The brothers are, therefore, a study in contrast: we can see Primo as the introvert and Secundo as the extrovert in every sense, from business to sexual politics. And yet they are united not just as buddies but by blood: they are, bottom line, brothers.

The comic climate of the film balances between warm humor and clearly etched irony. Directors Tucci and Scott manage to keep the pacing fast enough to hold our interest without turning the film into the pie-in-the-face food farce it could easily have degenerated into. In fact, Tropiano notes that part of the evolution of this script was from easy farce to character-centered comedy. "When we first started writing this, it was more of a farce. These brothers ran this restaurant, and there was this goofy Pascal guy across the street" (48). More specifically, the script took shape as they realized they wanted to go beyond the stereotypes of Italian gangster men in American cinema, such as in the films of Martin Scorsese and in the *Godfather* films by Francis Ford Coppola. "All these stereotypes are really insulting," comments Tropiano (48).

What emerged was a script that takes chances by going against the Hollywood wisdom of dumbing down comedy or bending to ethnic stereotypes. Thus Tucci and Tropiano were very much aiming for *an intelligent audience covering both the art house and the discerning mainstream theaters.* And they found it!

Highlights include:

1. A fine balance between ensemble group scenes and quieter small scenes, either between the brothers or, especially, between Secundo and his women or between Secundo and Pascal.

2. Well-constructed dialogue that rings true. The following scene sets up the whole core conflict of the film and suggests the fine comic insight and timing. It occurs after the brothers have just lost the only customers of the evening because Primo will not serve meatballs with spaghetti.

SECUNDO: What do you think about that? Take risotto off the menu?

PRIMO: I'm sorry, what did you say?

SECUNDO: Forget it.

PRIMO: No, I no hear what you say. Tell me what you say.

SECUNDO: Look. Risotto costs us a lot. And it take you a long time to make . . . I mean, you must work so hard to make, so, then we have to charge more, and . . . these customers don't understand really what is a risotto, and so there always is a problem.

A beat.

PRIMO: Sure. Good.

SECUNDO: OK. Good.

PRIMO: Yeah, that's good.

A beat.

PRIMO: Maybe instead we could put . . .

SECUNDO: Yeah, tell me, tell me . . .

PRIMO: I was thinking . . . uh . . . what do they call them . . . You know . . . hot dog? Hog dogs, hot dogs. Hot dogs. I think people would like that. Those.

Secundo stares at him.

SECUNDO: Fine.

He gets up and begins to gather the money.

PRIMO: If you give people time, they learn.

SECUNDO: I don't have time for them to learn. This is a restaurant. Not a fucking school.

Secundo leaves the frame. Primo goes back to his paper.

(*Big Night*)

Part of what we appreciate here is not just the comic repetition but the "jumps" in the dialogue caused by switches within the characters. Ultimately we sense that these brothers know each other so well that they play games. Thus Primo's surprise "OK," which turns out to be complete irony when he brings up "hot dogs," and then the straightforward exchange at the end that nails their differences exactly.

3. A carnivalesque balance between visual and verbal comedy. The film embraces the clever photography and montage presentation of food as a definite character in the film as well. This attention to detail immediately adds realism and fires the audience's taste buds. It is visual "comedy" when the brothers prepare and serve the food to Louis Prima's bouncy music and when the assembled group devours the food, dances, goes into ecstasy and finally fades away.

4. A bittersweet embrace ending that leaves the future open. If this were an anarchistic comedy in the Aristophanic tradition, we could close with a triumphant victory for the brothers, with Louis Prima in the Paradise, being photographed by the papers. The good nature and artistic talent of the brothers would have been rewarded.

But Tucci and Tropiano do not create such a fairy tale. Instead we are left in the kitchen with the sense that the restaurant has failed and the brothers have fought and offended each other. And yet, as Secundo quietly cooks an omelet and serves it to Primo, we have a beautifully written and realized "silent" comedy of renewed brotherhood and thus of hope for their futures, whatever they will be. The script says:

> *Without looking up from his plate, Secundo reaches over to Primo and places his hand on his back, tentatively. Primo looks at Secundo and Secundo looks up and meets his eyes.*

(*Big Night*, 46)

The actual film is even stronger: their eyes do not meet, but Primo reaches over too and places an arm around his brother. The camera pulls back as the brothers are still eating, embracing each other, silently.

That image says more than the pages of dialogue that most films feel they need to wrap a narrative.

And one final note: the last line of dialogue in the film is Secundo to Primo as he comes in: "Are you hungry?" Primo doesn't answer, just sits down, and then the above scene plays out. To end this at times joyful and at times bitter comedy about food and fellowship with a question about hunger is perfect!

Women and American Comedy: Penny Marshall's *A League of Their Own*

If we speak literally of women "in" comedy, we mean the actresses in front of the camera: bright and brilliant women such as Katharine Hepburn, Claudette Colbert, Jean Arthur, Barbara Stanwyck and Rosalind Russell. In more recent years we've seen smart and sassy comic performances from the likes of Shirley MacLaine, Whoopi Goldberg, Bette Midler, Goldie Hawn, Barbra Streisand, Diane Keaton, Melanie Griffith, Lily Tomlin, Jamie Lee Curtis, Amanda Plummer, Meg Ryan and Holly Hunter. But there is an equally long tradition of dumb blondes and actresses used and abused by the comic male leads. Where would Groucho be without Margaret Dumont to make fun of? Marilyn Monroe was that rare individual who, though cast as the sexy dumb blonde, managed through strength of personality to turn her roles upside down and inside out, so that we came off respecting her for who she was.

Women in comedy *behind* the camera becomes a much more problematic topic. There have not been many. Two of my choices in this section are a tribute to that rare and talented breed that one hopes will grow in number: women directors. Certainly Diane Keaton has jumped into the circle of the chosen few women who direct comedies, and we can also mention Susan Seidelman (*Desperately Seeking Susan*, 1984), Nora Ephron (*Sleepless in Seattle*, 1993), and Penelope Spheeris with *Wayne's World*.

Let us now examine one female-centered comedy up close. *A League of Their Own* is an ensemble character film that starts within a highly comic climate and moves toward a much more sober "embrace" conclusion.

Beginning as an actress herself, best remembered for playing Laverne in *Laverne and Shirley*, Penny Marshall has gone on to direct a number of highly successful films, including the comedies *Jumpin' Jack Flash* (1986), *Big* (1988), *A League of Their Own* (1992) and *Renaissance Man* (1994).

Based on a script by Babaloo Mandel and Lowell Ganz from a story idea by Kim Wilson and Kelly Candaele, *A League of Their Own* is clearly an *anarchistic ensemble comedy* grounded in a little-known page of American baseball history: during World War II, the lack of professional male ballplayers made it possible for a female pro league to catch on with moderate success. We could almost call this Aristophanes' *Lysistrata* goes to bat!

The audience is a very wide one: baseball lovers, women who wish to see at last an all-star female cast, and children as well. The film was rated PG, and ticket sales reflected a very diverse audience indeed.

The plot is the basic Aristophanic one of a crazy idea—creating a pro women's ball league—that gets carried out. Thus most of the laughs come from turning the typically male sports-centered story upside down: women in the locker room, women on the field stealing bases and hitting home runs, women swearing and riding the team bus around the country from game to game.

The script is structured as a circular tale, framing the World War II plot with a present-day gathering of the surviving "old ladies" in Cooperstown, New York, for the unveiling of a monument and exhibit dedicated to the team. This "then and now" set-up builds instant nostalgia by film's end, as we enjoy seeing the aged but familiar faces of Geena Davis, Madonna and others.

Within this overall narrative structure, two stories unfold. The primary tale is a sisterhood plot about Dottie (Geena Davis) and Kit (Lori Petty), two Oregon farm girls who are tapped for the big leagues. Dottie is the beauty and the apparent athlete, but Kit turns out to be the pro who goes the full distance, as Dottie drops out once her husband returns from the war, wounded but ready to start a family.

We see once more how comedy and melodrama cross, as the second half of the film concerns the rather somber development of Kit's growth and Dottie's departure from the pros. The ending becomes a solid embrace between sisters. Taking place in the present, the soulful hug is a "happy ending" that unites past and present and washes away all past antagonisms and hurt feelings in true sisterly concern—for the ending in the *past* is a World Series in which Kit's Racine, Wisconsin, team beats out Dottie's Rockford Peaches.

The second plot line revolves around Tom Hanks as Jimmy, their alcoholic ex-pro coach. He is both an *alazon* (buffoon) and an *eiron,* as he sarcastically manipulates the girls to get what he wants: a championship season. By film's end, however, he proves to be a Good Soul who takes the women's best interests to heart.

Highlights include a number of comic montages to suggest the passage of time and the growth of the women as players, and to cover their years on the road on buses and in boardinghouses.

Scatological slapstick is given a strong nod, especially in Tom Hanks's entry and hilariously long urination introduction to the team in their locker room. Penny Marshall plays the humor broadly enough to hold a large audience, and yet she avoids dwelling too long on such humor, since the final overall feeling the film leaves you with is a warm but tearfully nostalgic one.

The script manages the transition from humorous sports film to serious meditation on girls becoming women through sports with two particular touches. In the first, which we can place as the end of act 2, one of the women learns in a particularly moving scene that her husband has been killed on the front. And in the second, we realize that Tom Hanks has died several years before the "present" and thus is unable to be there to savor the success of his coaching. His absence makes his presence all the more powerful.

A League of Their Own manages to have its comedy both ways: the first half is often hilarious and very light and bright, often pure farce, but in the second half and particularly the last act the film has few laughs and a surprising number of tears, all wrapped in the banner of nostalgia and renewed sisterhood. While we laugh, we get a glimpse of changing values in American culture, as women who had previously defined themselves only as wives or working women in traditional roles now become more self-assured in their new "professional" images.

The screenwriters and Marshall deserve special credit for not overdoing the slapstick and for avoiding a simplistic romance between the Geena Davis and Tom Hanks characters. They come close, but the script resists such a cliché.

Race, Politics and Humor:
Spike Lee's *Get on the Bus*

The humor of any dominant culture in any country runs the risk of unfairly stereotyping other ethnic, racial or political groups. Conversely, humor and comedy become important ways in which a minority group can discuss its situation, in relation both to dominant cultures and to its own people.

African American comedians and actors have for years worked a wide spectrum of humor, ranging from the biting activist routines of Dick Gregory or Richard Pryor to the middle-class, image-conscious humor of Bill Cosby or the trendy youth laughter of Will Smith and Wesley Snipes.

At the center of commercial African American filmmaking over the past decade and more, however, is Spike Lee. Combining laughter with racial and sociopolitical insight, his films, beginning with *She's Gotta Have It* (1986), *School Daze* (1988) and most significantly *Do The Right Thing* (1989), have given voice to many concerns of contemporary urban African Americans.

Get on the Bus (1996), with a script by Reggie Rock Bythewood, is even more daring than Lee's previous work. Here, on a small budget of several million dollars raised entirely by fifteen African Americans, including Danny Glover, Will Smith and others, he successfully pulls off a very difficult assignment: making a fiction film about the Million Man March of 1995 without alienating either the Marchers or their detractors. I have watched the film a number of times now, and I must say I am deeply impressed with the concept, writing, and execution of this *anarchistic ensemble comic drama*. And Lee uses the element of improvisation (discussed in chapter 8) to make the very short shooting schedule a strength rather than a weakness.

Audience: targets the African American male, but the film "works" for audiences of all ages and races. Box-office receipts, however, and surveys did show that there was very little crossover to nonblack audiences.

Structure: Get on the Bus is a picaresque political road movie. The topic is the Million Man March, but much of the brilliance of the film is that instead of the typical dramatic story of a central character or two attending the March, perhaps experiencing both difficulties and transforming joy and then going home to make changes in their lives, Lee and scriptwriter Bythewood have made the journey *to* the March 85 percent of the film!

Given that the overall subject matter is a serious one, an even more important theme emerges through the film: the identity, role and significance of the African American male in American culture today. Bythewood and Lee have, furthermore, happily chosen to tackle this most serious topic with humor and pathos in such proportions that the humor keeps the pathos from ever turning into oversentimentality or easy melodrama.

I refer you back to our discussion in chapter 7 of Boccaccio and the Italian tradition of shaping comic narratives around a group telling stories. For Bythewood and Lee have similarly employed a *Decameron* structure in filling a bus with a wide spectrum of different black males, each of whom "tells" his own story. And in a spirit similar to both Boccaccio and Dante, *the overall sense of "comedy" comes from the celebration of the group as group and thus a microcommunity, ultimately tolerant of all its members.* The ending is thus very much an embrace.

Characters: This Noah's Ark of a bus has at least one of every kind of man we can imagine, including

> Evert, a truck driver and one-time deadbeat father who is now trying to come closer to Shmoo
>
> Shmoo, his hiphop teenage son, who has been picked up for shoplifting and allowed to come on the bus only chained to his father (the chains become a central ironic image for a "freedom" bus!)
>
> Xavier, a UCLA film student, a younger Spike Lee figure, out to capture the ride and the March on video as a class project
>
> Gary, a mulatto police officer with a white mother and a black policeman father who was murdered in the line of duty by a black man
>
> Jeremiah (Ossie Davis), a failed businessman, husband, father and man of the cloth with heart trouble, out to redeem himself
>
> An actor who claims he was "almost" cast in *Boyz N The Hood*
>
> A gay black couple who are trying to break up but remain friends (one, Mandell, is smooth, while the other is a rasta)
>
> A Black Muslim who used to deal drugs and has murdered a few brothers in the past

There are others as well, but the second most important member (after Ossie Davis, who functions as a wise grandfather figure for the group, leading them in prayer and in African drumming) is George, the bus driver (Charles S. Dutton).

The loose structure, wide variety of characters and finely tuned dialogue mean that there are nonstop opportunities for laughter, wise smiles and even tears, as Jeremiah dies in a Washington hospital as the March is beginning. Thus the film suggests that for many of the men onboard the triumph was not the actual March but the journey *to* the March and the humanity they have shown in being with Jeremiah.

The bus-ride structure and ample uses of confrontational humor among such a group also allow Bythewood and Lee to cover a multitude of important issues for black males (and ultimately for all Americans), as they discuss, argue, fight over and sometimes come together on topics such as black women, black Islamic vs. Christian movements, Southern vs. Northern or Western blacks, Jews and the African American community, drug violence in the black community, skin color among blacks, fatherhood and race, and relationships with women, including fidelity and infidelity.

By film's end, the sense of triumph required of comedy is apparent in each character, even Jeremiah, who dies knowing he has made a difference in the lives of those around him. No sudden miracles have taken place. But father and son do throw off the lock and chain and express their love for each other, and throughout the bus each takes back something of the spirit of the group.

George, the bus driver, gets to make a key speech near the end, much in the spirit of *Mr. Smith Goes to Washington,* as he tells the whole group, "God asks what you gonna do now. The real march ain't even started yet. We got work to do." Inside the Lincoln Memorial, they read a prayer written by Jeremiah.

Highlights would definitely include the "Roll Call" song that kicks off the ride in California as the group is immediately united through music, and a sequence in which a rich African American car dealer with an attitude gets thrown off the bus by the whole group before they reach Virginia.

Get on the Bus takes a lot of chances with humor in terms of character, story and theme, and I can't think of one of them that doesn't pay off handsomely in this small film that will find a larger audience over the years.

Children and Comedy:
The White Balloon, a Young Girl's
Comic Odyssey

Iran seems an unlikely place to look for an enjoyable and wise comedy about childhood. But *The White Balloon* (1995) is just one of many fine films "for children" that this Islamic nation with very strict limits on what can be shown or discussed has produced. Writers, pay attention: in a country that basically bans stories on politics, sex or religion, for starters, what do you write? Children's tales, of course! What we can learn from a film such as *The White Balloon* is both an engaging simplicity of story and style and a lesson or two about "Aesopian" storytelling. This is a term used for artists, writers and filmmakers in the former Communist regimes of the Soviet Union and Eastern Europe, where they learned the art of saying what they really wanted to say indirectly or metaphorically. An important part of the success of *The White Balloon*, therefore, is that this film, written by the famed director-screenwriter Abbas Kiarostami and directed by Jafar Panahi, is aimed not only at a children's market but at an attentive adult audience as well. Thus an important lesson for us all: how to craft a comedy that reaches both children and adults who have not forgotten the child within!

The plot is a picaresque journey story as a seven-year-old girl, Razieh (Aida Mohammadkhani), sets off from her home in a crowded Teheran neighborhood to buy a "dancing" goldfish as a New Year's gift. The plot twist involves the loss of the five-hundred-toman note her mother gave her and her tough-minded and clever determination to get it back.

Yes, this is anarchistic comedy, but like many we have discussed, it is anarchistic with a muted rather than Aristophanic ending. Razieh's idea to hunt out the goldfish is a crazy one, according to her older brother, who points to the goldfish she already has in their courtyard pond. Her answer is the classic one of childhood wishes and "pre-Oedipal" behavior: "Yes, that's true, but they are not the right ones!"

We adults laugh out loud (and definitely harder than the children in the audience) at this line, for we realize that Panahi and Kiarostami have hit upon a universal subject for comedy: all of us want that other goldfish, for we are not satisfied with the ones at hand!

This is the stuff of fairy tales, and yet from the opening shot we are in the streets of Teheran, teeming with life, sounds and probably odors. In fact, *the comic climate* is carnivalesque, since all happens during the festive period of an Islamic New Year celebration. The white balloon of the title is being sold in the street as part of the celebration, and it cleverly distracts us from the comic center of the film: Razieh's journey of initiation to beginning to come of age, travelling away from the safe and known confines of her home into the "real" world.

Definitely character-centered, this picaresque fish-out-of-water tale (she is definitely outside the environment she knows best, her home) opens up Razieh's multifaceted personality as both an innocent and an ironic instigator of trouble (comedy!), or, as Richard Corliss put it, "Razieh is a maven of curb-level politics, a born haggler. She'd be a demon at any yard sale" (46).

Screenwriters should study the film for the small details that slyly become significant. In the opening, for instance, we see Razieh heading home with her mother, but she breaks away for a moment to watch some old dervish snake charmers who have gathered an all-male crowd. We sense, therefore, that her desire for the dancing goldfish is simply the outer expression of a deeper burning to check out the exotic street life beyond her family's four walls.

It is to the filmmaker's credit that he and the script avoid making Razieh an overly cute Shirley Temple. In fact, we often feel like throttling her. She herself has a look beyond her years that suggests the middle-aged woman she might well become.

Highlights include an early scene in which a snake charmer reduces her to tears as he places her goldfish money in a box with his snake as a group of men watch on, as well as an extended sequence in which the money falls down a drain and we meet a cross-section of the population as she and finally her brother try to retrieve the money. It is in this way that a refugee boy selling white balloons enters the plot.

The ending is both an embrace—she obtains her goldfish and heads home with her brother—and a loner: the final shot is of the boy with the white balloon sitting alone. Subtly, the filmmaker ends not with an Iranian family celebrating the New Year together but with a homeless refugee, alone with nowhere to go, no one with whom to share the festivities.

Teens and Comedy: Amy Heckerling's *Clueless,* a Valley-Talking Anarchistic Romance

Amy Heckerling penned and directed *Clueless* (1995), one of the brightest, funniest teenage comedies in years, inspired, believe it or not, by Jane Austen's *Emma.* I've included *Clueless* as a shining example of how to write for and about teens without looking down on them and without reducing them to shallow stereotypes. Heckerling has a special talent for both spoofing teen culture and celebrating the joys of teenhood in America (specifically California, more specifically Beverly Hills) at the same time.

Heckerling has paid her dues, especially with her groundbreaking *Fast Times at Ridgemont High* (1982), which proved an early showcase for Sean Penn, Jennifer Jason Leigh and Judge Reinhold, among others. She is completely tuned in to the way Southern California teens talk, walk and act. We feel in both films that she is writing from the inside out.

The plot: Clueless is the reverse of Sturges's *Sullivan's Travels,* a romantic anarchistic comedy. Heckerling's comedy is an anarchistic romance. Her target audience is teens everywhere, but it speaks well for her talent that Heckerling's film brings laughter to audiences of all ages. During the first half the main character, Cher (Alicia Silverstone), has the "crazy" idea of being everyone else's matchmaker as an exercise in control and power. First she practices on her high school English teacher, with the selfish motive of wanting a higher midterm grade. And then she and her African American sidekick, Dione (Stacey Dash), pounce on the new girl in school, Tye (Brittany Murphy), for a make-over and a matchmaking session. This second half is absolutely a carnival of Aristophanic comedy, as Cher "rules" in her kingdom.

Heckerling's mastery of anarchistic comedy stems from the following elements:

1. A razor-sharp ear for teen talk and slang. Heckerling has made "As if!" and "Hello!" (accent heavily on the last syllable, please) everyday phrases for millions of viewers. Everyone has their favorite lines and exchanges, but no one can remember them all; thus the pleasure of repeated viewings this film brings. Here are just a few. When Cher reads a few lines of poetry she has copied for a false love letter from her English professor to her unsuspecting, troll-like guidance advisor, Dione asks where it is from.

> CHER: That's a famous quote.
> DIONE: From where?
> CHER: Cliff Notes!

When Cher's father finds a stack of parking tickets the licenseless Cher has run up, he exclaims, "I didn't even know you can get tickets without having a license." Or Cher on how she checks herself while dressing: "I don't rely on mirrors, so I always take Polaroids." Her disappointment in her big date with Christian, whom she does not yet understand is gay, is expressed with, "I guess it just wasn't meant to be. He does dress better than I do. What could I bring to the relationship?"

But clever lines alone do not a comedy make, as we know.

2. The creation of Cher as a comic protagonist who is half trickster and half innocent, and completely a clown. Yes, Jane Austen deserves credit for the original prototype. But Heckerling has leaped forward to turn Cher Horowitz into a sixteen-year-old gal whom we laugh both at (ridiculous) and with (ludicrous). Heckerling's use of *first-person voiceover* also does a lot for helping to establish Cher as a sympathetic "ditz with credit cards," or, in Tye's cruel words, "A virgin who doesn't know how to drive." Heckerling strikes a perfect balance between voiceover narration and simply letting her story roll.

3. Music-video-style pacing, editing and comedy. Heckerling helps keep this teen comedy light and bright in the first half, hitting us with music and images as well as sparkling dialogue. She thus incorporates teen culture into the style of her script.

The second half of the film becomes a screwball romance as all her carefully laid plans for Tye blow up, beginning when the intended boyfriend nearly rapes her in a parking lot dominated by a huge neon clown. All the formulas of screwball romance are touched on in this half, as Cher discovers she was wrong on all her "character" calls, but most of all, she was wrong about herself. And Josh, her "ex-stepbrother" (yes, as Cher's crazed lawyer father says, "You divorce wives, not children") emerges as the love interest.

Several critics paid *Clueless* the ultimate tribute when the film premiered in 1996: they noted that *Emma* was *Clueless* set in the nineteenth century but not as well done!

Blurring the Boundaries: Crime and Comedy in the Coen Brothers' *Fargo*

Quentin Tarantino caught the attention of a small dedicated audience with *Reservoir Dogs* (1992), and then the whole world with his irreverent *Pulp Fiction* (1994), blending laughter and murder in jarringly postmodern juxtapositions. American crime films have always had some very funny and ironic lines in them, especially since so many of them either came directly from or imitated great hard-boiled writers such as Dashiell Hammett and Raymond Chandler. These films can teach us much about laughter with an edge. We all remember Tarantino's snappy dialogue as John Travolta talks to Samuel L. Jackson about Big Macs in Paris as they're on the way to carry out an "assignment." The lines are funny enough in and of themselves, with Jackson playing the straight man to Travolta's wise guy. But what is distinctly "Tarantinesque" is the dark absurdity of the conversation, given that we know they are about to murder someone.

But for years before Tarantino began shooting his dark-humored films, the Coen brothers had been making us laugh in uncomfortable moments. Throughout their careers they have blurred the boundaries between cinematic genres as well as between independent and Hollywood productions. They have managed to keep an admirable independence in such quirky and original films as *Blood Simple* (1984), *Raising Arizona* (1987), *Miller's Crossing* (1990), *Barton Fink* (1991) and *The Hudsucker Proxy* (1994). With *Fargo* (1996) they not only walked off with Oscars for Best Original Screenplay and Best Actress (the amazing Frances McDormand), but they managed to mix crime and humor in a refreshing blend that had all audiences walking out with smiles on their faces and imitating Minnesota Scandinavian English, "Yah!"

What did they accomplish and how did they do it?

Start with *the strong sense of place, atmosphere and season:* the dead of a Minnesota winter. Ethan Coen, in his introduction to the published screenplay for *Fargo*, makes it clear that he and his brother, Joel (co-author and the director of their films), grew up in that bleak Minnesota landscape celebrated in the film. He builds on their experiences listening to tales by their Russian Jewish grandmother, which sounded true and exotic but which, on reflection, tested "credulity" (viii). In the spirit of their grandmother, they observe, "The stories that are not credible will occasionally, however, turn out to be true, and stories that ARE credible will conversely turn out to be false" (xix, x).

Nothing in the set-up of the film suggests the comic. As the film begins with a whited-out screen and an epic-sounding orchestra score, we might think we are in for *Dr. Zhivago, Part Two.* The tone is thus serious and mythic, as Ethan Coen suggests, and the iconic shot of a huge Paul Bunyan throughout the film alludes to other "myths" from the area. But as this dark tale of Jerry Lungegan, a simpleminded car salesman (an innocent little guy gone wrong) who hires two thugs (trickster *eirons*) to kidnap his wife in a hairbrained scheme to try to get out of debt, unfolds, laughter starts to become a distinguishing feature of this mixedgenre production. The Coens do blur the boundaries between what we normally think of as comic material and what should be offensive and gruesome as Jerry's whole scheme goes from bad to worse and then even worse still. Yet this story alone is not the heart of the film. The Coens skillfully present a *double tale,* each playing off the other. We wait a good thirty minutes to be introduced to Officer Marge Gunderson (Frances McDormand), the investigating police officer. At that point the whole focus and tone of the film shift to Marge, her artist husband Norm and their baby-to-be. In short, the crime plot is *not* what is at the center of the violence and the humor of this film; rather, family is. Jerry's world is one of failed marriage, failed fatherhood, a failed family in every sense: thus the spiral of violence, the crimes and murders, and the sad final arrest of Jerry in his underwear in a cheap motel. The flip side is our growing understanding of how good a marriage Marge and Norm have and what a truly happy family they will be after their child's birth. How do we know this? From the Coen brothers' careful attention to loving details, such as Norm's housekeeping and Marge's thoughtfulness in picking up worms for his fishing trips in the middle of her murder investigation (talk about role reversals!). And, the closing scene is a *strong embrace ending,* literally and figuratively. Marge and Norm are in bed, celebrating the news that Norm's painting of a duck has been accepted for a three-cent stamp. Once more, in a loving reversal of traditional roles, it is Marge, the real breadwinner of this duo, who comforts an insecure Norm. Listen to the humor and love and plain old good writing in that final exchange:

> NORM: They announced it.
> *Marge looks at him.*
> MARGE: They announced it?
> NORM: Yah.
> *Marge looks at him waiting for more, but Norm's eyes stay fixed on the television.*
> MARGE: ... So?

NORM: Three-cent stamp.

MARGE: Your mallard?

NORM: Yah.

MARGE: Norm, that's terrific!

Norm tries to suppress a smile of pleasure.

NORM: It's just the three-cent.

MARGE: It's terrific!

NORM: Hautman's blue-winged teal got the twenty-nine cent. People don't much use the three-cent.

MARGE: Oh, for Pete's—a course they do! Every time they raise the darned postage, people need the little stamps!

NORM: Yah.

MARGE: When they're stuck with a bunch a the old ones!

NORM: Yah, I guess.

MARGE: That's terrific.

Her eyes go back to the TV.

I'm so proud a you, Norm.

They watch TV.

. . . Heck, we're doin' pretty good, Norm.

Norm murmurs.

NORM: I love you, Margie.

MARGE: I love you, Norm.

Both of them are watching the TV as Norm reaches out to rest a hand on top of her stomach.

NORM: . . . Two more months.

Marge absently rests her own hand on top of his.

MARGE: Two more months.

Hold; fade out.

Pulp Fiction makes us laugh throughout its unfolding, but the final moment of Travolta and Jackson swaying out of the diner, having defused the robbery set up in the opening scene of the film, is a false "happy ending," for we already know that Travolta will be murdered while trying to pull his pants up. *Fargo*, on the other hand, begins bleakly, but subtly and surely the crime film becomes a family comedy.

Highlights: Too many to elaborate in a brief summary. But I would target five important comic levels in *Fargo*.

1. The double-story structure we have already mentioned succeeds in turning a crime film upside down and inside out. Just reverse the final scenes and think what a different film it would be if it ended with Jerry's pathetic arrest.

2. Character development: Jerry is stupid, but we don't hate him. The Coens shade his character so we have some sympathy for this sad fellow. And part of that sadness is that we never really understand what he is all about or what has gone wrong in his marriage. Similarly, Marge is brilliantly detailed. After all, we've never had a pregnant Minnesota police inspector on the screen before.

3. Visual humor: Take the scene late in the film when Grimsrud, the silent criminal (laconically played by Peter Stormare), is shoving Jerry's wife's leg into a wood-shredding machine. The scene is so bizarre and original that we can't help laughing, and yet the Coens have blurred the boundaries, for we know whose leg it is. As in all of their films, such a visualization of humor works well to capture a rather surrealistic level within the real world of the narrative.

4. Fine comic dialogue based on dialect: As mentioned in the beginning of this discussion, the Coens could write this dialogue because they grew up hearing it. Just imagine how false it would sound if someone who had never been to Minnesota had tried to write such lines: stereotyping or simpleminded caricaturing would probably result. The Coens, however, wound up with a Minnesota twang and laconic, loopy speech patterns that the whole nation enjoyed hearing and that even those I've interviewed who hail from those Scandinavian parts were not offended by.

5. And they created memorable minor characters! Who can forget the scenes with the two minor criminals, Showalter (perfectly realized by Steve Buscemi) and Grimsrud, especially the scene in which they are driving and Showalter can't stop talking, while Grimsrud says not a word. Once more, the Coens tread the thin line between caricature and character successfully, for there is a realism behind the exaggeration of the scene.

CHAPTER 10

Television Comedy:
Seinfeld and *The Simpsons*

You know, sometimes when I think you're the shallowest man
I've ever met, you somehow manage to drain a little more out
of the pool.

Elaine to Jerry in Seinfeld

I'll tell you about the time I got locked in the bank vault with
Mr. Mooney. It was another one of my harebrained schemes
. . . Wait a minute. That was a *Lucy* show!

Homer in The Simpsons

Our task in this chapter is to understand more clearly how two of the all-time most popular episodic television comedies "work." Then in chapter 12, it will be your turn to have a go at it.

Few shows make it past the five-year mark. Thus our two focal offerings in this chapter, *Seinfeld* and *The Simpsons,* should already command both our attention and our respect. As we go to print, *The Simpsons* is past the ten-year mark while *Seinfeld* continues to play strongly in reruns around the world. That alone says a lot about the quality of the writing and the staying power of good comedy. Our close-up on these shows will take us not only into the make-up of each series but also into a detailed look at representative scripts from the shows.

Do these two seemingly very different comedies share anything besides the ability to make millions laugh for twenty-six minutes at a time? The answer is "yes" on at least two fronts. Both are media- and audience-conscious, and each is fearless in experimenting with subject matter, format and the twisting and turning of narrative possibilities, including the use of dream, fantasy, flashbacks and flashforwards. Seinfeld the character is, after all, a successful comedian, and a number of episodes play with that reality, giving him total license to be a stand-up comedian within this sitcom. Similarly, every *Simpsons* episode begins with the imaginative credit sequence, showing each Simpson rushing home to watch . . . television. Each time, the Simpsons see "Created by Matt Groening" appear on the screen. The wink to both the medium and the audience, a prime characteristic of stage comedy since Aristophanes, is therefore definitely at play in both shows.

Seinfeld: Much Ado about Something

Jerry Seinfeld announced his resignation from the *Seinfeld* show after nine very successful seasons (1989–1998), doing what few actors, let alone comedians, have done: quit while they are ahead. "It's all about timing," said Jerry at the time, and in a real sense, he was absolutely correct (Handy, 77). For to watch any *Seinfeld* episode is to see a perfectly timed performance that *blends stand-up with ensemble anarchistic sitcom.* "Stand-up" because Jerry plays himself, a successful stand-up comedian; "ensemble" because it is a four-character series, with George, Kramer and Elaine sharing the spotlight from moment to moment; and "anarchistic" since each episode is propelled by several crazy ideas that usually, unlike Aristophanes' fantasies, go wrong, or at best astray. Note too that while there is a lot of dating and a lot of flirting and some sex, there really is nothing "romantic" about these late-twentieth-century New York singles.

One more classification: *Seinfeld* is also a *comedy of manners.* That is, like British comedies of the seventeenth century by William Wycherley and William Congreve, each *Seinfeld* episode brings up issues and customs of social interaction, examines them from a variety of angles and leads to some form of conclusion about them. We will follow a number of "manners" examined in the episode "The Kiss Hello," with the main plot being how and why and whom we kiss "hello" as a social greeting. In a comedy of manners, much of the laughter is generated by the characters' varying reactions to social manners and customs. Further, we follow the reactions to the conflict between individual desires and group pressures. Given that *Seinfeld* captures a culture in constant change, the possibilities for laughter are myriad.

Media critic Mike Flaherty has detailed seven principles that formed something of a backbone for the series from its beginning. Note how many of these dovetail with the observations on comedy offered in my introduction:

1. "The characters *playfully* do not grow," says Seinfeld writer Larry Charles (24). This factor is a clear thumbing of the nose not only at traditional family-oriented comedies and romantic comedy in general, but also at simplistic, feel-good "self-help" movements.

2. Nothing is sacred. The limits of taste are constantly pushed, as episodes treat everything from masturbation to making out while watching *Schindler's List.* How wide a range of material did the show embrace? Larry Charles, who wrote for *Seinfeld* for four seasons before moving on to the award-winning *Mad About You,* noted that just one season "went from *I Love Lucy* to Thomas Pynchon, from Al Hirt to John Coltrane" (Baldwin, 40).

3. No good ever comes from helping one's fellow man. In fact, if the worst could happen, it most likely did on *Seinfeld*.

4. Look to the past for inspiration. *Seinfeld* looked to the Abbott and Costello and Jackie Gleason TV shows of the 1950s in particular.

5. No reason is too trivial for breaking up. Note that Kramer gives up on Elaine's old friend Wendy in "The Kiss Hello" after one date because she changes her hairstyle, while Elaine breaks up with her friend because she doesn't give her a ride all the way to her apartment building after a day of skiing together.

6. A short, stocky, slow-witted bald man can be a chick magnet. For George, the opposite is usually the truth, but there are episodes when he does get lucky through no effort on his part.

7. The craziest person is the sanest of all. This one refers, of course, to Kramer, who as we shall see comes out on top in "The Kiss Hello."

The show's concept appeared simple: each episode is as much as possible about *nothing*, as *Seinfeld* often told us. But "nothing" is a very slippery term, as Western culture has known at least since the time Socrates claimed to be the wisest man because he *knew* he knew nothing. As critic Bruce Handy writes, if *Seinfeld* is "about nothing, then so are the works of Jane Austen and Noel Coward. If *Seinfeld* seems trivial, it is only because manners have so devolved over the course of our century" (79). A more accurate summary of the show's concept would be to say it is *character- and incident-driven rather than plot-oriented.* Most particularly, the show spotlights the absurdist humor of everyday life, of the little details that actually make up our lives and interactions, as opposed to any romantic or lofty idealism. Less definitely produces more in every *Seinfeld* episode. And Seinfeld often explained his strong debt to comics such as Gleason and Abbott and Costello, as well as to the New York Jewish tradition of stand-up humor from which he developed. In fact, *Seinfeld*'s much ado about nothing also reflected a lot about life in Manhattan and about self-absorbed relationships of the 1990s. In short, *Seinfeld* is actually much ado about a lot of things, but presented with such speed, lightness of touch, a nonjudgmental tone, and a balance between sarcasm and acceptance that a nation came to expect just about anything each week for half an hour.

The show is really about humor. "The goal was only laughter," wrote the *New York Times* (Carter, A15). And years of reruns surely validate this goal. With a watch or stopwatch, make this test yourself of any episode: count how many laughs there are per minute in any, say, five-minute stretch. I guarantee that almost every episode averages four laughs per minute! That's a lot of gag and joke writing, especially since most shows do not come close to such an intensity of laughter. But first a little more on the set-up of the show:

Characters: Consider the foursome who propel each episode—Jerry, George, Elaine and Kramer. They are about as unlikely a bunch of would-be friends as we can imagine. In fact, as many have pointed out, they are not friends at all. "The bond between these niggling, nudging four musketeers," writes critic Ken Tucker, "is a group dynamic rooted in jealousy, rage, insecurity, hopelessness and a touching lack of faith in one's fellow human beings" (Baldwin 22–23). Seinfeld himself, however, suggests that all of the picky bickering is carried out within an atmosphere of security: "There's a great warmth beneath the surface of these characters. Just the fact of what we forgive each other shows you that" (Baldwin, 24). The comic world created within *Seinfeld* is thus *sarcastic, cynical and seemingly uncaring on the surface, yet accepting and forgiving on the deeper level of a shared community.* Even if all appears to end badly, as in the episode we are about to examine, the characters are all back together in the next episode, ready to express themselves once more by being picky, trivial and vain.

Given our descriptions of comic characters in chapter 1, each character in *Seinfeld* except for Kramer rotates between being an *eiron* (ironic wise guy) and an *alazon* (pretentious, bragging fool), as well as rotating constantly between being a victim and a savior figure, and at times a mercenary figure as well. Kramer is a special case, however. Kramer is definitely a kind of holy fool, who functions completely according to the dictates of his own universe with no worries about how he fits into society. In true Aristophanic style, the universe must come to Kramer's vision and, as in "The Kiss Hello," often does!

Jerry Seinfeld plays a version of himself—a New York Jewish comedian who has become successful onstage but something of an aloof mess off. "I wanted to do a show about being a comedian," is how Jerry originally put it (Wild, 19). This position allows him to be something of a fall guy or straight man for the antics of the others, as well as something of a choral figure commenting on what's happening. It also allows him to throw in an onstage moment that comments on and expresses the themes or manners at play in that particular episode. He is the handsome lead who would be the romantic hero if this were screwball comedy, but instead is a thirty-something urban bachelor whose life is filled with the comic minefield of daily encounters that annoy, befuddle and amuse him.

Elaine (Julia Louis-Dreyfus) is the ex-girlfriend and now platonic friend, who by virtue of her position is able to make wry and sarcastic comments on all that goes on in Seinfeld's life, and for that matter the lives of the whole group. Like the heroines in screwball comedy, she is a professional and very bright, but unlike the Jean Arthurs and Katharine Hepburns of the past, her fears, insecurities and inability to commit emotionally mean that she, like Jerry and George, is condemned to hanging out with the guys and trying endlessly to find a Mr. Right who doesn't exist.

George Louis Costanza (Jason Alexander), Jerry's buddy since high school, cannot seem to get and hold a job or a woman, as he neurotically worries about everything. Alexander was the first supporting actor cast for the show once the concept of a Jerry-centered series was agreed upon, and this New Jersey–born actor notes, "Ever since I was little, I was crashing my bicycle into a tree to make people laugh" (Wild, 21).

Cosmo Kramer (Michael Richards) is the next-door neighbor who barges in and out, carrying out one eccentric scheme after another. He is the intruder figure, the unwanted guest you can't get rid of who is constantly affecting your life. But, as noted above, he is the one figure with visions that he tries to put into practice, inventions that actually would make sense if carried out by somebody else. Over the years, for instance, he comes up with notions of a pizza place where you make your own pizza, a cologne called "Beach" that smells like the real thing, "PB&J's," a restaurant that serves only peanut butter and jelly sandwiches, a mattress filled with sand to give you a "beach" sleep, and a garbage disposal unit in the bathtub so you can eat while showering.

Taken together, they are not exactly a group of friends. The show is called *Seinfeld,* and it is to Jerry that each other character relates, even when all are together in a scene. That group dynamic must always be kept in mind.

Let us now acknowledge four members of the principal writing team:

Larry David ran almost every detail of the show for eight years, including much of the writing. He conceived the show with Jerry and wrote about sixty episodes. According to David, much of the material came from real life, transformed to one degree or another, and he particularly appreciated that NBC never really censored the show.

Jerry Seinfeld was involved in much of the writing as well as being cofounder of the series and its star. We have in the United States a long tradition of comedians who write, produce and sometimes direct themselves, from Chaplin and Buster Keaton down to Woody Allen, Mel Brooks and beyond, but once more, Seinfeld stands out in the medium of television comedy as that rare bird that does it all.

Larry Charles wrote for the first four seasons, penning many of the dark episodes with neo-Nazis and serial killers and the homeless as topics. What did he enjoy most in writing for the show? "So many places they ask you to shave the edge off. At *Seinfeld* they asked you to sharpen it." Biggest challenge in writing? Writing for Elaine—until he was told he did not have to treat her "like a woman" but just "as neurotic and troubled as the rest" (Baldwin, 40).

Peter Mehlman wrote the first freelance episode ("The Apartment," first season) and eighteen after that. His background? Journalism, including the *New York Times,* where Jerry spotted him through one of his articles. He had never written dialogue before and found the biggest challenge writing for Kramer. His solution? "My strategy is to come up with very sane stories and then let his personality take it to crazy places" (Baldwin, 42).

"The Kiss Hello" Up Close

"The Kiss Hello" (labeled as Episode 100 and dated January 5, 1995, though it actually aired on February 16, 1995, as episode 97), written by Seinfeld and Larry

David, follows the two acts with a final "show close" scene. There are twenty-eight scenes, averaging two to three pages apiece, or about a minute a scene. For starters, it will be useful to see the scene and character breakdown so we can refer back to it. Note that scenes are lettered, not numbered, and that there is no Scene I, since "I" would be confused with the number one, or scenes F, O, Q, U and X for similar reasons. Finally, once you have run through the alphabet, scenes become AA, BB and so on. The numbers in parentheses are the page number on which that scene begins in this seventy-one-page script.

Scene Breakdown for "The Kiss Hello"

ACT 1 SCENE A (1)	*Int. Jerry's Apartment—Day One* Jerry, George, Ted	
ACT 1 SCENE B (5)	*Ext. New York Street—Day One* Jerry, George, Elaine, Wendy	
ACT 1 SCENE C (10)	*Int. Coffee Shop—Day One* Jerry, George, Elaine, Kramer	
ACT 1 SCENE D (16)	*Int. Nana's Apartment—Night One* Jerry, Uncle Leo, Nana	
ACT 1 SCENE E (20)	*Int. Jerry's Apartment—Day Two* Jerry, Elaine, Kramer	
ACT 1 SCENE G (24)	*Int. Morty & Helen's Condo—Day Two* Morty, Helen	
ACT 1 SCENE H (26)	*Int. Jerry's Apartment—Day Two* Jerry, Elaine, Kramer, Wendy	
ACT 1 SCENE J (31)	*Int. Wendy's Car—Day Two* Elaine, Wendy	
ACT 1 SCENE K (33)	*Int. Wendy's Office—Reception Area—Day Two* George, Wendy, Receptionist	
ACT 1 SCENE L (37)	*Ext. New York Street—Day Three* Jerry, Elaine	
ACT 1 SCENE M (38)	*Int. Jerry's Lobby—Day Three* Jerry, Elaine, Kramer, Joel, Louise	
ACT 1 SCENE N (41)	*Int. Jerry's Apartment—Day Three* Jerry, Elaine	
ACT 2 SCENE P (42)	*Int. Jerry's Lobby—Day Four* Jerry, Joan, Mary, (Woman)	
ACT 2 SCENE R (44)	*Int. Jerry's Apartment—Day Four* Jerry, Kramer	
ACT 2 SCENE S (46)	*Int. Morty & Helen's Condo—Day Four* Morty, Helen	
ACT 2 SCENE T (47)	*Int. Jerry's Apartment—Day Four* Jerry, George, Kramer	

Comic Narrative Structures

For a show supposedly about nothing, there are at least five subplots woven around the main plot of Jerry's anarchistic idea to stop kissing people hello, because as he explains:

> JERRY: Well frankly, outside of a sexual relationship, I really don't see the point to it. And I'm not thrilled with all the handshaking either. But one step at a time.

(Act 1, Scene C)

Thus the front story revolves around the social "manners" of how we greet each other. Seinfeld is announcing his protest of traditional custom, and we recognize of course that he is absolutely headed for trouble. In terms of the story arc for the whole episode, Jerry's stance puts him in direct conflict with Kramer, who decides to help everyone become one big "family" in the apartment building by placing a sign board up in the lobby with everyone's photo and name on it. This leads to perhaps the key exchange of the episode:

KRAMER: You should be thanking me for liberating you from your world
    of loneliness and isolation. Now you're part of a family.

JERRY: Family? You think I want another family? My father's demanding
    that my uncle pay him interest on fifty dollars he was supposed to
    give my mother in 1941. And my uncle's put my grandmother in a
    home because of it.

(Act 2, Scene R)

The grandmother story involves two subplots, as Jerry is initially called to
Nana's house to help her open a bottle of ketchup. Once there, he discovers that
Uncle Leo has also been called over, and Nana, drifting in time, asks if he ever paid
the fifty dollars to Jerry's mother he was supposed to. It seems that Jerry's grandfather won at the races one day and gave Leo one hundred dollars with the stipula-
tion that half of it would go to Helen, Jerry's mother.

Going on the narrative and comic impulse that things will go from bad to
worse, this leads Uncle Leo to have Nana put in an old folks' home to keep her
quiet and leads Jerry's father, Morty, to begin figuring out the compounded interest on fifty dollars over forty-three years. He finally calculates that Leo owes him
$20,320 if it had been invested in a 12-percent-yielding account!

We can say, therefore, that part of the comedy of manners at play in this
episode has to do with defining family and simple acquaintances within an apartment building. Comedy thrives on contradiction, and Jerry is nothing if not a
bundle of contradictions. He does not wish to kiss hello, but he rushes to help his
grandmother open ketchup. Yet it is hard: even this effort to help a relative is less
"love" than "duty," a polarity Jerry is caught between.

The main arc of the episode leads to Jerry's nonkissing experiment blowing
up in his face. Kramer's efforts to bring the apartment building residents together
has paid off handsomely. Not only do we see everyone beginning to call each other
by their first names, shaking hands and kissing, thanks to Kramer's photo and
name board, but they all shun Jerry for not being "civil." The final blow comes in
the end tag scene of the show: Jerry asks Kramer if he can use his shower, since the
building super won't fix Jerry's because of his unneighborly aloofness. And Kramer
refuses, because he has a party of all the neighbors going on at the moment.
Kramer closes the door, Jerry is alone, clearly *not* understanding, and the show is
over. *Note how such an ending appears to violate the traditions of comedy, which
thrive on acceptance and either romantic union or anarchistic celebration.* Jerry is
alone. But Kramer is not, and therein lies the anarchistic comic ending: he has created a "new world." Jerry's solitude, on the other hand, adds an ironic twist to it all.
We have a double ending.

But we have left out at least four more subplots in the episode.

1. George wants to date Wendy, Elaine's physical therapist friend, and so
    schedules an appointment to see her at her office.

2. But this leads to a comedy of manners about how one handles cancellations, as George is billed for missing his appointment.

3. And Elaine and Wendy have a falling out when returning from a ski trip. Wendy refuses to drive Elaine all the way to her apartment building, insisting that Elaine get out three blocks from home, a distance too short for a taxi but long enough to be a major burden when one is carrying ski equipment.

4. Finally, Elaine and Jerry have one of their many bets going, this time to see if they can get Kramer and Wendy together not as a dating couple but for the sole purpose of having Kramer tell Wendy her hairstyle is terrible and should be changed.

Seinfeld celebrates the failure of most of its characters' efforts. Thus George and Elaine both wind up dumping Wendy as a date/friend, as does Kramer, who actually liked the awful hairdo and does not like the new cut she gets. And Jerry gets the goods on Uncle Leo by finding Buddy, a fellow in the old folks' home who remembers Leo and what happened. We are even left with the possibility of a new friendship, as Buddy and Nana appear to be getting on famously.

Four points we can learn about the construction of sitcom writing from a *Seinfeld* episode:

1. *Comic density.* We used this term to describe Preston Sturges's comedies of the 1930s and 1940s, and the term applies equally to *Seinfeld.* Each episode is packed, not only with the four main characters but with all of the others who fill up each frame, from the other residents in the apartment building to Jerry's Nana, parents and Uncle Leo. Much more than a three-ring circus, *Seinfeld* is more like an eight- or ten-ring circus.

2. *Overlapping scenes.* More so than other shows, *Seinfeld* delights in having conversations spill over from one scene to the next. This signifies that not a whole lot of time has passed between scenes; but also there is the pure pleasure of seeing and hearing how wrapped up these characters get in their discussions, which interest them immensely but appear trivial and inane to anyone else. The interlocking dialogue between scenes simply highlights the intensity of their discussions.

3. *Short scenes.* The economy of good television comedy is to be respected. Take the very brief appearance in two scenes of Jerry's parents. A lot of the humor comes from the absolute brevity of their appearance for the mere point of showing Morty figuring out the amount of money owed him according to varying interest rates. There is no need for a lengthy dialogue about Nana and how Uncle Leo is a scoundrel. The simple figuring of interest over so many years becomes funny in and of itself, as we realize Morty's cause is not justice but good old profit!

4. *One long scene near the beginning to set up the whole show.* On *Seinfeld* the coffee shop proves ideal. It is, first of all, neutral territory outside the apart-

ment and therefore acceptable to all and open to outside influences. A "long" scene in *Seinfeld* is defined as six pages. That's less than three minutes of screen time, but that's enough for Scene C to establish Jerry's no-kiss-hello campaign, for George to make it clear he is after Wendy, for Elaine and Jerry to cook up an effort to bring Wendy and Kramer together so he can tell her that her hair is all wrong, and for Kramer to announce his good-neighbor photo and name board plan. The rest of the script is spent developing all that happens over coffee in this early sequence.

Put it all together and we keep on laughing at and with Seinfeld, because he does make us a little wiser about how much of our lives are spent on little details that mean nothing . . . and everything. It's all a matter of perspective, distance, context.

The Simpsons:
"We're a Nice Normal Family!"

Walt Disney revolutionized cartoons and features for children by exploring the seemingly limitless resources of animation. And *The Simpsons* has revolutionized television in general and the sitcom in particular by proving that those ageless 'toons can make millions from the laughter of millions everywhere, representing a much larger audience age span and demographic than, say, *Seinfeld*. Creator Matt Groening puts it best: "*The Simpsons* is a show that rewards you paying attention" (9). Disney's approach was to present fairy-tale narratives about both people and animals and aimed at children, from *Snow White and the Seven Dwarfs* and *Cinderella* to *Bambi* and *Dumbo*. Groening and *The Simpsons* development staff, including James L. Brooks and Sam Simon, passed up the sweetness-and-light school of animation offered by Disney and took a chance, aiming for a family sitcom that would use humor in very sneaky ways to attract audiences from three to ninety-three. That is its overwhelming accomplishment, and "sneaky" is, as Groening admits, the operative word and concept. As he says, the show is "full of sneaky details, hidden jokes, and annoying catchphrases. The book contains vital statistics, not-so-vital statistics, and important factoids" (9). It's got memorable lines and even the hard-to-decipher background signs.

At dead center, of course, is the seductive pleasure of animation. There is just something about 'toons that is nonthreatening and invites us all to be kids again. Add to this that the kind of animation is "line animation," using cartoonish, broadly done figures and scenes as opposed to the lush detailed work of Disney, which was often, as in the case of *Snow White*, rotoscoped (a process of using a live model on film and then drawing from the film version). A lot of the humor, of course, is the 'toonish exaggeration of the characters, making them more caricatures than fully developed characters.

In terms of comedy, we should note how broad a path Groening and team cut across the landscape of humor. Remember our delineation of the comic spectrum in the introduction. We explored comedy in terms of the following:

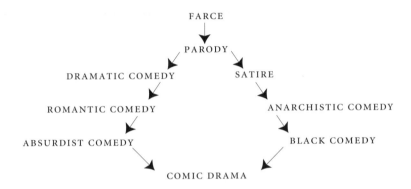

FARCE

PARODY

DRAMATIC COMEDY   SATIRE

ROMANTIC COMEDY   ANARCHISTIC COMEDY

ABSURDIST COMEDY   BLACK COMEDY

COMIC DRAMA

The Simpsons chalks up all of the above except for comic drama and perhaps romantic comedy, which is drained of real non-comic emotion on the show.

Take the sneaky level of parody and satire, for instance. *The Simpsons* is a kind of ludic encyclopedia of winks to those in the know about movies, music, books, headlines and other television and media events. Start with the titles of many of the episodes, which immediately blend satire and parody: "Homer Alone," "Lisa the Greek," "Mr. Lisa Goes to Washington" or "A Streetcar Named Marge." For adults especially (how many of us laugh when our children don't and then have to explain each *Simpsons* gag or allusion that they missed?), these gag/ allusions pepper each episode.

Our chosen episode is an early one, "There's No Disgrace Like Home," written by veteran *Simpsons* writers Al Jean and Michael Reiss (labeled First Draft, May 10, 1989, and aired January 28, 1990). The scene near the end in Dr. Monroe's family therapy laboratory is described in the script as looking like a scene from Kubrick's *Clockwork Orange,* while an early shot in which the Simpsons approach Mr. Burns's mansion for the annual company picnic has us (the camera) going through the iron fence and past a NO TRESPASSING sign as we pan up to the mansion on the hill in exact imitation of the opening of Welles's *Citizen Kane.*

How else does the show reward paying attention? As Groening comments, even the background signs become "throwaway" gags that add much to the comic texture and density of the show. In Groening's excellent book, *The Simpsons: A Complete Guide to Our Favorite Family* (1997), the Simpson fan is given a key to such intentional playful trivia. We learn that various episodes have had signs such as PUPPIES FOR FREE OR BEST OFFER; WE CRAM FUN DOWN YOUR THROAT (at Wall E. Weasel's Pizzeria/Arcade); and COME FOR THE FUNERALS, STAY FOR THE PIE (at the Springfield Cemetery). In short, the strong anarchistic bent of the show absolutely suggests that, as we have often noted about pure comedy, nothing is sacred, as religion, minorities, races, politicians (remember when George Bush moved to town?), marriage, sex and even motherhood are called into playful question. In the carnivalesque world of the Simpson family, everything and anything in American culture is fair game for the show.

Start with the family itself: in the sitcom tradition, each member is a strong individual, and taken together they form a unit that agrees to disagree each week over the situation at hand. In this sense the show supports the idea that in an age of increasing divorce and single-parent households, sitcoms reinforce the notion of a nuclear family. But even though Homer wants to believe they are a "normal" family, the whole decade of *The Simpsons* celebrates if not a dysfunctional group, at least the nuttiest family in the history of sitcom.

Homer J. Simpson, age 36, over 250 pounds, works at a nuclear power plant, is best known for saying, "D'oh!" when mad and "Mmmmm" when happy, and struggles to survive as a father and husband in a zany household. He is more buffoon than ironic figure, more victim than instigator.

Marge Simpson, 34, beehive blue hairdo, is the mother and wife who somehow holds the family together, listens to Tom Jones's music, cooks marshmallow squares, has webbed feet and has in the past been convicted of shoplifting.

Bart Simpson, age 10, is a hell-raiser, trickster and practical joker who once sold his soul for five dollars and destroyed Australia's ecosystem with a single bullfrog.

Lisa Simpson, age 8, is the brain and moral center of the family. Her first word as a baby was "Bart!" and she loves to play the saxophone in the style of Bleeding Gums Murphy.

Maggie Simpson, age one, sucks constantly on a pacifier and gets put through the supermarket price scanner (she's worth $847).

Put them together and commedia dell'arte meets vaudeville plus one stand-up line after another.

"There's No Disgrace Like Home" Up Close

When will I learn? The answers to life's problems aren't at the bottom of a bottle. They're on TV!

Homer Simpson

This early episode concerns the Simpsons attending the annual company picnic given by Mr. Burns at his estate. Of course everything goes wrong: Bart makes a nuisance of himself, especially when he almost beats Mr. Burns in the sack race, and Marge gets quite drunk with the wives. This leads Homer to Moe's Bar to drown his sorrows about what a mess his family has become. But in the midst of his self-pity, he sees a television ad for Dr. Marvin Monroe's Family Therapy

Center, and after hocking the family television set at the local pawn shop, he drags his reluctant family into therapy. The comic plot is thus *central character with a difficult task or quest.* Not only do the Simpsons prove incurable, however; they drive Dr. Monroe so crazy by show's end that he gives them double their money back. Thus two more comic plots have kicked in: a *parody and burlesque* of family therapy and *reductio ad absurdum* as the therapy becomes a carnival of destruction. Fade out with a happy ending: the Simpsons leave as a family in harmony at last, now that they have enough money for frosty chocolate milkshakes and their television. Lisa's take? "It's not the money as much as the feeling that we earned it."

Structure: Three acts, twenty-eight scenes. Act One is Mr. Burns's party; Act Two deals with the Simpsons spying on other families to see what they are like and contains the longest scene in the episode, the Moe's Bar sequence (seven-and-a-half pages); and Act Three is the attempted therapy at Dr. Monroe's office and lab.

Comic climate and comic density: The Simpsons is, as always, wildly inventive, extremely packed with sneaky (and we could say "cheeky"!) comic details that create a climate that ranges from pure farce to hilarious satire and parody. The major object of satire and parody in this episode? Family therapy! The gang on the writing staff at *The Simpsons* often takes swipes at psychotherapeutic jargon and trendy self-improvement movements, and this is one of the first (if not the first) episodes to do so.

Let's use *Seinfeld* as a comparison here. While both shows are *dense* in terms of being full of jokes and multiple stories, *The Simpsons* is less verbally (read: joke) centered than *Seinfeld,* as one can immediately see from the page lengths: seventy-one pages for *Seinfeld,* fifty-two for *The Simpsons.* But note that part of the "brevity" of the *Simpsons* script has to do with how totally cinematic it is, making more use of visuals and montage editing effects than *Seinfeld.* The final *Clockwork Orange* family therapy electro-shock scene in Dr. Monroe's lab, for instance, is complete slapstick farce on a visual and sound level, thus requiring a lot less script space than a series of jokes:

> INT. LABORATORY—CONTINUOUS: *The Simpsons are now zapping each other with wild abandon—at least three of them are being electrified at any one time. The room is full of smoke.*

On-screen such a brushstroke description becomes a hilariously worked-out scene, as each in turn zaps the others, acting out their aggressions in an orgy of catharsis.

Four Elements of Vintage *Simpsons* Writing to Admire

1. Sharp nutty dialogue. The opening scene sets the tone and theme of the whole episode. Lisa and Bart are fighting as usual. But why?

HOMER: Hey! What's the problem here?

LISA: We were fighting over which one of us loves you more.

Homer sniffles. There is a tear in his eye.

HOMER: Go ahead. Some things are worth dying for.

The fight starts again, with the same cloud formation.

BART: You love him more!

LISA: No, you do!

The writing team for *The Simpsons*—Al Jean and Michael Reiss in this episode—
delights in raiding all of American humor for its material, and this fighting over
love reworks a classic W. C. Fields routine, in which he is about to hit his son at
the breakfast table when the boy claims W. C. doesn't love him. Fields, his arm
raised: "No child of mine is gonna get away with saying I don't love him."

Whether this *Simpsons* episode is consciously beginning with a Fields routine is not the point. I am simply reiterating the fun the writers are having, working in a rich comic tradition that includes everything from vaudeville and silent
comedy to old TV shows and movies. More importantly, the opening sets up the
comic tension between family—that is, love—and violence. And the dialogue is
wonderfully upside down, reversing our expectations: each feels the other loves
him more.

2. Numerous details in the script for the animators that may or may not
"appear" on-screen. At the party, Mr. Burns (called Mr. Meaney in this early
script) is described as "a doddering, dignified Reagan type" (5). That is, in fact,
how he looks, and yet not everyone will "get" the Reagan note.

3. Carnivalesque moments that allow characters to act out of character. In
this episode it's a howl to watch Marge get drunk and start singing:

> *Marge continues to drink with the other women. They are all singing.*
>
> **MARGE:** (*singing*) Here we sit, enjoying the shade.
>
> **OTHER WOMEN:** (*singing*) Hey, brother, pour the wine!
>
> **MARGE:** (*singing*) Drink the drink that I have made.
>
> **OTHER WOMEN:** (*singing*) Hey, brother, pour the wine!

And while on the one hand this is a comic moment in and of itself, it fits into the
general theme of the Simpsons being a dysfunctional family.

4. Finally, the episode portrays the Simpsons as being as dysfunctional
as can possibly be imagined, only to bring them all together again by the closing. Homer sets the tone for act 2 when he calls a family meeting in the living
room—that center of all family sitcoms, but also the room in which the Simpsons watch . . . television. Homer announces there is not enough love in their
family. They have already disgraced themselves at Mr. Burns's party. What follows is the parody of family therapy at Dr. Monroe's clinic as they electrocute

and zap each other. But a happy family ending follows, as Monroe doubles the refund, and they leave not only pleased that they will be able to repurchase their television set, but looking forward to the chocolate milkshakes Homer offers to buy everyone.

Earlier on, however, perhaps the key line of this family sitcom is uttered by Lisa: "The sad truth is all families are like us."

IV

WRITING COMEDY

CHAPTER 11

The Fifteen-Week
Feature Comedy Screenplay

Comedy resolves the contradictions and rights the balance by showing us our failings, and if we consider them failings, we recognize
higher standards.

Harry Levin

Humor hasn't the time to be hypocritical, it hasn't the patience to be
polite, it hasn't the tolerance to be timid.

Sol Saks

Let's start writing comedy.

But take seriously the basic pitch of the book: *allow yourself the pleasure and
freedom to be a clown or to fool yourself.* Don't try to second-guess the market, audiences or producers. One film to watch before jumping in? Very hard choice, but
what the hell, if you haven't seen it, invite over some of your friends, open a good
bottle of wine and rent a South African comedy: *The Gods Must Be Crazy* (1981).
After you've seen it, ask yourself this: what Hollywood producer would ever fund
a film that would have to be described as a story about a Coke bottle that falls out
of a plane over Africa and lands in a tribal village that has never tasted the drink of
the twentieth century? Take it from there.

Getting Started

Why fifteen weeks for a feature comedy? Simple. That is the length of the av-
erage American college semester. This chapter presents a comfortable pace for students to get through a term without anxiety attacks and with, finally, a complete
script of which they can be proud. Your pace depends, of course, on your own
frame of mind and time commitments. Some may find they can do a feature script
in a month, and others may need a year. Fifteen weeks is only a convenient starting point that can be adjusted to please your own particular needs.

Writing a feature-length comedy brings up all of the issues of writing any feature screenplay. You must necessarily tackle the intertwining of story, character, structure, pacing, genre, texture, subplots and minor characters with theme and atmosphere. And whatever screenwriting skills you have acquired on your own, or through courses or the bookcases full of screenwriting books, should serve you in comedy as well. I refer you to my previous book for more on the basics of screenwriting, including format: *Writing the Character-Centered Screenplay* (University of California Press).

Our particular mission, however, is to focus on comedy and the capturing and developing of the comic spirit in your script.

Good luck, enjoy the journey, and here goes!

Week 1: Comic Explorations

Use this opening week to begin to explore comedy more fully. Read this text, and follow some of the suggestions in chapter 2, Exercises to Nurture the Comic Muse. Also make a commitment to watch two or three feature comedies you haven't seen or haven't watched in years that are mentioned in the text or in appendix 1 *each week*. That's right. This should be an ongoing assignment, to keep that comic stimulation going as you work on your own project.

ASSIGNMENT:
1. Complete the comic self-portrait called for in chapter 2.
2. Get hold of at least two screenplays for films mentioned in this text and read them carefully, with an eye to all of the issues discussed in this text. If a script is not published in book form—as are Preston Sturges's scripts, for instance, and *Fargo, Smoke* and *Kolya*—you can purchase a photocopy of any American script by contacting Script City at (800) 676-2522.
3. Start a comic journal in which you brainstorm ideas and jot down observations, lines of dialogue heard and reactions to comedies seen or read.

Week 2: Humorous Brainstorming, or Three Ideas Are Better than One

Use this week to begin to brainstorm on a comic concept, but do not narrow your ideas down to the one you think you will do. Surprise yourself and keep your options open, exploring more fully and winding up the week with at least three ideas.

Where do comic feature film ideas come from? Everywhere. Just look at the films discussed in this text. But consider the following sources:

1. Your life and that of those around you.
2. True life stories from the news, journals and television. We explored this one in chapter 2. Keeping a file of stories from the paper or news is definitely worthwhile.
3. History. Buster Keaton's *The General* (1927) features great gags involving trains and chases, but the actual story was based on a historical event during the Civil War. Humor and history cross paths and illuminate each other. Another example from appendix 1 would be George Roy Hill's *Butch Cassidy and the Sundance Kid,* from William Goldman's script. Goldman did his homework and became fascinated with these two fellows from New Jersey who wound up out West and then disappeared in South America (Horton, *The Films of George Roy Hill,* 124).
4. Adaptations, remakes and spinoffs. In this area you are counting on an "original" source in another creative work that you can inject your humor and imagination into to make it yours. This can be a rich area, especially for beginners, for you do not have to come up with everything and yet the opportunities for true creativity are there.
5. An imaginative cross-fertilization of several of the above.

ASSIGNMENT:

Building on the suggestions in chapter 2, make sure you have either a comic "partner" who will prove supportive in devoting time to you both for brainstorming and for reacting to your writing. Spend an evening over a tasty meal or an afternoon with a full coffee pot, brainstorming comic ideas. Even better, if you develop a comic story circle, devote one session to you and ideas you are thinking about. Draw up three comic possibilities on the following scale: a "safe" comic idea, a slightly outrageous idea, and a third one that is really out there. Where are the boundaries? Only you know for sure, and that is all that matters. For instance, we could say *Dumb and Dumber* is very safe because it simply goes for pure farce. *Clueless* is more daring because it takes a chance on adapting a British classic in a hip California mode and tone (not to mention accent!). And *The Full Monty* and *There's Something about Mary* (1998) are very much over the edge.

On Creating Truly Zany Script Ideas

Most of us play it too safe most of the time. For at least one of your ideas, allow yourself the freedom to follow outrageous ideas for the fun of it. How will you know how humorous you can be unless you are in the playful realm of experimentation.

I give you one clear example. My friend and colleague Srdjan Karanovic of Yugoslavia, mentioned in chapter 2, began his feature career with a film called *Social Games* (1974). What was his concept? Simple: to write a script based on the responses to an ad placed in many Yugoslav newspapers: "Anyone who wishes to be in a feature film, please send in a photo, describe your occupation, and explain what role you wish to play in a film." He received more than four thousand letters. He and his writing partners and staff chose the one hundred they found most interesting and invited those hundred letter-writers to Belgrade for interviews.

One person explained that he was a bricklayer from Zagreb and wished to be a detective like Humphrey Bogart. Another said he was a minor employee in his twenties who had hated his mother's lover since his father died and wished to murder him with a knife. And someone from the countryside explained that he had always wanted to be a messenger for Tito's Partisans fighting the Nazis during World War II but had been too young at the time.

Once the interviews were completed, Karanovic wrote the script and used about thirty of the actual people he had interviewed to play themselves. He started his "documentary fairy tale" with each person facing the camera and explaining who they were, what they did and what role they wished to play. Then the film "begins" and they become the parts: a young man murders his mother's lover with a knife, a detective investigates the murder, a messenger in a Partisan uniform delivers messages throughout the film for no reason at all.

The ending? A completely festive embrace: all the "actors" come together on a boat and begin singing while floating down the Danube River. The laughter in *Social Games* cuts in a variety of directions, as we laugh in part *at* these folk making fools of themselves on camera, but most of the laughter is sympathetic rather than ironic, for each comes through as a person as well.

Week 3: Constructing a Comedy-Centered Treatment

You have your concept. Now you must spin it into a treatment that does justice to the humor, characters and story you wish to write. Nothing about screenwriting is harder than writing a treatment that jumps off the page and grabs our attention. Why? Because the treatment is the whole story squeezed into a few pages. And that is doubly frustrating, because to write you must assume both that you know your story and that you have the magical ability to condense said masterpiece into humorous prose. That's asking a lot. Especially when we are speaking about comedy; you are, in effect, trying to suggest why what you are *really* going to write will be humorous, or side-splitting, or scandalous, or warmly amusing.

You may wish to plunge in and begin writing without a treatment. But my years of experience have taught me that the effort expended on the initial treatment is worth it for at least three reasons. First, you do confront the whole project—characters, story, tone, genre and theme—and work out at least your initial belief in where and why the comedy will become what you wish it to be. Next, the treatment gives you practice in synopsizing your tale, which you are going to have to do many times anyway, so you might as well begin your "act" at the beginning. Finally, writing the treatment allows you the freedom to think about what you wish to change in it as you go along, for the treatment is not written in marble, just ink that can be altered. *Particularly because comedy is a special form of storytelling, I think such "pre-writing" of the script is necessary.*

I emphasize spending some time on a treatment for yet another reason: it might be what gets you a contract, a grant or some development money. The last three scripts I've been paid to write have been on the basis of short treatments. Local, state and national media funding organizations rely as much on treatments as commercial film and television outfits, so do polish your treatment skills. Treatments can be registered with the Writers Guild (see appendix 2) or simply mailed to yourself and left unopened as a form of "self-registration" to prove it is your own if the need ever arises.

Study the treatment below for structure and format. There is no set formula, but I recommend the concept paragraph as an overview of genre, main character, theme and story. Then tell the story, with characters' names set in capital letters the first time, just as in a script. Events are told in the present tense, and you write what we see and hear, just as in a script. There is also a treatment for an anarchistic comedy in the Week 9 section below.

A Romantic Comedy Treatment

The following is a first-draft treatment of a romantic comedy written by Laura Coroianu, a Romanian student at the International Academy of Broadcasting, Montreux, Switzerland. Laura had never written a feature script before, and of course she was writing in a foreign language—English—for this assignment. At first she told me she had "no ideas" and then, when pressed, came up with an extremely complicated film about the fall of communism in Romania that no one outside of the country would be able to fully appreciate. Then a smile and this six-page treatment emerged. Note the absolute simplicity of her set-up, a basically two-character idea that is full of comic and romantic potential. As this goes to press, she has completed a revised script under contract with a European company that wishes to shoot this as a television feature. I have made no changes in her English as it was originally written.

Sub Sub-Let

CONCEPT: This is a romantic comedy about a Romanian orthodox girl studying in Switzerland on a scholarship who finds herself alone in a sub-let Geneva apartment of a schoolmate for the Christmas holidays. She sub sub-lets one of the rooms to a young fundamentalist Turkish guy for only one week, and then she cannot get him out of there anymore, and while fighting each other, they fall in love.

STORY:

(ACT 1)

MARIA is a 24-year-old Romanian girl who has graduated from a Business school in Bucharest and has got the chance of a lifetime: to do an MBA in hotel management at one of the most famous hotel schools in Switzerland, the Hotel Institute of Montreux. Maria is good-looking though not beautiful, the type of "pal" accepted in the all-male entourage, she has a strong sense of humor and takes religion with a grain of salt: the "God is out there somewhere, let's not disturb him" attitude. But she is rather short for money and cannot afford to go home during the Christmas holidays. A solution comes her way when her schoolmate ERNESTINE offers her Geneva apartment in exchange for substantial help with writing her graduation thesis.

MEHMET is a 28-year-old once-was rock 'n' roll kid, now a young adult fallen into a second-puberty religious crisis. His mentor, the Imam, has converted him to the rightful fundamentalist path of religion in which he has plunged headlong. He is an extremely attractive man, that lethal Oriental combination of sea-green eyes and chocolate skin. He wears now only the traditional Islamic clothes culminating with the turban on top of his head. He comes to Switzerland to visit his brother HASSAN, a once brilliant Istanbul physician, now a shop-assistant in a Geneva pharmacy, who has married MARIE-LOUISE, a typical dry blonde Swiss woman of a rather frigid disposition who works in a jewelry shop.

Maria arrives in Geneva to this lavish three room flat which overwhelms her but soon she finds out that the glamour of the place and of the city cannot warm her heart; the only person she is able to befriend is AZIZ, the concierge, an understanding middle-aged man, who happens to be Hassan's best pal. Only Aziz can understand how lonely poor Maria can feel, and how upset she is that she cannot afford the wonderful Tissot watch that lies in that shop window down the road.

In the meantime Mehmet is quite fed up with Swiss society and his sister-in-law's embodiment of it, and he spills out his guts over dinner to the astonishment of his brother, Aziz, and several other guests. Darling Marie-Louise asks him to leave at once, and proud Mehmet will not waste a moment. But where to go with not enough money in his pocket and a return ticket to Istanbul on a fixed date? Aziz is the God sent salvation: he will set Mehmet up in Maria's flat for peanuts—

300 francs. Maria will get to buy her watch and have some good company . . . perfect arrangement!

(ACT 2)

First shock: introductions!

A Turk with a turban and a fierce fundamentalist gaze is not Maria's idea of a perfect tenant. She sets the house rules and they go to bed in their separate rooms.

Cut to her dream in Medieval Romania. This is only one of the many visions they start having of each other, set in Medieval times, Maria seeing him as the Muslim predator, and Mehmet picturing her as beauty in his harem. This is Maria's first vision: a long line of girls in folk costumes go down to the river to fetch water in their buckets. All of a sudden a gang of ruthless Ottoman soldiers headed by Mehmet himself storms the group of helpless girls. Maria and two others are kidnapped on horseback and taken to this dungeon at the top of a tower. Looking out of the window, she realizes in dismay that beneath her lies a Turkish city with its minarets and mosques, and the shrill voice of an Imam is filling the air with the morning prayer.

She wakes up covered in sweat just to realize that the awful noise is still going on at 5:00 am in real life. Mehmet, dutifully facing Mecca on his little carpet, is voicing the first out of his five daily prayers. And this is only the beginning. They both get on each other's nerves with their different customs, traditions and mentalities: he hates her woman's lib behavior and the pork fillets in the fridge, the pork sausages and tzuika (ethnic dish) DHL-ed by her concerned parents; she despises his zealot and the wax dripping from the numberless candles in his "altar-room" right on her friend's furniture. And she freaks out at his deafening prayers that make old MS. SCHROEDER, their neighbor, poke her nose into their affairs and complain to Aziz, who is over his head in trying to keep the situation cool and he ends up in the hospital with a stroke one day before Mehmet's "contract" expires: i.e., on Christmas Eve.

Maria wants him out of the house even before, but he refuses to go. Christmas day comes and goes in a tense and depressed atmosphere, with Maria having a long walk around a city of happy strangers. In the evening she lies on the couch to watch Laurel and Hardy in the living room, and starts laughing louder and louder and is joined eventually by a reluctant Mehmet who is engulfed in the cheerful atmosphere and becomes his own old self for a short while.

Romance is in the air.

The next morning it's time to leave, but without Aziz to help, he has nowhere else to go. So he refuses to split, and there is no way she can legally evict him. So it's war between them and any dirty tricks are allowed. She fills the flat with burnt sausage smell, sticks a huge Jesus-on-the-Cross poster on his door with the words, THE REAL THING. She plays blaring rock 'n' roll alternating with Gregorian monks' songs, etc.

He retaliates in drawing moustaches and a turban on the Christ poster, and cutting to shreds her fancy underwear. The roaring conflict summons nosy Ms. Schroeder's attention and she is pleased to report the situation to the local police. Maria has a rough time hushing up the scandal while Mehmet plays hide-and-seek in the apartment.

No sooner have the police departed than once again the bell rings. Total chaos: relatives of the owners appear on the scene to spend one night at the flat: mama, papa and scheming little junior: all three of solid Swiss German extraction.

Maria and Mehmet are thus forced to spend the night together in her room which turns out to be impossible due to the mounting sexual tension. So Mehmet ends up sleeping in the bathtub where he is discovered by Junior. Confusion, explanations. Mehmet has to pretend he is the concierge and is blackmailed by Ms. Schroeder into walking her three Yorkshire terriers every morning, a disgusting occupation that draws him in front of Marie-Louise's shop. She follows him back and finds out where he lives.

Remorseful Hassan comes to his brother's rescue and the war is over. Maria is left alone and sad in a messed-up apartment, just in time to clean it up before the owners arrive the next day. She also finds the Koran in "his room."

Mehmet leaves for Istanbul in a dreamy mood. He has other visions of Maria. Cut to Maria meeting Ernestine at the railway station, coming back to Montreux.

(ACT 3)
Cut to Istanbul. Mehmet is in his old rock 'n' roll clothes, getting out of his house and heading for the nearest club. A silhouette is approaching him from behind: it's the Imam full of reproaches for his falling from faith.

In the club, Mehmet drinks heavily while watching the strip show. Suddenly he notices a woman in traditional Muslim clothes with a veil on her face sitting at the other end of the bar, an impossible sight, of course, in such a place. She comes round and offers him an open Koran with an underlined passage against drinking, prostitution, etc. He is in utmost confusion while she takes her veil off and we discover a smiling Maria who has not bought her Tissot watch, but got a bargain holiday deal on a ticket to Istanbul.

They kiss passionately and leave the bar as Mehmet puts the veil back on her face.

THE END

ASSIGNMENT:
Write a comedy-centered treatment of five to eight pages, double-spaced. Be sure to have a title, a concept statement and the story, written not too dryly, but sparkling with the kind of tone and flavor you hope to capture in your script. Yes, you must have a title. Work in a line or two of dialogue, so we can get your style, concept, approach.

Week 4: Fade in Laughing

Start writing. But how to begin? Beginnings need to accomplish so much in comedy, especially in clueing us into what flavor of comedy we should be preparing ourselves to enjoy. I've written in my previous book on approaches to opening scenes, but I'd like to rephrase the possibilities with a different focus for comedy. Ask yourself at least three questions: (1) Do I want a quiet or a noisy opening? (2) Do I wish to begin immediately with my main protagonist(s) or delay an entrance while a comic environment is established? (3) Am I trying for a laugh right from the beginning, or am I easing into my story?

Consider some of the openings we have covered in earlier chapters:

1. *Quiet opening. Big Night* begins and ends very quietly. No laughs, no noise. In between are both, as well as anger, joy and that delicious food.

2. *Noisy opening. Sullivan's Travels* jumps in with the loud action of the two fellows killing each other atop a speeding train. We quickly realize that we are watching the ending of a serious film that the comic filmmaker Sullivan wishes to complete. Much of the rest of the film will be quiet, even silent. But Preston Sturges wanted to grab us with this action-packed beginning.

3. *Comic character up front. Clueless* hits us immediately with Cher, talking to us, as she will, nonstop, throughout the film. She is the narrator, the main character, the endless fountain of humor as we observe and listen to her efforts to control the lives of everyone around her.

4. *Delayed entrance of comic protagonist. The White Balloon* has a noisy and crowded opening on a New Year's Eve street in Teheran, but it is several minutes before we actually see the young girl with the blue balloon who is to be our comic protagonist. Why the delay? We are asked to begin to experience the whole city—that is, the girl's environment—before we meet her, for this is a comic tale of her journey into the city.

5. *A laughter-oriented opening.* We are laughing during the opening minute of *Kolya* as Louka, our fifty-something cellist, flirts with the female singer during their performance at a funeral. That opening scene immediately establishes character, as well as a special "Czech touch," mixing laughter and an awareness of death.

6. *Delayed-laughter opening. Fargo* has a lot of laughter in it, but the opening is solemn, as the richly orchestrated theme music plays over a bleak winter snowscape in Fargo, North Dakota. The Coen brothers clearly wanted to frame the dark humor of their script with the humorless winter landscape within which the tale unfolds.

A final example. Wayne Wang's *Smoke* was written by novelist Paul Auster and is very much a film about friendship, New York City, storytelling and, yes, smoking. It is an ensemble anarchistic comedy but also a buddy film, both focused on Auggie (Harvey Keitel), the owner of a Brooklyn smoke shop, and Paul

(William Hurt), a writer recovering from the death of his wife. The opening establishes all of these themes and story elements, as all of the regulars meet and talk in Auggie's tobacco shop. The whole theme of the film is laid out clearly once Paul arrives to buy some supplies and tells the following story:

> PAUL: That's the man. Well, Raleigh was the person who introduced tobacco in England, and since he was a favorite of the Queen's— Queen Bess, he used to call her—smoking caught on as a fashion at court. I'm sure Old Bess must have shared a stogie or two with Sir Walter. Once he made a bet with her that he could measure the weight of smoke.
>
> DENNIS: You mean, weigh smoke?
>
> PAUL: Exactly. Weigh smoke.
>
> TOMMY: You can't do that. It's like weighing air.
>
> PAUL: I admit it's strange. Almost like weighing someone's soul. But Sir Walter was a clever guy. First, he took an unsmoked cigar and put it on a balance and weighed it. Then he lit up and smoked the cigar, carefully tapping the ashes into the balance pan. When he was finished, he put the butt into the pan along with the ashes and weighed what was there. Then he subtracted that number from the original weight of the unsmoked cigar. The difference was the weight of the smoke.
>
> TOMMY: Not bad. That's the kind of guy we need to take over the Mets.

See how perfect this opening is for what Auster wishes to do. We meet a group of storytellers, but within that group, the only one who is a novelist has told an especially good tale, which happens to be true and which also relates directly to what binds them all together: tobacco and "smoke." The story itself draws laughs from us and amazement from those in the shop, and the scene is capped with a joke, as Tommy ties this tale into the previous conversation about baseball. For the next hour and a half we will deal with "smoke," that substance, like their souls, that is everything and nothing.

Your turn.

ASSIGNMENT:
Write your first ten pages and make a date with your designated writing partner/friend to go over them.

Week 5: Focus on Scene
and Sequence Construction

How to construct a comic scene?

My whole study has led up to such questions. The answer depends on the kind of comedy you are writing and the part of the script you are currently tackling. In putting together any scene—for drama, action thriller or comedy—there is the need for a level of tension between protagonists, or between our comic figure and his or her environment, or between the scene and what has come before and will follow.

But there is a basic need for that tension to be exaggerated in comedy, and if there are two or more characters in the scene, there is a need for one at least to be the straight man or woman to the other's antics. Also, keep in mind how much of comedy depends on reversal of expectation. And think what "cap" you can put to the scene to top the humor you have already honestly won.

Consider three examples.

A dialogue-centered scene: In *Four Weddings and a Funeral,* Hugh Grant asks Andie MacDowell, in a rare quiet moment before all the events surrounding her actual wedding begin, how many lovers she has had. Our expectation is that she will list a handful and then he will hint at several dozen. But the scene completely reverses this stereotype as she begins to list her lovers, one by one and name by name, as Grant becomes the straight man, reacting with increasing discomfort as the list passes thirty and continues. There are laughs as she goes on and on, as we watch Grant's reactions, and even more as the scene is capped by Grant's embarrassed response when she asks about his lovers.

A physical humor–based scene: In *Sherlock Jr.,* Buster Keaton milks one set-up for all it's worth in a scene that might more accurately be described as a sequence of short scenes. He plays a small-town movie theater projectionist who falls asleep and, in "dream" form, moves out of his own body and onto the screen, climbing into the film being projected. The set-up is simple: how does someone—even in dream form—walk into a screen and become part of a movie? The answer is also simple: with great difficulty, and with a lot of humor. The first time, he is bounced out of the film as if it were a live theatrical piece; the actors simply shove him out. Then he actually enters the frame, only to become a victim of film editing. When he appears to be standing on a rock in the sea, he dives into the water—but while he is in the middle of his dive, the film cuts to a new scene, so he ends up diving into a snow bank. And when he starts to lean against a tree in one frame, the scene cuts to a treeless garden and he falls once more. With more than ten such gag cuts, Keaton pushes the set-up as far as he can before his "Sherlock" figure is finally assimilated into the movie on screen. Note that if you have a clever set-up for physical comedy, the audience can take a lot of variations, for both the pleasure and the mental stimulation of it. As numerous critics have pointed out, there is almost an existential dimension to Keaton's physical humor (see Horton, *Buster Keaton's "Sherlock Jr."*). Such repetition would be lame and boring if it were only the throwing of custard pies, for instance. Keaton's physical gags tickle our imagination because ultimately we "get" that he is playing with film language in a way we have never seen it done before.

An extended monologue scene: Matt Damon and Ben Affleck picked up the 1997 Oscar for Best Original Screenplay with their first script, *Good Will Hunting*. The film mixes psychological drama, refreshingly nutty screwball romantic comedy and anarchistic comic and dramatic elements.

Humor is used throughout the film, both to reveal character and to highlight the emotional dimensions of the narrative. The script sparkles with well-written dialogue, but some of the biggest laughs come from extended monologues, one in which Will (Matt Damon) verbally humiliates a Harvard student in a bar who is flirting with a student (Minnie Driver) he is interested in, and another, late in the film, when Will turns his verbal laser beam on a nameless and faceless NSA recruiter.

Audiences in theaters where I've seen the film break into applause, after first laughing throughout Will's passionate and sarcastic attack on all that the NSA stands for. The applause, of course, is for Will's outlandish skill and for the complete silence maintained by the straight man, the NSA rep. Note that we do not even get a final reaction shot but rather cut to the next scene, simply imagining how confused and angry the executive must be.

Once again: if a whole series of monologues were launched in the film, we would tire swiftly and head out for more popcorn. But the careful planting of only two major speeches helps punctuate the film emotionally and comically. Would a long monologue be effective in your script? Once more, examine your story and characters to see what effect you are striving for.

Two more areas of comic scene construction should be mentioned at this point: *the counterpoint of foreground and background* and *the counterpoint between sound and image.*

Think about the humor that can arise from the clash between what is happening in the background and the foreground activity. In *Babe* (1995), the Australian farmer (James Cromwell) who seems so stern and grim cuts loose in one scene and joyfully dances his heart out, thinking he is alone, only to discover, in the background, all of his farmyard animals peering through the window in bewildered awe. And in *The Full Monty*, as the gang of unemployed steel workers stand in the unemployment line in the foreground, our "dancers" begin to do a little disco shuffle as they stand in line. The humor comes not because they are dancing again but because of the incongruity of where they are dancing.

When you think about the play between sound track and image, think not just about music but about sound. Humphrey Bogart gets our laughs early in *African Queen* when his stomach growls endlessly during Robert Morley's impossibly formal tea in an isolated African mission. No amount of dialogue could accomplish what the simple sound of a growling stomach conveys about how impossibly wrong the gin-swigging, free-living riverboat captain Bogart is for such sedate society.

The same is true of music. We have pointed out how the serious funeral hymn that opens *Kolya* stands in clear opposition to the "behind the scenes" activities of Louka, who is both flirting with the singer and trying to make a cup of coffee while a funeral is in progress.

Sequence Construction and Comic Rhythm

I suggest that during this week you outline how many sequences your treatment indicates given the story you are telling. By "sequence" we mean those scenes that clearly work together to create a certain mood or a narrative part of your script. The Coen brothers' *Raising Arizona,* for instance, uses Nicolas Cage's opening voiceover narration as a unifying element for the whole opening sequence of short scenes. Similarly, in George Roy Hill's *The World According to Garp,* the section in which Garp (Robin Williams) imagines one of the stories he is writing becomes a separate sequence, united in tone and effect.

The benefit of such an exercise is that you will begin to see your comedy as *a series of movements that have a purpose and rhythm of their own,* beyond any sense of a "three-act structure." *Sullivan's Travels,* for instance, in loosely following Jonathan Swift's *Gulliver's Travels,* has at least four major sequences, defined by the four journeys Sullivan takes from Hollywood, and smaller related sequences within those major divisions, each with its own distinct visual style and pace. The first journey, for instance, is a slapstick silent comedy sequence, while the later café scene with Veronica Lake begins a romantic comedy sequence.

To be able to identify sequences in your script means that you will better understand your comedy as not just one comic tale, but as a pleasingly complex crossroads of various segments, each with its own possible degree and form of humor and laughter.

Thinking of your scenes as belonging to sequences also helps you understand your need for those quiet moments along the way in a noisy comedy, or vice versa. Jules Dassin's glorious *Never on Sunday* (1960) is a very boisterous comedy, as he plays an idealistic American who attempts to reform an Athenian prostitute (Melina Mercouri) with no lasting success. But in the center of all of the carnival-esque activities, the film slows down for a quiet sequence: Mercouri, alone in her apartment, sings a quiet song that becomes the theme song of the film. Even within the almost complete anarchy of a Marx Brothers film, all comes to a quiet halt when Harpo plays his harp, lyrically and well. Simply ask yourself if you too have hit a rhythm and variety of moods and tones that allow for the humorous sections to be even more humorous and the quieter moments to have their value.

ASSIGNMENT:

1. Write pages 11–20.
2. Surprise yourself big time this week, in your writing and in your daily life!

Week 6: Focus on Comic Dialogue

Unless you are writing a silent physical comedy, you will be in the business of writing dialogue that you hope will make us laugh out loud. Where to begin? Nothing is healthier than the kind of exercise suggested in chapter 2, in which you spend some time each day or each week simply *listening to others talk* in a park, a restaurant, a mall, on the street. People are often very funny without knowing it. Training our ears to listen—to *really* listen—and our eyes to pick out telling details is at least half the carnival of writing lively dialogue. How do you capture that quality of really nutty speech on paper?

Start with character and context. If you know your character, you should know how she or he will react and speak in any given situation. That said, the same principles we've outlined elsewhere hold true here as well. Look for comic exaggeration, the combining of opposites, and upping the stakes of a comic "crisis." Remember that we meet many conversations already in progress, that sentences rarely get finished because characters often interrupt each other, and that especially in comedy *characters speak at cross-purposes, with large misunderstandings* that the audience is in on and thus laughs with and at. Finally, consider accent, dialect and vocabulary. Remember *The Little Rascals* (*Our Gang*) from the 1930s? They got laughs for one whole episode based on the fact that none of the kids knew what the word "divorce" meant but none of them wanted to admit it. Thus everybody from Spanky to Buckwheat claimed they had a divorce in their family too.

Let's examine a few set-ups:

1. Original romantic comic dialogue: Do whatever you have to do to destroy stereotypical romantic dialogue. We have already looked at the crackling dialogue in James L. Brooks's *As Good As It Gets*. Add this short exchange from Preston Sturges's script for *The Good Fairy* (1935, directed by William Wyler). Margaret Sullavan is a clueless innocent "orphan" turned loose in decadent Budapest. Dr. Sporum is a clueless doctor who has fallen for her. In this case the humor comes from a romantic couple in which neither is smooth with language, not to mention courtship.

LU: I'm an orphan.

DR. SPORUM: There should be more orphans.

LU: I never heard anybody say that before.

If Dr. Sporum were being ironic, that would be one matter, but the fact that he is actually attempting a compliment adds to the humor, capped by Lu's simple rejoinder.

2. Dialogue centered on some basic misunderstanding: Half the laughs in *Forrest Gump* arise because Gump says whatever comes into his mind, without a clue as to what others are thinking. When asked why he is jogging across America, he answers that he likes to run. A similar fish-out-of-water tale of a total innocent in a world full of shattered innocence would be George Roy Hill's *Slaughterhouse Five,* based on Kurt Vonnegut's darkly satirical novel. Billy Pilgrim, like Gump, takes everything at face value; we laugh at the dialogue scenes, knowing what Pilgrim doesn't. And 80 percent of the laughs in *Tootsie* or *Mrs. Doubtfire* come from the comic misunderstandings generated by gender-switching, echoing the fun Shakespeare used to have with hidden and mistaken identities. Add *Some Like It Hot* to the list too.

3. Dialogue in comic conflict or contrast to surroundings: What is happening while your characters are talking? In comedy, even more than in drama, we usually want our characters to be up to something, or to generate laughter by the conflict between speech and act. In Preston Sturges's *The Palm Beach Story* (1942), Claudette Colbert is discovered hiding (in her dressing gown) in the shower of a fancy apartment she is trying to sell. The man who discovers her is a very rich old man who makes "weenies." The dialogue between the self-proclaimed Weenie King and Colbert becomes both ludicrous and suggestive in a very nutty way, and finally borders on touching, as the old man gives her money since he is too old to do anything else. We laugh all the more because they both look particularly ridiculous standing together in a bathroom. More surrealistically, Woody Allen talks to his "enlarged" mother hovering over Manhattan, as if just to embarrass him personally, in Allen's section of *New York Stories* (1989). Finally, touching on wickedly surrealistic comedy, Luis Buñuel has his discreet bourgeoisie chatting away in a restaurant while the body of the owner lies on the table behind them in *Discreet Charm of the Bourgeoisie.*

4. One-sided "dialogue" with one partner silent: Look how funny the two crooks in *Fargo* are because one does not speak.

5. Dialogue at cross-purposes: The famous closing moment in Billy Wilder's *Some Like It Hot,* in which Jack Lemmon tries to explain that he is not a woman, does not faze Joe E. Brown. Why? They are at cross-purposes: Lemmon wants to come clean and end the charade, but Joe E. Brown is intent on marriage and will be stopped by nothing or no one—not even by reality! "I'm a man," says Lemmon. "Nobody's perfect," quips Brown, in one of the most delicious endings of an American comedy.

ASSIGNMENT:

1. Yes, roughly ten more pages.
2. Look at appendix 1 and rent a foreign comedy you haven't seen for the pleasure and instruction of it. Invite your comic partner over to see it too.

Week 7: Focus on Comic Subplots and Minor Characters

Review your own script and see if you have enough minor characters, and whether you have the *right* ones. This goes for subplots as well. Are you being too predictable? Do you need to include other figures not to simply fill up ninety minutes of screen time but to comically explore a dimension of your tale you have left underdeveloped?

Comedy celebrates diversity. Embrace a bevy of characters in addition to the main protagonist(s), and embrace smaller stories beyond the driving narrative. Look at so many of the comedies covered in previous chapters. Each of Aristophanes' chorus of brightly feathered birds in *Birds* is his own character, while a wealth of scoundrels (priests, fortune-tellers and gods such as Hercules) attempt to crash Cloudcuckooland. Or take any Marx Brothers or Fellini or Frank Capra comedy: we delight not only in following Groucho, Marcello Mastroianni or Jimmy Stewart but the wacky array of secondary characters and interwoven subplots.

As in any story, the so-called minor characters and subplots reflect some dimension of our main protagonist or some aspect in contrast to the protagonist. In ensemble comedy such as *M*A*S*H*, we begin with a comic landscape that is crowded from start to finish. Which characters in Spike Lee's *Get on the Bus* are major or minor? Each adds to the mosaic of African American males on a journey to a march and on a voyage of self-discovery.

Look at some more of the films we've reviewed. *The White Balloon* takes us through the streets of Teheran so that our young protagonist comes across every kind of person you can imagine. Each is important to how our seven-year-old heroine will deal with life, from snake charmer to tailor, from a soldier on leave to a teenager selling balloons. And each character within the carnival of teens in Amy Heckerling's *Clueless* suggests the wide world of Beverly Hills and greater Los Angeles—Cher's comic environment.

Note that "minor" characters and "sub" plots are only loosely useful terms. Two examples: The Coen brothers' *Fargo* would still be a powerful film without developing Norm, Marge's quiet homebody artist husband. But the "minor" details of his character and story, including the final scene of the film, tell us so much about Marge and allow the film to be clearly taken as a comedy, given the happy ending of a loving twosome about to become a family of three. Similarly, *Kolya* would be touching and hilarious with just Louka and Kolya attempting to get on together in their Czech and Russian and with their opposite needs. But the comedy becomes much warmer and funnier with the addition of Louka's girlfriends, mother and graveyard-operating friend Boz, with his home full of children, animals and noise.

ASSIGNMENT:

1. Sail joyfully through pages 31–40.

2. In your comic journal, name a few comic "minor" characters who have added to the spice in your life.

Week 8: Are You Surprising and Entertaining Yourself As You Write?

I do get calls, letters and e-mails from stressed-out writers working on comedies. And I must admit I am always a bit baffled. Stressed-out authors working on comedy? Shouldn't this be a contradiction in terms? Isn't the whole point to enjoy the experience? Isn't your comic partner close by, on the phone or across the table with a coffee cup or glass of Merlot to lighten you up, challenge you playfully and give you hell if you begin to take yourself too seriously?

But my question remains: are you surprising and entertaining yourself with your own comedy? If not, turn off the computer and go fishing, shopping, jogging, on a trip, on a walk, to sleep, to a friend's, or pick up the phone and call someone you haven't seen in five years. That will surprise you and them. Meanwhile, let's be honest and admit one more time: writing good comedy can be tricky. What can go wrong? Anything and everything, but here are three danger points:

1. You are following your treatment too mechanically, so that you are being true to the outline but missing the spirit of the comedy you originally enjoyed. Your treatment should be a magic carpet to what you write rather than a straightjacket closing you off from changes and fresh insights. Particularly in comedy, if one element "takes off" on you, follow it through and see where that character, that idea, that twist is headed! Do you need to see a comedy that runs out of gas early on and then painfully follows a plot outline that should have been opened up or thrown out? Rent Tom Schulman's *Eight Heads in a Duffel Bag* (1997) and try to stick with it long enough to see what goes wrong in timing, story, characterization—did I leave out anything?

2. You are not allowing yourself to be crazy enough in dreaming up a world turned upside down, characters who are carnivalesque, situations that pit opposites playfully against one another. *The Full Monty* could have settled for a

mildly amusing social comedy about the unemployed. Instead, Simon Beaufoy
gave himself the total freedom to create a gaggle of oddly shaped misfits who
were willing to humiliate themselves all the way and in the process regain their
own self-esteem. Nothing is "too crazy." Write it and share it, then decide if it
needs pulling in, toning down, redefining. But redefining is very different from
*con*fining. Go for total carnival and see what happens! Put on a Monty Python
film just to remind yourself how nutty comedy—anarchistic comedy especially—can be.

   3. You are actually beginning to change the kind of comedy you are writing. Cervantes began *Don Quixote* as a comic parody, and it wound up as one of
the most touching novels Europe has produced. What happened? Cervantes discovered he had a bigger tale to tell than he originally thought. If your vision of
the project is changing, take time off and think it through. Perhaps it needs to
change! Take the Oscar-winning Italian comedy *Mediterraneo* (1991, Gabriele
Salvatores), for instance. This tale of six inept Italian soldiers stranded on a
Greek island during World War II could have faded out with their rescue at the
end of the war, and it would be seen as a warm and often hilarious ensemble anarchistic comedy with romantic touches. But the postscript scene that caps the
film has one of the soldiers returning to the island in the present, in his late sixties or early seventies. He meets up with two more of the original group, and the
three old men sit quietly peeling eggplants for a moussaka, full of memories of
the past and with a shared friendship continuing in the present. The tone of the
ending? Nostalgic and muted. And it is an ending with a bit of social criticism attached, since the returning veteran says he left Italy because the dream of building a better society after the war didn't work out. That jump-to-the-present ending changes the whole impact of the film, making it a more serious work even
though our memories include much laughter throughout. If your sense of your
comedy is changing, does that reflect several levels of comedy that could, as in
Mediterraneo, be combined skillfully and effectively to deliver laughter and a few
tears too? This is a good week to take stock.

   ASSIGNMENT:
   1. Pen pages 41–50.
   2. Check out a few websites on comedy (appendix 2) to see if there are any
   of interest to you.

Week 9: Reviewing the Treatment

   ASSIGNMENT:
   1. Write on with good humor to roughly your halfway point, pages 51–60.
   2. Treat yourself to several days off to read and think over what you have

accomplished, and to recharge your comic batteries with whatever activity you wish.

There's nothing sacred about taking stock of your whole project at roughly the halfway point, for you are in a real sense constantly reviewing and replaying your story, structure and characters as you write. But it is good to take a day or two off at what feels like a significant point and review the whole picture with an honest eye, and hopefully with a partner's or friend's feedback.

Begin with your treatment. Nine times out of ten, you are making real and perhaps radical changes as you go along, and you better understand what your characters and story are up to. You may wish to take a day and simply *revise your treatment*. In that spirit, I offer one of my own treatments for a script still waiting to be written.

A Sample Anarchistic Romantic Treatment

What follows is a sample anarchistic romantic comedy treatment I wrote with two Russian friends a few years ago. I do wish to make this film someday. It is offered simply as an example of how to present enough story, character and suggestion of comedy in under five pages for a producer to get the gist and flavor of the whole project.

In this particular case, the story grew out of a very real situation in New Orleans. Since the late 1970s, many of the Mardi Gras groups ("krewes") have used Russian tractors to pull their floats on Mardi Gras day and in the parades leading up to it. But while these tractors are inexpensive, they are also cheap and continually break down. Thus the need for Russian mechanics to fly over during the Mardi Gras season to help service them! So we cooked up this idea as the simple "what if" connected to one simple clueless mechanic—a fish out of water—who is suddenly and unexpectedly dropped into the festive world of carnival.

Tractor Blues, *an original screen treatment by Andrew Horton, Marina Drozdova, and Sasha Kiselev*

CONCEPT: *Tractor Blues* is an offbeat anarchistic screwball romantic comedy involving a Russian tractor mechanic and a young Creole girl, set in New Orleans during the Mardi Gras season. East meets West as the spirit of carnival helps this unlikely couple enjoy some unexpected pleasures before their real lives resume.

THE STORY: In the dark we hear Louis Armstrong sing "When It's Sleepy Time Down South." Opening shot: A wolf howling in close-up. We continue to hear Louis Armstrong throughout this scene. The flat landscape of Siberia, as a handsome young engineer, IVAN (28, give him another name you feel works!), is fixing a tractor. THREE OF HIS CHILDREN watch their father as he works. Their simple house in the background as the mother hangs up clothes to dry. The wolf howls again as he comes closer to the few houses that make up the Siberian farm village. Ivan calmly puts down his tools, picks up a rifle and shoots the wolf. He goes back to work as the kids run over to see the wolf.

From far away we see the dust of an approaching jeep coming toward them. It seems to take forever because the distances are so great. When the jeep arrives, there is a "novi" Russian businessman in a suit, who hands Ivan a sealed envelope. "Where must I go this time?" Ivan says. "New Orleans. Tonight," says the businessman.

Cut to: Credit montage sequence as we see Ivan at the Moscow Airport, with crosscutting to New Orleans shots of the beginning of Mardi Gras season and back to Ivan on a jet as we continue to hear Louis Armstrong. Sequence ends with Ivan getting off the plane in New Orleans and being greeted by several men, including an almost-fat man, DAVE (45), who wears a cap saying BELARUS TRACTORS. As the music ends, Ivan can see as they leave the airport that the Louisiana landscape is as flat as his native Siberia!

As they drive into New Orleans and Ivan looks at this strange and wonderful city, Dave explains Ivan's job through an interpreter, LEON, black, educated, fluent in Russian and finishing his Ph.D at Tulane University with a thesis on Pushkin! In fact, as they drive into the city, Dave has a small video player in his large car, and we see shots of Russian tractors pulling Mardi Gras carnival floats through parades. Dave explains (through Leon) that it is Ivan's job to supervise the American mechanics as they take care of the tractors during the two-week season that includes all the parades leading up to Mardi Gras day and that day itself. "These Russian tractors," says Dave, "are like our Louisiana women: they look good but you ride them too hard and they break down!"

Of course the "surface" plot will involve this fish-out-of-water or stranger-comes-to-town story of a Siberian farm engineer coming up against the crazy world of the pagan/Catholic/southern/African/Creole season of carnival, with all of its festivity, sexuality, music, humor, danger and sense of renewal of the human spirit! Leon, of course, will constantly quote Pushkin to Ivan. Ivan, on the other hand, has not read much Russian literature but knows all of Jack London by heart.

Ivan should be a socialist realist hero. Serious but not stupid. Not given to pleasure. In fact, he is a really good guy who has done everything "right" and yet has never had a good time. It will take New Orleans to teach him how to let go and enjoy. Ivan should also be not a communist but not a democrat either. He feels very mixed about the changes in Russia today. He doesn't want Stalin, but he feels capitalism will "rob the spirit of us all."

Of course we can have many funny scenes with the tractors and parades and costumes (Ivan will have to be in costume to work on the tractors!!!). But also se-rious moments too, as he comes to see and understand black New Orleans culture, music, food. Leon is his window to this world. Leon is also gay! There should be funny/serious scenes as Ivan deals with this and as Leon expresses his fears: AIDS, being black, etc. But a true friendship (with one big blow-up) should develop that helps both of them. Dave, meanwhile, is a "good old boy" who wants wine, women and . . . tractors (money), but with a good soul too.

Now for the subplot, which is really the heart and soul of the film. Leon's sis-ter: ROBYN. Light-skinned Creole girl of 18 who, we learn, has been tapped by the family to be a voodoo priestess, in an old tradition (which really exists) of grand-mothers who are priestesses passing it on to their granddaughters. She is not sure about becoming a priestess (this is not a "job" but something one does for family and friends), and she wants to have a serious musical career. The family has jazz musicians who want her to continue with jazz, but she dreams of classical music.

The unlikely happens, of course. Ivan and Robyn become close and, one night, lovers. It is a beautiful moment when it happens, a calm in the midst of a carnival hurricane of emotions. For Robyn also has a jealous boyfriend, MR. FAITH, who is the owner of a jazz club, The Bottom Line.

There will be another subplot that puts everyone in danger: a right-wing re-ligious/political outfit, American for Americans (modeled on David Duke), wants to rid New Orleans of all foreign influences, including especially Russian tractors at Mardi Gras. They sabotage a number of tractors and put all of Mardi Gras in danger. But Ivan, Dave and Leon are able to find a solution after Robyn, using voodoo powers, discovers who the bad guys are. Dave, meanwhile, has sold his Russian tractor business, fed up with it all, to a Japanese businessman. Dave is go-ing into the women's clothing business . . . "to meet more women!"

"What goes up, must come down," says Robyn, and so Ivan must leave the morning after Mardi Gras. It is a gray cold morning. The streets are empty. A few drunks sleeping in strange costumes, but basically no sign of Mardi Gras.

Robyn and Ivan part. Louis Armstrong plays but it becomes Robyn's voice as he walks off to Leon's car.

Cut to: Siberia. Same as opening shot. Ivan is again working in front of his house. His kids play. His wife cooks. A jeep approaches. It takes forever. It ar-rives. Leon gets out! He has come to stay . . . for a while, while he finishes writing his thesis.

THE END

If I followed this treatment and reached approximately the halfway point, I would indeed wish to pause and go over a number of points. For instance, while I'm happy with the general shape of the film as a "circular" tale that ends where it begins but with changes in between—the New Orleans experience of our comic protagonist—I still have questions and areas that need work: is the ending too simple? Have I fallen into the trap of making my subplot too formulaic? How can I open up the temporary romance that develops? What if Ivan doesn't go back? And a number of other points I will deal with when I get there.

Week 10: Focus on Comic Texture and Tone

So you are back on the job, ready to buckle down and enjoy the second half of your script. Congrats!

Take a few moments to think over the texture and tone of your comedy. Let's review three quite different comedies for our assignment of the week.

John Huston's *African Queen* meets the requirements of screwball romantic comedy. But it is something of an action-adventure film as well. The tone therefore hovers between these two poles as Humphrey Bogart and Katharine Hepburn negotiate their way down an African river, confront a Nazi gunboat and simultaneously come to appreciate each other as man and woman. The texture of the film has to do with the rugged and often dangerous beauty of Africa—including the animals and birds they encounter—which really shares the spotlight with the characters. Put another way, the texture of this romantic adventure comedy has much to do with a feeling of being *outdoors.* And this should strike us as a refreshing switch from so many romantic comedies set in cities and taking place inside houses, buildings and cars. Yes, shooting on location *did* make a difference to the look, tone, and texture of this American classic, which made it to the AFI Best 100 Films list.

Kevin Smith's debut, no-budget comedy *Clerks* (1994) also gained much by being shot on location. In this case, however, the location is a convenience store in Smith's suburban New Jersey, where he actually worked at the time he made the film. Truly an anarchistic buddy film, *Clerks* is fun to a large degree because the low budget helps create the texture of a kind of clever home movie, complete with black-and-white cinematography and often rough camera shots or set-ups. The absurd tone of the film comes from our feeling that the scene is so real that the "actors" must be making up half their lines as they go along. The texture is thus as far from that of a Hollywood studio film as possible. And the results of such a consciously chosen rough texture? Leonard Maltin speaks for many critics when he notes that *Clerks* is "certainly more provocative and entertaining than many glossy Hollywood movies of the 1990's" (245).

Benny and Joon (1993) creates yet another atmosphere and comic climate. Director Jeremiah Chechik aims for a tone evenly balanced between wry comedy and very real pathos in this fable about a mentally unhinged young woman (Mary Stuart Masterson) and a young social misfit who sees himself as a reincarnation of

Buster Keaton (Johnny Depp). Yes, it could technically be called a romantic comedy, but the underlying seriousness generated by the "case history" tone of many scenes means that we come away from the film feeling it to be equally a psychological drama that skates very close to melodrama. Also important to the texture and climate of the film is the strong echo of silent comedy, especially that of Keaton and Chaplin, as Johnny Depp acts out old slapstick routines and mime performances. In short, many mimes explode before film's end.

Considering tone and texture helps you define what it is in your script you are up to beyond laughter. What determines these twin elements? Everything: characterization, your particular genres of comedy (or comedy mixed with other genres), minor characters, locations and subplots.

ASSIGNMENT:
1. Write pages 61–70.
2. You are in charge of the movie poster for your own comedy. Dream up what you want to be your poster image or images. Besides the title and credits, what one-liner might appear on it?

Week 11: Balancing Fantasy and Festivity

Fantasy and festivity: twin elements of comedy that are important to whatever particular form of the muse you are writing. The question of the week is: what kinds of festivity and fantasy have you made use of, and are you satisfied with the degree and mixture you are cooking up in your comic recipe? Remember our basic distinction: *fantasy* celebrates the freedom of an individual's imagination and embraces any "magical" element in a script, and *festivity* is a shared and therefore communal celebration. Anarchistic comedies by definition suggest a great freedom to indulge in these twin elements. But romantic comedies may invoke large doses of each as well.

Consider the following examples:

Penny Marshall's *The Preacher's Wife* (1996) has Denzel Washington as an angel sent down to help a troubled African American gospel church who falls in love with Whitney Houston, the preacher's wife. An anarchistic gospel screwball comedy, it is actually a remake of the 1947 comedy *The Bishop's Wife*. In Marshall's update, the fantasy element—an African American angel—blends humorously and joyously with the festive gospel hand-clapping scenes for a true carnival of a Christmas-season film.

Dona Flor and Her Two Husbands was a Brazilian hit comedy in 1978, starring Sonia Braga as a very sensuous cooking instructor who is haunted by the ghost of her hard-drinking, hard-loving young husband (Jose Wilker) while she tries to live a quiet middle-class life with her chubby and very conservative middle-aged second husband (Mauro Mendoca). In the tradition of South American "magic realism," the presence of the dead first husband, who is only visible to Dona Flor, is the clear fantasy element. Festivity breaks out everywhere throughout the film, beginning with the opening scene, since the setting is a carnival culture (the first husband dies during a carnival parade). Food itself becomes festive in the scenes in which Dona Flor is cooking. Add the carnival music to the sound track and you have a film that is a carnival pure and simple from beginning to end.

But what of films that do not introduce such obvious "magical" fantasy elements? *Big Night,* we have suggested, is one of the most festive celebrations of good food in American cinema: the whole narrative revolves around the preparation and consumption of a "to die for" meal. Festivity? Absolutely: it is a shared experience that brings a very diverse group of people together for an evening they will never forget. And fantasy? The biggest fantasy is simply the two brothers' dream that they can save the restaurant. But this outward goal covers a deeper inner need: for Primo to be taken seriously as an Italian chef and for Secundo to feel he is succeeding in America.

Finally, in an ensemble male-bonding anarchistic feel-good comedy of the early 1990s, Ron Underwood's *City Slickers,* fantasy and festivity cross paths constantly. Billy Crystal, Daniel Stern and Bruno Kirby live out their fantasies of escaping middle-class, middle-aged suburban life on their getaway holidays. We meet them in the opening credit sequence being chased by bulls down the streets of Pamplona, Spain, in a funny takeoff on their Ernest Hemingway fantasy. The comedy shifts to Out West, as they become cowboys under the mentorship of a stone-faced Jack Palance. The comedy in the film is generated from watching not only the obvious slapstick of city slickers trying to be cowboys but a group of friends needing to redefine themselves and readjust their fantasies. The festivity is therefore reflected in the shared experiences of this group of urban cowboys.

Look over your script. Are you happy with the intertwining of these elements in your tale? What would happen if you added more or less? Woody Allen begins *Annie Hall* (1977) by looking out at us, standing alone, like the stand-up comedian he used to be. He ends speaking to us once more, in voiceover, but the camera is trained on a busy New York street near Lincoln Center. The street with its passersby is not an actual carnival, of course. Yet I would argue this is a "festive" ending, for Allen has shifted our attention from just himself onto the passing world outside. This is an embrace and celebration of a much wider world.

ASSIGNMENT:

1. Deliver, playfully, pages 71–80.

2. Take a few minutes to do a fantasy/festivity check on the major players in your script. What are the fantasies of each, and to what degree have they or

have they not fulfilled them? Similarly, what is the relationship of each of your characters to festivity, and have you increased or decreased that character's "festivity threshold"?

Week 12: A Few Words on Tears and Laughter

If you are writing a purely anarchistic farce along the lines of *Austin Powers* or *There's Something about Mary* or *Duck Soup* or *Blazing Saddles,* then keep writing and pass on to Week 13. But for many of you, comedy may well include moments if not a whole overall tone that calls for both laughter and a few tears along the way. We have discussed a number of genre-bending examples and suggested that such border-crossing films have become more numerous, be they *Fargo, Pulp Fiction, Kolya, Get on the Bus, Good Will Hunting, Cinema Paradiso* or *My Life as a Dog.* Comedy and serious drama often cross in unusual ways, as even Socrates has pointed out. Realize further that to talk of tears and laughter is to suggest several possibilities. Think about which may apply to your script.

A strongly comic film with one or more scenes that reach an emotional level. Four Weddings and a Funeral keeps us laughing 90 percent of the time as a romantic comedy with strong farcical underpinnings. But the funeral packs an honest tearful punch, in large part because of the contrast with the laughter we have experienced before it (and will experience again afterwards).

A film more dramatic than comic that becomes even more emotional because of the humor. John Hughes's best film may well be *The Breakfast Club* (1985), as Emilio Estevez, Molly Ringwald, Judd Nelson, Anthony Michael Hall and Ally Sheedy spend a Saturday together in high school detention. The film turns increasingly dramatic as the story progresses, yet the comic moments keep even the soul confessions of this cross-section of teen culture from falling over into sentimentality.

A film that mixes humor and pathos and can hit those moments that can make you simultaneously laugh and cry. Of the films discussed in earlier chapters, *Kolya* would be the best example. We can safely say that European films in general are much more successful at blending tears and laughter than Hollywood products. Look at the scene, for instance, of Kolya making a toy out of a shoe box and other scraps in Louka's apartment. As we close in to see what it is, we realize that he has constructed a coffin and is playing a cremation game. That is the world Kolya has known living with a musician who earns his living playing funerals.

One filmmaking friend judges the emotional punch of a film by how many handkerchiefs you need to get through it. Thus it's up to you to decide if yours is a one-handkerchief comedy (*Four Weddings and a Funeral*), a two-handkerchief comedy (*Kolya*) or a three-handkerchief "weepie-comedy" (*Life Is Beautiful*) or comic drama (*Il Postino/The Postman*, 1994).

ASSIGNMENT:

1. Write pages 81–90.

2. If indeed you are interested in exploring how to find the balance between tears and laughter, rent an Italian drama full of comic moments, *Three Brothers* (Francesco Rosi, 1980), and enjoy how surprising humor comes from three very different brothers returning to their small Italian home for their mother's funeral.

Week 13: Comic Endings versus Endings of Comedies

You are approaching the ending of your comedy, and you've obviously had a game plan about how you see your film wrapping up. But has that vision shifted as you come down to the wire?

Take a moment and *draw up at least three or four endings* for your script before you get there, just to make sure you are happy with the one you are aiming for. It goes without saying that you want to bounce these ideas off your comic partner, for he or she may also have some thoughts on the matter. Comedy, remember, ends in some form of triumph and some degree of an embrace in which our comic protagonist is not alone. In short, comedy celebrates the birth of a new community of two or more individuals who have new possibilities because they are united in some way. Furthermore, we have said the anarchistic comedies of Aristophanes end in dance and song with the whole community taking part, while romantic comedy ends with the young couple united, if not by marriage then certainly by love and commitment. The fun of finding your ending is perhaps best summed up in saying you are in search of a fresh variation on either of these two classic closings.

Consider five variations on romantic and anarchistic themes.

1. A non-marriage romantic ending: *Four Weddings and a Funeral* ends with Hugh Grant and Andie MacDowell in a loving embrace, having promised each other they will never marry each other. Part of the pleasure of this ironic take is that we have just watched a romance that has blossomed in spite of all the set rituals of conventional weddings.

We can point to many romantic comedies that do not end in marriage, but simply with the couple together. *Tootsie* leaves us on a New York street with Dustin Hoffman and Jessica Lange walking into the crowd, arguing playfully about a dress of Dustin's that Jessica wishes to borrow.

2. A flash-forward "dream" ending: *Raising Arizona* is framed by Nicolas Cage's voiceover, which makes this very much his story. It is fitting, therefore, that the ending is a dream of himself and Holly Hunter as aged grandparents, welcoming the tribe of their children and grandchildren in a festive family-holiday scene bathed in golden light. The dream is a wonderful blending of fantasy and festivity, a triumph of family for a couple who have had to steal a baby to get started.

3. Ending on strong comic irony: The "I'm a man" ending of Billy Wilder's *Some Like It Hot* is a prime example of an ironic ending. But my favorite of all time is still Buster Keaton's closing shot for *Sherlock Jr.* (1924). Remember, he is the small-town projectionist with two interests, getting the girl and becoming a detective. At film's end, the girl is in the projection booth with him while he looks out at the film he is projecting for clues as to how he should act. Following what he sees on the screen, he kisses her, puts a ring on her finger and then looks back at the screen to see the couple now have twins. The closing shot is Buster framed in the projection booth window scratching his head, as if to say either "Do I really want to go down this path?" or "Where do babies come from?" or . . . both!

4. Ensemble festive ending: *The First Wives Club* (1996, Hugh Wilson) teams up Goldie Hawn, Bette Midler and Diane Keaton as three school chums who meet years later, after they have each been dumped by husbands. Predictably, they put their lives back in order and begin to have some fun. And to cap it all off, by film's end we see them begin to dance together to a pop song down a New York street. *The Full Monty* goes out in an even more gloriously festive style, as our group of unemployed steelworkers finally get it together to take it all off before wives and girlfriends and other appreciative women.

5. A quiet ending to a comedy rather than a comic ending: *Big Night* best exemplifies this brand of closing shot. The simple cooking and sharing of an omelet, each brother with an arm around the other's shoulder, is the way this generally noisy and festive comedy about food, love, brotherhood and dreams made and lost closes. Softly, tenderly, quietly, and fade out.

ASSIGNMENT:
1. Write pages 91–100, keeping your ending in mind!
2. What are half a dozen films you really admire? Consider how they end. Do any of them suggest ways you might handle your own script?

Week 14: Share the Laughter

A hearty congratulations! You are finishing your script either this week or next. Either way, I offer my handshake and salute at this point. Put "The End" on the last page and think how best to celebrate. Any way except alone. Share the joy and the laughter, and explode even more mimes in appreciation of the work you have done. Yes, your partner deserves a treat too for having put up with you this long. Make the celebration special, and do *not* immediately rush to rewrite or try to call an agent!

Toward a Comic Out-Loud Reading of Your Script

Take it easy, come back to planet Earth, and think about anything else except screenwriting. Best to let several weeks at the least go by without touching it. Then organize a reading with friends you know can read well enough to give some life and color to your lines, and turn this event into a working party rather than a dry run-through. You may even wish to have someone videotape this event, if the recording doesn't get in the way of the fun of the evening.

Should you read or just listen? That's entirely up to you. But if you are reading, you are listening as well, for this is your big chance to test your script and to hear what works and what doesn't, what gets laughs and what lies there on the page wishing to hide away.

Then roll 'em, and enjoy hearing your own work performed. What happens if you skip this exercise? A lot. You may completely mistake what you are doing really well or very badly if you depend on just your reading or your partner's. The group response counts, and your reaction to the group matters a lot as well. You did so much to get to this point, so you deserve to have the best testing of your material possible.

Follow the reading with a discussion—even an informal one—afterwards. As with a story circle (see chapter 2), such a wrap on the evening may well net a number of significant insights from those participating.

Should you invite some other friends as well? Up to you, once again. Some scriptwriting programs advertise public readings of scripts as part of a student's degree requirements. You might want to pull in some people you know or even go for some strangers showing up too, as in a public reading.

ASSIGNMENT:

1. Write pages 101–110 and keep on writing if this is not yet the end!

2. Go out to a very serious film that appears not to have a stroke of humor in it. Remind yourself of the power of pure drama, but also perhaps of the reasons you feel good about writing comedy.

3. You have exercised your talent. Now look for and take advantage of any "luck" that comes your way.

Week 15: Retaining Your Humor from Page to Screen

You've recovered from the comic reading and tossed out the last of the left-over pizza. Now what? Lock the script away for a few weeks or a month, minimum, and take a long-deserved vacation. A real one if you can, or otherwise a fantasy "few days off" around the house or the neighborhood.

The rewrite is the next step, but especially since you are working on comedy, you want to be fresh again. So whatever you do, please don't rush into the revision before you have regained your humor, sanity (or parts thereof), and some sense of the pure pleasure of it all again.

Meanwhile, turn to appendix 2 and see what items may prove useful to you as you begin to think of Life After the Rewrite. Realize that a whole other world awaits you as you head toward seeing your laughter transformed to the screen. Yes, it can be a hard, cruel and humorless set of hurdles, obstacles, roadblocks and land mines. All the more reason to hold on to your unexploded mimes and let them go whenever you need one to explode the most. For I would not be writing these words if that route wasn't also filled with memories of new friendships, hilarious meetings and exhilarating experiences. If you don't see this next step as a grand comedy too (OK, it may often become a farce as well!), then it is time to consider other pursuits.

ASSIGNMENT:

1. Finish your comedy!

2. And do a hearty rewrite after the input of your partner and friends from the comic reading, and from readings by those chosen few whose opinions you trust.

3. Then on to appendix 2 and the wide world beyond.

CHAPTER 12

The Seven-Week Half-Hour
Television Comedy Pilot Script

*Man plays only when he is in the fullest sense of the word a human
being, and he is only a complete human being when he plays.*

Schiller

I have strongly urged you to write whatever feature comedy you wish and enjoy the process of doing so. Of course, my hopes are that you will find lasting sat-
isfaction in coming up with episodic television comedy as well. But we would be
kidding ourselves if we did not from the beginning acknowledge the much more
restricted and swiftly shifting world of television production. Translation: this is
the chapter in danger of being "out of date" upon publication. Television changes
that fast. Keeping that in mind, however, I've tried to focus on general advice that
should transcend the shifting sands of trends and hype.

Yes, it is relatively easy to get your own work on local cable access channels if
you are living in the United States. But the moment you begin to think about network half-hour comedy shows, you are speaking of a very highly competitive ball
game that is difficult—but not impossible—to break into. That said, let's let the
televised laughter begin.

CHAPTER ASSIGNMENT:
Write a pilot script for an original half-hour comedy series.

Week 1: Conceiving Episodic Comedy

ASSIGNMENT:
1. Tape a half-hour comedy show that means a lot to you and study that
episode carefully, perhaps watching it three or four times. Get hold of the
script from Script City or the Internet (see appendix 2), and go over the
script for format and set-up and to see what changes may or may not have
been made between script and the broadcast episode.
2. Plan out a "spec" script for the show you have studied in a two- to three-
page treatment.

3. Write one-paragraph concepts for three original series ideas, without ranking them, and test them on your comic partner and trusted friends to refine or redefine them and then, finally, to select one of them as the one you wish to develop.

Start with a simple question: What recent episodic comedy has worked for you? Is it *Frasier*'s "psycho-com" series, which seems, at this writing, to have gained millions of new fans as well as Emmys each year? Perhaps it is *Ally McBeal* that appeals, with its surrealistic flashes of fantasy, irony and humor about the problems of a bright and good-looking female lawyer in balancing relationships and career. Or does *Everybody Loves Raymond* tickle you as a subtly subversive family sitcom in a way that *Home Improvement* can't? Perhaps you wish to pen an animated series that will take off where *King of the Hill* and *The Simpsons* stop, outrageous to a degree that live-action sitcom could never get away with? Or do you see a show like *Ellen* as your mentor for pushing the envelope of sitcom, not only in Ellen DeGeneres's "coming out" episode but in the show's constant celebration of creative freedom?

Despite television's seasonal shifts in tastes, it is worth taking a closer look at one or two shows that work for you so that you can better understand how they do it, so you can get hold of exactly what the show is doing to and for you.

Try your hand at writing a *sample script for a popular comedy series* as your "passport" sample. And in fact it is not a bad idea to have both the original pilot script we are targeting in this chapter *and* a spec script for an existing show as a writing sample when you go to shop your project around. Which one to write for? That depends on what is hot at the moment you decide to take a shot at it. Choose a show that is clearly on the rise. As longtime comic writer John Vorhaus notes, "Be the first on your block to write a spec script for a smart new show" (140).

But note that many television producers would be just as happy, or even more so, to see one of your original feature scripts to prove to them that you have the imagination and talent to go the whole route. Part of the logic of setting up the feature film comedy script in a chapter before this one is to meet such a demand. If you are capable of completing the script you created as outlined in chapter 11, then you should find this chapter's assignment—a half-hour episodic comedy pilot script—easier going.

As with the feature comedy assignment, see if you can dream up three concepts for comedy series, ranging from (1) fairly safe to (2) slightly outrageous to (3) completely out there and over the top.

Take the following four points into consideration as you brainstorm, both alone and with your trusty comic partner:

1. There is absolutely no predicting what will and what will not work in episodic comedy. Try to imagine the original pitch for *Seinfeld* (four characters who talk about and do "nothing"), for *Northern Exposure* (a Jewish doctor in an Alaskan village), or for *Cheers* (a bunch of characters who hang out in a Boston

bar). And given that America is a "middle-class" nation, how did *Roseanne,* a show about a working-class woman and her family, capture our imaginations for so many years? I would suggest the results are not that much different in other countries I have visited either. *Mork and Mindy* launched Robin Williams, so even aliens in a middle-class household can make us laugh. The message is thus clear: anything goes when it comes to comic concepts!

2. Build on concepts that you connect with, either through experience or passion or, best of all, both. Ray Romano, star of *Everybody Loves Raymond,* drew from his own life situation of living near his parents in New York and dealing with an obsessive brother who is a cop. A concept you have passion and knowledge about is going to take you further than something you are only guessing about. There are qualifications to this point, of course. Almost none of the writers on *Northern Exposure* ever went to Alaska. But everyone "got" that Cicely was a mythical never-never land in which everyone was free to be him- or herself. It was from the start conceived as a "fantasy" Alaska.

3. Does your concept involve the interweaving of characters and potential situations that will have "legs" to go for season after season? Shows that last more than a few years plan on major changes or events taking place in the characters' lives to suggest "growth" each season. The idea is not to simply repeat set guidelines and situations but to actually have characters and situations that are strong enough to encourage and allow for such growth. *The Full Monty* was enjoyable as a feature comedy, but would it work week after week and season after season on the small screen? I don't think so. It's a one-shot, one-punch-line comedy. On the other hand, one of my students came up with the idea of a successful middle-aged husband-and-wife team—both professionals with good salaries—who quit and move to a small town to run a bed and breakfast (B & B). In fact, that was her title for the show: *B & B,* for the characters were named Bob and Barbara. Clearly this concept has legs: you have the ever-changing guests who come through and the fish-out-of-water structure as the couple adjust to country life and to themselves once more.

4. Is your concept on a timely curve of popular needs or interests? Producer/writer Barbara Hall (*Northern Exposure, Chicago Hope, I'll Fly Away* and more) notes that pilot scripts, whether for comedy or drama, succeed most often when they are in sync with the perceived "hot" trends of the moment in television. She comments:

> What networks are looking for in a pilot is anything that vaguely resembles a successful series from the previous season. Sometimes, too, they want to see pilots that reflect some successful movie. So if someone has a pilot idea that can be compared to *Good Will Hunting* this year [1998] and pair it with something like *Buffy the Vampire Slayer,* then you probably have a hit. And I'm only being half facetious. *Also, pilots sell far more often from an oral pitch*

than from a script, but that doesn't mean one shouldn't go ahead and write a
pilot, because they are excellent "samples" and good practice too.

(Personal interview, April 13, 1998.
Emphasis added.)

So end the week knowing which pilot you wish to go ahead with, but save the other ideas too. You never know what you might be able to do with them later when more comic lightning strikes, like an unexploded mime going off.

Week 2: Structuring Your Pilot

ASSIGNMENT:

1. Do a story outline for your pilot, breaking it into a two- or three-act structure.
2. Identify your "A" story and "B" story, possibly with a "C" and maybe even a "D" if you are writing something as dense as *Seinfeld*.

Half-hour episodic comedy is structured in either two-act (*M*A*S*H, Mad About You, Seinfeld*) or three-act (*The Simpsons, Murphy Brown*) divisions. What is the difference between the two? Both add up to 23 to 25 minutes of total screen time, but the three-act allows for two major shifts in story in half an hour while the two-act depends on that one big jolt halfway through. What you are trying to accomplish either way is to Disrupt the Status Quo in act 1. If you are doing three acts, Follow the Disruptions Further in act 2 (the bar scene, for instance, in the *Simpsons* episode discussed in chapter 10). And in the final act, Re-establish an Equilibrium. In other words, we start with the "normal" set-up, whatever that is for your show, then undergo a Disruption that turns into an Eruption followed by a Readjustment that leads to a Re-establishment of "normal" once more. That story sense—the Completed Circle That Is Not Quite Round—is necessary for television episodic shows, of course, since no radical change can take place without doing damage to the show's basic concept. The characters in *M*A*S*H* don't leave Korea or go beyond the time period of the Korean War; Lucy never moves out of the suburban home we came to memorize the floor plan and furniture of; Homer Simpson never leaves his job at the nuclear power plant; Seinfeld always lives in his own apartment and keeps his job as a stand-up comedian.

Television requires that comfort zone of the predictable within which small surprises and changes can take place over time.

Decide which is your main, or "A," story and which one or more narratives are your subplots, or "B," "C" or even "D" stories. We can say that *Seinfeld* really is a four-character, four-story show, with one being foregrounded each week as

the "A" story and each of the other characters having his or her own preoccupa-
tions as well. Other comedy shows function well with just one subplot, or two at
the most.

Whatever your choice of how many subplots, *make sure that your minor stories reflect some aspect of the main story,* either in contrast or as a variation. The "B"
and "C" plots allow you a range of the comic. If your "A" story is romantic, your
"B" might be more farcical; if "A" is quite anarchistic, your "B" and "C" might
reflect more conservative forms of humor, including one story that goes for some
pathos.

Week 3: Outlining Five to Ten Episodes for Your Series

ASSIGNMENT:
You have the series concept you like best. And you know what you want for
your pilot episode. But before writing the pilot, sit down and in brief outline
form map out five to ten episodes.

Why not just jump into writing the pilot? Simple. This series outline assignment helps you determine whether or not your idea has staying power. It can help
you sharpen your pilot as well.

This is also the time to review any chapters of this text that caught your
eye in a first reading. Was there something about Aristophanes or Shakespeare
that might influence your soon-to-be hit comedy? Or should you look at a Czech
or Yugoslav comedy before writing dialogue for your sitcom about a dentist in
Des Moines who with his wife has adopted four children, each from a different
country?

Finally, have you made someone close to you laugh recently? That's a good
check-up on whether or not you are ready to write the comedy pilot that all the
networks will be beating down your door to produce.

Week 4: Writing Act 1

ASSIGNMENT:
Make sure you have gone over the simple basics of television format, then—
write act 1!

If you've covered everything in the text up till now, you don't need me to repeat advice. But remember that everything happens at least twice as fast in tele-

vision. *As Good As It Gets* or *The African Queen* have almost two hours to develop romance and comedy, but you have less than half an hour to work with. So make it all happen faster. (But don't be afraid to write whatever you wish at first and then trim back.)

If feature comedy is epic, then series comedy is much closer to haiku! The structure and length are set. What you must master (and what the audience enjoys) is what you can do within such restrictions. In fact, taking the haiku analogy one step further, the brevity and tight structure should be viewed in series comedy as in Japanese poetry, as your invitation to creativity and novelty.

More easily said than done, of course. But worth remembering nevertheless.

End the week watching one of your taped shows once more, so that you can be proud of how much you have done so far.

Week 5: Writing Act 2

ASSIGNMENT:

Write act 2, making sure that even though you think you know where the story is going, you still manage to surprise yourself daily with a plot wrinkle, a really good line you had not come up with before, or a bad joke that works perfectly for your episode.

If you are writing a two-act pilot, then this is it. If you have a three-act comedy, you are enjoying seeing your carnival of clashing forces unfold. Is there anything left for you to consider at this point? Always! Ask yourself these three questions:

1. Am I "pushing the envelope" at least a few inches in this episode? No, I don't advise doing something like the "coming-out" *Ellen* episode as your pilot for a new show and hope to sell it to a major network. But this question is asking you to consider if in fact you might be guilty of the opposite: are you playing it too safe and thus giving us the same-old-same-old in a version that does not let your originality and talent shine through. Don't be afraid to try out a character, a situation, an idea that has a bit of an edge to it. If I were doing a show set in a New Orleans, where I have lived the last twenty years, I would in part want to smash stereotypes of the proverbial city of jazz and good food—by, say, adding one character who is Vietnamese. Why? Because New Orleans has one of the largest Vietnamese populations in the United States, and they have become an important part of the culture and economics of the city. And I would also enjoy writing such a character because I don't remember such a figure in a major American comic series.

Ask yourself what your pilot is offering us that we haven't seen before! Take some chances for the pure fun of it.

2. Am I having fun with some "sneaky" details that reward, as *The Simpsons* does, those who pay attention? What cereal does Seinfeld eat, what messages are on the blackboard in Bart Simpson's classroom, and what musical groups are they talking about in *Fresh Prince of Bel-Air?* Comedy does thrive on detail, and you have a wonderful opportunity to sneak in some details for the unadulterated pleasure of it. Teenage girls used to make a run on libraries the day after each episode of *Northern Exposure* aired, asking for those "guys" that Chris, the highly literate deejay, had mentioned that week, ranging from Proust to Hemingway, Sartre to Socrates.

3. Is there at least one moment, one scene, that even by my own standards seems a little bit over the top? Comedy invites excess, and in fact demands it. Forget this at your peril. And yet comedy that is excessive nonstop becomes a bore. How to *orchestrate* and *build* to the excess is the question. Often you can build to the moment when one or more of your secondary stories crashes into your main story. In *The Simpsons,* excess is the operative word, in large part because of the freedom granted the show by the limitless world of animation. As we explored in chapter 10, Marge doesn't just get drunk at Mr. Burns's picnic, she gets really *really* drunk and then tops that when she begins to sing. You can always pull a scene back in a rewrite, but let carnival rule as you write some scenes that go for flat-out comedy.

Week 6: Writing Act 3
or Polishing the Two-Act Pilot

ASSIGNMENT:

1. Wrap up your comedy.
2. Go over chapter 11 to review details on everything from minor characters and comic texture to the need for balancing fantasy and festivity in your pilot.
3. Fine-tune rather than completely rewrite your comedy.

Go for the swift ending with a final wink, joke or line that seals it all. In our *Simpsons* episode covered in chapter 10, the family is expelled from a family therapy clinic as a newly reunited group that the good Doc just can't handle. But the perfect cap that takes it one step further is that the Doc gives them double their money back so they can retrieve the family television set. The Simpsons can now return home to the activity that has always drawn them together as a family: watching television.

Our other sample show, *Seinfeld,* had a very simple set-up and close for many episodes, bookending the action with snippets from Jerry's stand-up routines, thus allowing him the chance to be both the central protagonist and the nar-rator/wise-guy commentator. I've often run into folks who watched the show just for those moments.

In both cases, the endings are what we could call "trademark" closings, for they are emblematic and repeated actions—the family watching television and Jerry joking about the events he has just lived through. Thus, even with your pilot, you are not just figuring out how to reach "The End" but thinking about what might become an expected motif or theme for your closings for audiences to look forward to.

Rewrites? Don't do any major overhauling before the "performance" in week 7. But comedy even more than drama needs a fine-tuning of lines and scenes to heighten laughter and shade character. No wonder so many stand-ups and gag men and women have worked in television. A rewrite is always a chance for, "Oh, that reminds me of the joke my mother used to tell . . ." or "Perhaps your slapstick biz on page ten is too close to what *Saturday Night Live* did three years ago." In short, the first rewrite is more a going-over to brush out clinkers and see if you can build in fresher lines, livelier moments, even more comic anarchy that will bring on more honest laughter.

Week 7: A Performance and Celebration Evening

Bravo, folks! Another television comic series has been born.

Savor the moment, then prepare to share it through a celebratory evening and reading as outlined in chapter 11. Think particularly of the fun you can have with such an evening if you have, as suggested in chapter 2, set up a comic story circle that meets on some kind of regular basis. Even if you don't have such a "home team," not to worry. A reading with friends or those you know with some acting talent and those who, best of all, may fit the parts will certainly tell you much about what you have accomplished and what can be made even better.

Then a rewrite. *Double-check television script format.* I have advised you to get hold of several television scripts to study them, but it is also useful to refer to some of the standard works on format and screenwriting that cover these topics more thoroughly. Individual shows make particular changes according to their needs, and thus you have a certain degree of flexibility, since you are creating your own pilot. In general, however, note that the format is similar to feature screenplay format with these differences: Include labels for acts; number or letter scenes. Most shows have a top-of-page heading that includes the title of the show, the title of the episode, the number of the draft, the date of the draft and a page number. For a pilot, however, I would have the show's name, the pilot's title and a page number only. Some shows underline slug lines (<u>EXT. NEW YORK STREET–DAY</u>) and others don't. Some, such as *Seinfeld*, capitalize all directions, while others don't. Some shows underline all entries and exits of characters, many don't. Bottom line: be consistent.

What next? Because television comedy can change so swiftly, you must be prepared to take some chances as outlined in appendix 2 and to be ready to follow through on any breaks or contacts that come your way. At a minimum, you should not bat an eye at picking up and flying to New York or Los Angeles and staying there for several weeks if nibbles begin to come, or even to begin knocking on doors. Remember, "they" will not be calling you if you do not first get "their" attention!

Do not forget two important items once you start in on placing your script: be most grateful and gracious to those who do help you, and above all, be yourself.

Beyond Happy Endings:
Toward a Comic Conclusion

> The cheerful doling out of futures which takes place at the conclu-
> sion of most comedies is not in any secure sense "happy." Rather it
> is sublimely arbitrary.
>
> Walter Kerr, *Tragedy and Comedy*

> Laughter lifts our spirits, surprises and sometimes shocks our ex-
> pectations, allows us to cross boundaries, reorders our priorities,
> and gives us access to ideas and associations we rarely ever thought
> to have.
>
> Jean Houston, *A Mythic Life*

That's all, friends . . . almost.

We've looked into writing screenplays that shine with humor and the comic spirit. But we should end as we began, realizing that in real life comedy plays its daily role and at times makes history as well as laughter.

That comedy and carnival are a state of being beyond the borders of genres was very clear to all who participated in the Belgrade protests after the Bosnian war ended and the socioeconomic situation continued to worsen in Yugoslavia. I quote from a Serbian friend's letter:

> What has happened these days in Belgrade and in the other towns of Serbia
> is a completely new form of human communication. It has happened at a
> moment when we are confronted with a total break of communication. Ser-
> bian TV has destroyed real information.
>
> Yet communication among the people in the towns was never so close,
> so live, so direct. We have been communicating with each other in a new
> way: with whistles, leaflets, jokes, passwords, gazes, meetings, by drumming
> on pots and pans every evening at 7:30 to block out the TV newscasts. Stu-
> dents and citizens have made a real democratic carnival. And carnival, as
> Bakhtin writes, destroys the existing order and establishes a new one. . . .
> Every day people go into the streets to purify themselves mentally and to de-
> fend their hope through laughter and humor.
>
> (Slobodanka Pekovic, letter, January 1997)

At such a point, there is no script, no scenario other than the spontaneous one of a mass carnival. Such comedy-of-the-streets goes beyond festivity in the community and personal release to reach, as the Russian theoretician Mikhail Bakhtin suggests, its "meaningful philosophical content" (5).

Let us sign off by wishing you well in all of your comedies, written, lived, re-membered and yet to come. I call on Milan Kundera to offer the final appeal: "I beg you, friend, be happy. I have the vague sense that on your capacity to be happy hangs our only hope!" (156). And, of course, to top off even such an invitation, bring on Groucho Marx in *A Night at the Opera,* giving his approval to the carni-val of fantasy and comic chaos that, in the film, follows his words:

> And now on with the opera. Let joy be unconfined. Let there be dancing in the streets, drinking in the saloons, and necking in the parlor.

A Recommended Viewing List of American and Foreign Feature Comedies

I started out this list modestly, proposing some twenty-five titles that I thought cut across the whole band of comedy. The list quickly grew to 101, but I kept adding, and finally—wisely, I trust—said the hell with it and let the list take on a carnival of its own! Then, at last, I trimmed, knowing my editor would not approve of an extra twenty pages of listings!

This list brings together many of the feature comedies discussed in this book and others from around the world. The list is meant to be suggestive or even provocative and offbeat rather than exhaustive. Not all these films would be recognized as comedies, but their inclusion here merely means there are enough comedic elements and moments to make them worthy of study and enjoyment. And I've squeezed in several other categories as well. Enjoy!

Silent Comedy

Safety Last (1923) Director: Fred Newmeyer. Screenplay: Hal Roach, Tim Whelan, Sam Taylor. Cast: Harold Lloyd, Sam Taylor, Mildred Davis, Bill Strothers.

Charlie Chaplin, all, but especially: *The Gold Rush* (1925) Director and screenplay: Charles Chaplin. Cast: Charles Chaplin, Georgia Hale, Mack Swain, Tom Murray.

Buster Keaton, all, but especially: *The General* (1927) Director: Buster Keaton. Screenplay: Buster Keaton, Clyde Bruckman, from *The Great Locomotive Chase* by William Pittinger. Cast: Buster Keaton, Marion Mack, Glen Cavender, Jim Farley, Joseph Keaton; and *Sherlock Jr.* (1924) Director: Buster Keaton. Screenplay: Clyde Bruckman, Jean Havez, Joseph Mitchell. Cast: Buster Keaton, Kathryn McGuire, Ward Crane, Joseph Keaton, Erwin Connolly.

Anarchistic and Black Satirical Comedy

Ace Ventura: Pet Detective (1994) Director: Tom Shadyac. Screenplay: Jack
 Bernstein, Tom Shadyac, Jim Carrey. Cast: Jim Carrey, Courteney
 Cox, Sean Young.

After Hours (1985) Director: Martin Scorsese. Screenplay: Joseph Minion.
 Cast: Griffin Dunne, Rosanna Arquette, Verna Bloom, Thomas
 Chong, Linda Fiorentino.

Bananas (1971) Director: Woody Allen. Screenplay: Woody Allen, Mickey
 Rose. Cast: Woody Allen, Carlos Montalban, Louise Lasser.

Being There (1979) Director: Hal Ashby. Screenplay: Jerzy Kosinski, from
 his own novel. Cast: Peter Sellers, Shirley MacLaine, Melvyn Doug-
 las, Jack Warden.

Blazing Saddles (1974) Director: Mel Brooks. Screenplay: Mel Brooks,
 Norman Steinberg, Andrew Bergman, Richard Pryor, Alan Uger.
 Cast: Cleavon Little, Gene Wilder, Harvey Korman, Madeline Kahn.

Court Jester (1956) Director: Norman Panama. Screenplay: Norman
 Panama, Melvin Frank. Cast: Danny Kaye, Melvin Frank, Glynis
 Johns, Basil Rathbone, Angela Lansbury, Cecil Parker.

Dr. Strangelove: Or How I Learned to Stop Worrying and Love the Bomb
 (1964) Director: Stanley Kubrick. Screenplay: Stanley Kubrick,
 Terry Southern, Peter George, based on the novel *Red Alert* by Peter
 George. Cast: Peter Sellers, George C. Scott, Sterling Hayden, Keenan
 Wynn, Slim Pickens, Peter Bull.

The Marx Brothers in anything, but especially: *Duck Soup* (1933) Director:
 Leo McCarey. Screenplay, music and lyrics: Bert Kalmar and Harry
 Ruby. Cast: The Marx Brothers, Margaret Dumont, Louis Calhern.

A Fish Called Wanda (1988) Director: Charles Crichton. Screenplay: John
 Cleese, based on a story by John Cleese and Charles Crichton.
 Cast: John Cleese, Kevin Kline, Jamie Lee Curtis, Michael Palin.

Good Morning, Vietnam (1987) Director: Barry Levinson. Screenplay:
 Mitch Markowitz. Cast: Robin Williams, Forest Whitaker, Tung
 Thanh Tran.

Harold and Maude (1971) Director: Hal Ashby. Screenplay: Colin Higgins.
 Cast: Ruth Gordon, Bud Cort, Vivian Pickles.

A League of Their Own (1992) Director: Penny Marshall. Screenplay:
 Lowell Ganz, Babaloo Mandel, from a story by Jim Wilson and Kelly

Candaele. Cast: Tom Hanks, Geena Davis, Madonna, Lori Petty, Jon Lovitz.

M*A*S*H (1970) Director: Robert Altman. Screenplay: Ring Lardner Jr., based on the novel by Richard Hooker. Cast: Elliot Gould, Donald Sutherland, Tom Skerritt, Sally Kellerman.

Mr. Smith Goes to Washington (1939) Director: Frank Capra. Screenplay: Sidney Buchman, based on the novel *The Gentleman from Montana* by Lewis R. Foster. Cast: James Stewart, Jean Arthur, Claude Rains, Edward Arnold, Guy Kibee.

My Dinner with Andre (1981) Director: Louis Malle. Screenplay: Wallace Shawn, Andre Gregory. Cast: Wallace Shawn, Andre Gregory.

National Lampoon's Animal House (1978) Director: John Landis. Screenplay: Harold Ramis, Douglass Kenney, Chris Miller. Cast: John Belushi, Tim Matheson, John Vernon, Verna Bloom.

Nobody's Fool (1994) Director: Robert Benton. Screenplay: Robert Benton, based on the novel by Richard Russo. Cast: Paul Newman, Jessica Tandy, Bruce Willis, Melanie Griffith, Gene Sacks, Dylan Walsh, Pruit Taylor Vance.

The Paleface (1948) Director: Norman Z. McLeod. Screenplay: Frank Tashlin, Edmund Hartman, Jack Rose. Cast: Bob Hope, Jane Russell, Robert Armstrong, Iris Adrian.

The Pink Panther (1964) Director: Blake Edwards. Screenplay: Blake Edwards, Maurice Michlin. Cast: Peter Sellers, David Niven, Capucine, Robert Wagner, Claudia Cardinale.

The Producers (1967) Director and screenplay: Mel Brooks. Cast: Zero Mostel, Gene Wilder, Kenneth Mars, Dick Shawn, Lee Meredith.

Slacker (1991) Director and screenplay: Richard Linklater. Cast: Richard Linklater, Rudy Basquez, Jean Caggeine, Jan Hocky, Stephan Hocky, Mark James.

Slap Shot (1977) Director: George Roy Hill. Screenplay: Nancy Dowd. Cast: Paul Newman, Strother Martin, Michael Ontkean, Jennifer Warren, Lindsey Crouse.

Smoke (1995) Director: Wayne Wang. Screenplay: Paul Auster. Cast: Harvey Keitel, William Hurt, Stockard Channing, Forest Whitaker, Harold Perrineau Jr.

To Be or Not To Be (1942) Director: Ernst Lubitsch. Screenplay: Edwin Meyer. Cast: Carole Lombard, Jack Benny, Robert Stack, Sig Ruman.

Trading Places (1983) Director: John Landis. Screenplay: Herschel Weingrod, Timothy Harris. Cast: Dan Aykroyd, Eddie Murphy, Ralph
Bellamy, Don Ameche.

Wayne's World (1992) Director: Penelope Spheeris. Screenplay: Mike
Myers, Bonnie Turner, Terry Turner, from characters created
by Mike Myers. Cast: Mike Myers, Dana Carvey, Rob Lowe,
Tia Carrere.

Romantic Comedy

The African Queen (1951) Director: John Huston. Screenplay: James Agee.
Cast: Humphrey Bogart, Katharine Hepburn, Robert Morley, Peter
Bull, Theodore Bikel.

Annie Hall (1977) Director and screenplay: Woody Allen. Cast: Woody
Allen, Diane Keaton, Tony Roberts, Paul Simon, Shelley Duvall.

As Good As It Gets (1997) Director and Screenplay: Richard L. Brooks.
Cast: Jack Nicholson, Helen Hunt, Greg Kinnear.

Atlantic City (1980) Director: Louis Malle. Screenplay: John Guare. Cast:
Burt Lancaster, Susan Sarandon, Kate Reid.

Benny and Joon (1993) Director: Jeremiah Chechik. Screenplay: Barry
Berman, from a story by Berman and Leslie McNeil. Cast: Johnny
Depp, Mary Stuart Masterson, Aidan Quinn.

Bringing Up Baby (1938) Director: Howard Hawks. Screenplay: Dudley
Nichols, Hagar Wilde, based on a story by Wilde. Cast: Cary Grant,
Katharine Hepburn, Charlie Ruggles, May Robinson.

Desperately Seeking Susan (1984) Director: Susan Seidelman. Screenplay:
Leora Burish. Cast: Rosanna Arquette, Madonna, Aidan Quinn,
Mark Blum.

His Girl Friday (1940) Director: Howard Hawks, Screenplay: Charles Led-
erer, based on the play *The Front Page* by Charles MacArthur and
Ben Hecht. Cast: Cary Grant, Rosalind Russell, Ralph Bellamy, Gene
Lockhart, Helen Mack.

Anything by Frank Capra, but particularly: *It Happened One Night* (1934)
Director: Frank Capra. Screenplay: Robert Riskin, based on the story
"Night Bus" by Sam Hopkins Adams. Cast: Clark Gable, Claudette
Colbert, Walter Connolly, Roscoe Karns, Alan Hale.

Preston Sturges's films as writer and as writer/director, especially: *The Lady Eve* (1941) Director and screenplay: Preston Sturges. Cast: Henry Fonda, Barbara Stanwyck, Charles Coburn; and *The Palm Beach Story* (1942) Director and Screenplay: Preston Sturges. Cast: Claudette Colbert, Joel McCrea, Rudy Valee.

The Quiet Man (1952) Director: John Ford. Screenplay: Frank Nugent, from the story by Maurice Walsh. Cast: John Wayne, Maureen O'Hara, Barry Fitzgerald, Victor McLaglen.

Tootsie (1982) Director: Sydney Pollack. Screenplay: Larry Gelbart, Elaine May, Murray Schisgal (uncredited), based on a story by Don McGuire and Larry Gelbart. Cast: Dustin Hoffman, Jessica Lange, Teri Garr, Dabney Coleman, Charles Durning, Bill Murray, Sydney Pollack.

Trouble in Paradise (1932) Director: Ernst Lubitsch. Screenplay: Samson Raphaelson, Grover Jones. Cast: Miriam Hopkins, Kay Francis, Herbert Marshall, Charlie Ruggles.

Magical Realism in Romantic Comedy

Dona Flor and Her Two Husbands (1978) Director: Bruno Barreto. Screenplay: Bruno Barreto, based on the novel by Jorge Amado. Cast: Sonia Braga, Jose Wilker, Mauro Mendoca, Dinorah Brillanti.

Michael (1996) Director: Nora Ephron. Screenplay: Peter Dexter, Jim Quinlan. Cast: John Travolta, Andie MacDowell, William Hurt, Robert Pastorelli, Bob Hoskins, Jean Stapleton, Teri Garr.

The Preacher's Wife (1996) Director: Penny Marshall. Screenplay: Nat Mauldin, Leonardo Bercovici. Cast: Denzel Washington, Whitney Houston, Courtney B. Vance, Gregory Hines.

Half 'n' Half
(Anarchistic and Romantic)

Forrest Gump (1994) Director: Robert Zemeckis. Screenplay: Eric Roth, based on the novel by Winston Groom. Cast: Tom Hanks, Robin Wright, Gary Sinise, Sally Field, Mykelti Williamson.

Mighty Aphrodite (1995) Director and screenplay: Woody Allen. Cast: Woody Allen, F. Murray Abraham, Claire Bloom, Olympia Dukakis, Michael Rappaport, Mira Sorvino.

Raising Arizona (1987) Director: Joel Coen. Screenplay: Ethan & Joel Coen. Cast: Holly Hunter, Nicolas Cage, Trey Wilson, John Goodman, Frances McDormand.

Sullivan's Travels (1941) Director and screenplay: Preston Sturges. Cast: Joel McCrea, Veronica Lake, William Demarest, Robert Warwick, Margaret Hayes.

The World According to Garp (1982) Director: George Roy Hill. Screenplay: Steve Tesich, based on the novel by John Irving. Cast: Robin Williams, Mary Beth Hurt, Glenn Close, John Lithgow, Hume Cronyn, Jessica Tandy.

Buddy Comedy

Blues Brothers (1980) Director: John Landis; Screenplay: John Landis, Dan Aykroyd. Cast: John Belushi, Dan Aykroyd, Cab Calloway, John Candy, Henry Gibson, Carrie Fisher.

Butch Cassidy and the Sundance Kid (1969) Director: George Roy Hill. Screenplay: William Goldman. Cast: Paul Newman, Robert Redford, Katherine Ross, Strother Martin.

City Slickers (1991) Director: Ron Underwood. Screenplay: Lowell Ganz, Babaloo Mandel, based on a story by Billy Crystal. Cast: Billy Crystal, Daniel Stern, Bruno Kirby, Jack Palance, Patricia Wettig.

The First Wives Club (1996) Director: Hugh Wilson. Screenplay: Robert Harling, from Olivia Goldsmith's novel. Cast: Goldie Hawn, Diane Keaton, Bette Midler, Maggie Smith.

Ghostbusters (1984) Director: Ivan Reitman. Screenplay: Dan Aykroyd, Harold Ramis, Sheldon Kahn. Cast: Bill Murray, Dan Aykroyd, Harold Ramis, Sigourney Weaver.

Some Like It Hot (1959) Director: Billy Wilder. Screenplay: Billy Wilder, I. A. L. Diamond, from a story by R. Thoeren and M. Logan. Cast: Marilyn Monroe, Tony Curtis, Jack Lemmon, George Raft, Joe E. Brown.

Teen and Youth Comedy

The Breakfast Club (1985) Director and screenplay: John Hughes. Cast: Emilio Estevez, Molly Ringwald, Judd Nelson, Anthony Michael Hall, Ally Sheedy.

Clueless (1995) Director and screenplay: Amy Heckerling. Cast: Alicia Silverstone, Stacey Dash, Brittany Murphy, Phil Rudd, Donald Fairson, Breckin Meyer.

Fly Away Home (1996) Director: Carroll Ballard. Screenplay: Bill Lichman, Robert Rodat. Cast: Jeff Daniels, Anna Paquin, Dana Delany, Terry Kinney.

A Little Romance (1979) Director: George Roy Hill. Screenplay: Allan Burns, based on the novel $E = mc^2$ *Mon Amour* by Patrick Cauvin. Cast: Laurence Olivier, Diane Lane, Thelonious Bernard, Arthur Hill, Sally Kellerman.

Children's Comedy

The Great Muppet Caper (1981) Director: Jim Henson. Screenplay: Tom Patchett, Jay Tarses, Jerry Juhl, Jack Rose. Cast: The Muppet Performers (with voices by Frank Oz, Jerry Nelson, Jim Henson, Richard Hunt), Charles Grodin, Diana Rigg, John Cleese.

Home Alone (1990) Director: Chris Columbus. Screenplay: John Hughes. Cast: Macaulay Culkin, Joe Pesci, Daniel Stern.

Snow White and the Seven Dwarfs (1937) Director: Ben Sharpsteen. Screenplay: Ted Sears, Otto Englander, Earl Hurd, plus five others. Cast: voices of Adriana Caselotti, Harry Stockwell, Lucille laVerne.

Space Jam (1996) Director: Joc Pytka. Screenplay: Herschel Weingrod, Leo Benvenuti, Steve Rudnick, Tim Harris. Cast: Bugs Bunny, Michael Jordan.

Toy Story (1995) Director: John Lassetter. Screenplay: Andrew Stanton, Joel Cohen, Alec Sokolow, Joss Whedon. Cast: voices of Tom Hanks, Tim Allen, Don Rickles, Jim Varney, Wallace Shawn.

Comedy in Drama

Brazil (1985) Director: Terry Gilliam. Screenplay: Terry Gilliam, Tom Stoppard, Charles McKeown. Cast: Jonathan Pryce, Kim Greist, Robert De Niro.

Casablanca (1942) Director: Michael Curtiz. Screenplay: Julius J. Epstein, Philip G. Epstein, Howard Koch, based on the play *Everybody Goes to*

Rick's by Murray Burnett and Joan Alison. Cast: Humphrey Bogart, Ingrid Bergman, Paul Henreid, Claude Rains, Conrad Veidt, Sydney Greenstreet.

Clockwatchers (1997) Director: Jill Sprecher. Screenplay: Jill and Nan Sprecher. Cast: Toni Collette, Parker Posey, Lisa Kudrow, Alanna Ubach.

A Clockwork Orange (1971) Director: Stanley Kubrick. Screenplay: Stanley Kubrick, from the novel by Anthony Burgess. Cast: Malcolm McDowell, Patrick Magee.

The Crying Game (1992) Director and screenplay: Neil Jordan. Cast: Stephen Rea, Miranda Richardson, Forest Whitaker, Jim Broadbent, Ralph Brown, Adrian Dunbar, Jaye Davidson, Breffini McKenna, Joe Savino.

Dead Man Walking (1995) Director: Tim Robbins. Screenplay: Tim Robbins. Cast: Susan Sarandon, Sean Penn, Robert Prosky, Raymond J. Barry.

Heavenly Creatures (1994) Director: Peter Jackson. Screenplay: Peter Jackson, Fran Walsh. Cast: Melanie Lynskey, Kate Winslet, Sarah Peirse, Diana Kent.

Lenny (1974) Director: Bob Fosse. Screenplay: Julian Barry, from his own Broadway play. Cast: Dustin Hoffman, Valerie Perrine, Jan Miner, Stanley Beck, Gary Morton.

Pulp Fiction (1994) Director and screenplay: Quentin Tarantino. Cast: John Travolta, Samuel L. Jackson, Uma Thurman, Harvey Keitel, Tim Roth, Amanda Plummer.

Thelma and Louise (1991) Director: Ridley Scott. Screenplay: Callie Khouri. Cast: Susan Sarandon, Geena Davis, Harvey Keitel, Michael Madsen, Brad Pitt, Stephen Tobolowsky.

Trainspotting (1996, UK) Director: Danny Boyle. Screenplay: Irvine Welsh, John Hodge. Cast: Ewan McGregor, Ewen Bremner, Jonny Lee Miller, Kevin McKidd.

Witness (1985) Director and screenplay: Peter Weir. Cast: Harrison Ford, Kelly McGillis, Joseph Sommer, Lukas Haas, Jan Rubes, Alexander Godunov.

Comedy from around the World

Australia and New Zealand

Adventures of Priscilla, Queen of the Desert (1994, Australia) Director and screenplay: Stephan Elliott. Cast: Terrence Stamp, Hugo Weaving, Guy Pearce, Bill Hunter, Sarah Chadwick.

Babe (1995, Australia) Director: Chris Noonan. Screenplay: George Miller, Chris Noonan, based on the novel *The Sheep-Pig* by Dick King-Smith. Cast: James Cromwell, Magda Szuzbanski, and the voices of Christine Cavanagh, Miriam Margolyes, Danny Mann, Hugo Weaving.

Bad Taste (1988, New Zealand) Director and screenplay: Peter Jackson. Cast: Peter Jackson, Pete O'Herne, Mike Minett, Terry Potter, Craig Smith.

Green Card (1990, Australia-France) Director and screenplay: Peter Weir. Cast: Gerard Depardieu, Andie MacDowell, Bebe Neuwirth, Gregg Edelman.

Shine (1996, Australia) Director: Scott Hicks. Screenplay: Scott Hicks, Jan Sardi. Cast: Geoffrey Rush, Armin Mueller-Stahl, Noah Taylor, Alex Rafalowicz, Sonia Todd, Lynn Redgrave, John Gielgud.

Czechoslovakia/Czech Republic

Closely Watched Trains (1966) Director: Jiri Menzel. Screenplay: Jiri Menzel, Bohumil Hrabal, based on Hrabal's novel. Cast: Vaclav Neckar, Jitka Bendova, Vladimir Valenta, Libuse Habelkova.

The Firemen's Ball (1967) Director: Milos Forman. Screenplay: Milos Forman, Jaroslav Papousek. Cast: Josef Kolb, Marie Jezkova, Jan Vostreil.

Kolya (1996) Director: Jan Sverak. Screenplay: Zdenek Sverak. Cast: Zdenek Sverak, Audrey Chalmon, Libuse Safranokova.

Denmark

Babette's Feast (1987) Director: Gabriel Axel. Screenplay: Gabriel Axel, from a story by Isak Dinesen. Cast: Stephane Audran, Jean-Phillipe Lafont, Gudmar Wivesson.

Finland

Leningrad Cowboys Go America (1989) Director and screenplay: Aki Kauris-
    maki. Cast: Marti Peliopaa, Karl Vaanaenen, Jim Jarmusch, Nicky
    Tesco.

France

Boudu Saved from Drowning (1932) Director: Jean Renoir. Screenplay: Jean
    Renoir, based on the play by Rene Fauchois. Cast: Michel Simon,
    Charles Granbal, Marcelle Hania, Severine Lerczynska.

Day for Night (1973) Director and screenplay: François Truffaut. Cast:
    François Truffaut, Jacqueline Bisset, Jean-Pierre Aumont, Valentina
    Cortese, Jean-Pierre Leaud.

Mr. Hulot's Holiday (1953) Director: Jacques Tati. Screenplay: Jacques Tati,
    Henri Marquet, Pierre Aubert, Jacques Lagrange. Cast: Jacques Tati,
    Nathalie Pascaud.

Pauline at the Beach (1983) Director and screenplay: Eric Rohmer.
    Cast: Amanda Langlet, Arielle Dombasle, Pascal Dreggory.

Pierrot le Fou (1965) Director and screenplay: Jean-Luc Godard. Cast:
    Jean-Paul Belmondo, Anna Karina.

Rules of the Game (1939) Director and screenplay: Jean Renoir. Cast:
    Marcel Dalio, Nora Gregor, Mila Parely, Jean Renoir.

Great Britain

The Captain's Paradise (1953) Director: Anthony Kimmin. Screenplay: Alec
    Coppel, Nicholas Phipps, based on a story by Alec Coppel. Cast: Alec
    Guinness, Yvonne De Carlo, Celia Johnson, Bill Fraser.

Four Weddings and a Funeral (1994) Director: Mike Newell. Screenplay:
    Richard Curtis. Cast: Hugh Grant, Andie MacDowell, Kristin Scott
    Thomas, Simon Callow, Rowan Atkinson, James Fleet.

The Full Monty (1997) Director: Peter Cattaneo. Screenplay: Simon Beau-
    foy. Cast: Robert Carlyle.

The Horse's Mouth (1958) Director: Robert Neame. Screenplay: Alec Guin-
    ness, from the novel by Joyce Cary. Cast: Alec Guinness, Kay Walsh,
    Renee Houston, Mike Morgan.

Local Hero (1983) Director and screenplay: Bill Forsyth. Cast: Burt Lancaster, Fulton MacKay, Denis Lawson, Norman Chancer, Peter Capaldi, Jenny Seagrove.

Monty Python's The Meaning of Life (1983) Director: Terry Jones. Screenplay: John Cleese, Graham Chapman. Cast: Graham Chapman, John Cleese, Terry Gilliam, Eric Idle, Terry Jones, Michael Palin.

The Mouse That Roared (1959) Director: Jack Arnold. Screenplay: Roger MacDougall, Stanley Mann, based on the novel *The Wrath of Grapes* by Leonard Wibberly. Cast: Peter Sellers, Jean Seberg, David Kossoff, William Hartnell.

Greece

Never on Sunday (1960) Director and screenplay: Jules Dassin. Cast: Melina Mercouri, Jules Dassin, Georges Fondas, Titos Vandis, Mitsos Liguisos.

Hungary

Mr. Universe (1988) Director: Gyorgy Szomjas. Screenplay: No credit given. Cast: Mariska Hargitay, George Pinter, Micky Hargitay.

My Twentieth Century (1989) Director and screenplay: Ildiko Enyedi. Cast: Dorotha Segda, Oleg Jankovskij, Paulaus Manker.

Iran

The White Balloon (1995) Director: Jafar Panahi. Screenplay: Abbas Kiarostami. Cast: Aida Mohammadkhani, Mohsen Kalifi, Fereshteh Sadr Orfani, Anna Bourkowska, Mohammad Shahani.

Italy

The Bicycle Thief (1947) Director: Vittorio de Sica. Screenplay: Cesare Zavattini, based on a novel by Luigi Bartolini. Cast: Lamberto Maggiorani, Lianella Carell, Enzo Staiola.

Cinema Paradiso (1988) Director and screenplay: Giuseppe Tornatore. Cast: Philippe Noiret, Jacques Perrin, Salvatore Cascio, Mario Leonardi.

Mediterraneo (1991) Director and screenplay: Gabriele Salvatore. Cast: Diego Abatantuono, Claudio Bigagli, Giuseppi Cedema, Vanna Barba, Claudio Bisio.

Swept Away (1975) Director and screenplay: Lina Wertmuller. Cast: Giancarlo Giannini, Mariangelo Melato.

Russia/USSR

Cloud Paradise (1991) Director: Nikolai Dostal. Screenplay: Georgi Nikolajev. Cast: Andrei Zhigalov, Sergei Batalov, Irina Rozanova.

Fountain (1988) Director: Juri Mamin. Screenplay: Vladimir Vardunas. Cast: Asankul Kuttubayev, Sergei Dontsov, Shanna Kerimtayeva.

South Africa

The Gods Must Be Crazy (1981) Director and screenplay: Jamie Uys. Cast: Marius Weyers, Sandra Prinsloo, N'xau, Louw Verwey.

Spain and Mexico

Luis Buñuel, the master of comic surrealism! All, including *The Discreet Charm of the Bourgeoisie* (1972) Director: Luis Buñuel. Screenplay: Luis Buñuel, Jean-Claude Carierre. Cast: Fernando Rey, Delphine Seyrig, Stephane Audran, Bulle Ogier.

Viridiana (1961) Director: Luis Buñuel. Screenplay: Luis Buñuel, Julio Alejandro, based on a story by Luis Buñuel. Cast: Sylvia Pinal, Fernando Rey, Margarita Lozano.

Sweden

My Life as a Dog (1985) Director: Lasse Halstrom. Screenplay: Lasse Halstrom, Reidar Jonsson, Brasse Brannstrom, Per Berglund, based on the novel by Reidar Jonsson. Cast: Anton Glanzelius, Tomas von Bromssen, Anki Liden, Melinda Kinnaman.

Switzerland

Jonah, Who Will Be 21 in the Year 2000 (1976) Director: Alain Tanner.
  Screenplay: John Berger, Alain Tanner. Cast: Myrian Boyer, Jean-Luc
  Rideau, Miou-Miou, Roger Jeandy, Jacques Dennis.

Taiwan

Eat Drink Man Woman (1994) Director: Ang Lee. Screenplay: Ang Lee, Hui
  Ling Wang, James Schamus. Cast: Sihung Lung, Kuei-Mei Yung,
  Chien-Lien Wu, Yu-Wen Wang.

Yugoslavia

Innocence Unprotected (1966) Director and screenplay: Dusan Makavejev.
  Cast: Dragoljub Aleksic, Bratoljub Gligorijevic, Vera Jovanovic.

Something in Between (1983) Director: Srdjan Karanovic. Screenplay:
  Srdjan Karanovic, Andrew Horton, Sasha Marinovic. Cast: Miki
  Manolovic, Drago Nicholis, Carris Corfman.

Time of the Gypsies (1989) Director: Emir Kusturica. Screenplay: Emir
  Kusturica, Gordan Mihic. Cast: Davor Dujmovic, Bora Todorovic,
  Ljubica Adzovic, Sinolicka Trpkova, Husnija Hasi.

APPENDIX 2

Networking, Marketing and Making Your Own Comedy

Remember, the first step in marketing your wares is to be good.
Gene Perret

So you have written the funniest television pilot, the wittiest new screwball feature comedy or the fall-down hilarious independent farce that will make *Clerks* look like Greek tragedy. Now how do you sell it, how do you get it produced, filmed, distributed, and set up for healthy returns on video and television reruns? Gene Perret, whose television credits include a lot of work for Bob Hope, Carol Burnett, Bill Cosby and others, put it best: "Acquiring the skill is the easiest part because you are in control. You depend on no one else. If it takes six hours of practice a day for three years to become a proficient jazz drummer, you can arrange your life to do that. Convincing others of your proficiency, though, can be frustrating because you're not in control. They are" (219).

This book has focused on the writing of comedy and the traditions and elements involved in that writing. But I do wish to close with at least some suggestions of what happens next, when you are not in control.

Networking and Sharpening Skills

No crossed legs during a pitch.
Jurgen Wolff

At the center of "what happens next" is the gathering of information, both about who is who and how to reach them and also about new ideas, perspectives and techniques that could serve you well in your writing and efforts to move your scripts into production. Consider the following sources of information:

192

Newsletters

Orben's Current Comedy, 1200 N. Nash St, #1122, Arlington, VA 22209
Gene Perret's Round Table, PO Box 13, King of Prussia, PA 19406

The Internet

No one needs to be told, "Hey, check the Net." All you need is to dedicate some time to exploring sites that could be immensely helpful to you. Wherever you start, you are sure to find another hundred paths opening up before you. But, for starters, here are a few:

Sites for Writers

Writers Guild of America: http://www.wga.org

This site provides special links with a variety of sites to help writers, including sites on children's literature, sites on Shakespeare, and screenwriting sites such as Hollywood Writers Network and Tip Sheet for Low Budget Scripts.

Screenplays On Line

There are a number of websites that give you access to complete screenplays, some of which you can download and others you cannot. Drew's Scripts-O-Rama and all the others can be reached via a listing on Cinemedia after you type in "Screenplays":

http://www.afionline.org/cinemedia/welcomes/you.html

On a recent check of Drew's site, I found the following as just a sampling of comic scripts on line: *The Blues Brothers, The Breakfast Club, Home Alone, Clueless, Annie Hall, Dr. Strangelove, Brazil, Barton Fink, Fargo* and many, many others.

Comedy On Line

Any search engine on the Net will come up with over eight thousand sites, but here are a few that are recommended:

The American Association for Therapeutic Humor:
http://www.callamer.com/itc/aath/steves.html

Chris Rock and His Talk Show: http://www.hbo.com/chrisrock

How to Be Annoying & Humorous:
http://www.math.fau.edu/klotzbach/amusing/annoying.html

Jim Carrey: http://www.geocities.com/Hollywood9090/index.html

Men Jokes (many of which actually make fun of the male species!):
home3.swipnet.se/~w-37418/menjokes.html

Odd Dancing Baby: http://hgabweb.cit.cornell.edu/cha.html

A computer-animated baby doing a very weird funky chicken dance.
Anarchistic? Completely!

Randomized Punchlines: http://www.yahoo.com/Entertainment/
Humor_Jokes_and_Fun/Randomized_Things/

Stand-up Comedy Bingo: http://www.fadetoblack.com/bingo.html

Yes, a bingo card with bad jokes and groaners rather than letters and
numbers!

Tony Kornheiser, columnist for *The Washington Post*:
http://www.geocities.com/Athens/1603/korn.html

Workshops and Conferences

There is an increasingly wide variety of comedy-oriented workshops and
conferences being organized around the country (and indeed around the world)
that may very well be useful to you. As with any conference, it's not just what you
learn but who you meet that counts.

One of the most respected is the annual Conference on the Positive Power of
Humor & Creativity, put together for over a dozen years by the HUMOR Project.
No, this is not a film- or television-centered outfit. Rather, the focus here is on including businesses, corporations, institutions and organizations within a world of
humor. Participants in the past have come from IBM, AT&T, AARP, Procter &
Gamble, Xerox as well as many other professions and walks of life. For information contact:

THE HUMOR PROJECT, INC.
480 Broadway, Suite 210
Saratoga Springs, NY 12866
Phone: (518) 587-8770 Fax: (800) 600-1242
http://www.wizvax.net/humor/

Film, TV and Comedy Festivals

There is no better way to make contacts swiftly with people from around the
world than at some of the major film festivals. This goes particularly for foreign
producers, directors and filmmakers, but ironically it is often easier to catch a Hollywood producer in Toronto than in Los Angeles. Think about it: on their home
turf they are working nonstop or playing tennis. In Montreal, Montreux or else-

where, however, they are more relaxed and more apt to have free time to chat, share a café au lait and give advice.

Your best bet? A festival most Americans don't know about but should: the Rose d'Or International Festival of Television Comedy, held in Montreux, Switzerland, each April. The Rose d'Or (Golden Rose) brings together the shakers and makers of sitcoms, stand-up comedy, variety comedy, musical comedy, game shows and arts specials from around the world to display, screen, sell and buy comedy. And that's no joke. Thousands have been laughing all the way to the bank for forty years each April in Montreux. Their actual title for the whole list of offerings is "light entertainment television programming." For information if you are in North America:

> John E. Nathan
> Deerfield Green, Montauk Highway
> PO Box 1285
> Water Mill, NY 11976
> Phone: (516) 726-7500   Fax: (516) 726-7510

The headquarters in Switzerland is:

> Rose d'Or
> Television Suisse Romande
> Case postale 234
> Quai Ernest Ansermet 20
> CH 1211 Geneve 8, Switzerland
> Fax: 41 21 963 88 51

There is a market at which videos can be screened, along with seminars and presentations, but best of all is simply the chance to meet those interested in comedy from all over the world.

Marketing Your Comedies Abroad

If you are American, you most likely are thinking about writing for an American market. But in the spirit of exploding a few more unexploded mimes, take a moment to realize how much comedy is written abroad that may well need someone like you to help out. No matter what country you are from, the message is the same: laugh locally but think globally! For instance:

Writing for Foreign Television

According to *Variety,* one-fifth of German television programming is written by American writers. "American writers have a firm grasp of character development and sitcom structure," comments one executive working with the Germans (Hills, 46). Think about it. And think about the number of countries in the world that are, like Germany, beginning to realize there is gold and laughter in hiring American writers, who can continue to live in the States but who can pen comedy that can entertain the home country writing the checks.

Co-Writing or Writing for Foreign Film Productions

As I complete this book, I am also finishing a new feature comedy. But it is not an American film at all. Rather, I am at this moment in New Zealand, co-writing with Russell Campbell a nutty sheep-farm jazz comedy that brings together an African American jazz band and an all-girl bagpipe band in the isolated sheep country on the South Island of New Zealand. And in the past three years I have written feature comedies under contract in Norway, Greece and Hungary. The satisfactions have been tremendous, including the pure fun of travel, meeting new people and catching on to how universal most humor is.

How do you sign up to write an Argentine or Dutch or Polish comedy? Of course there is no 1-800-COMEDIES-ABROAD number. But partially it is a matter of getting in touch with countries and filmmakers from countries you admire. My work with noted Hungarian filmmaker George Szomjas came about because I met him at the Montreal International Film Festival after seeing one of his nutty social comedies that I particularly loved. That led to a visit to Hungary, and to his visit to New Orleans; the rest is an ongoing history and, yes, carnival. Similarly, my interest in New Zealand films, ranging from the powerful drama of *Once Were Warriors* and *The Piano* to Peter Jackson's absurdist humor in *Bad Taste* and other films, led eventually to an exchange teaching assignment in Wellington, which in turn opened up opportunities such as my current sheep-farm comedy.

The lesson from such experiences? Be open to meeting people whose work you admire, and to attending film festivals. Also consider living abroad in a country you enjoy! Most countries do have script development funds, through either a film commission or some kind of arts and culture funding, so that it may very well be possible to make proposals with a filmmaker from that country to write your comedy for the big screen or for television.

Studying Screenwriting Abroad

There are also fine film and broadcasting programs abroad. Consider the following four:

The Summer Screenwriting Program in Croatia, run by Ohio University. Filmmaker Rajko Grlic of Zagreb is now a filmmaking professor at Ohio University in Athens, Ohio, and runs a splendid script seminar on the Adriatic Coast in Croatia each summer, bringing over faculty such as Lew Hunter of UCLA and Yvette Biro of NYU. Students now come from the States, Croatia, Bosnia and other countries. Well worth checking into. Contact: Rajko Grlic, Film Department, Ohio University, Athens, Ohio 45701.

Screenwriting and Filmmaking Program, FAMU, the film school of Prague in the Czech Republic. It's hard to imagine a more pleasant city in the world than Prague. FAMU is the school that produced so many well-known directors, including Milos Forman and many Yugoslav directors, such as Emir Kusturica and Srdjan Karanovic. Contact Director of the English Language Screenwriting and Filmmaking Program, FAMU, Akademie Muzekych Umeni, Smestanova NA 3.2, Prague 1, The Czech Republic. Fax: 422-24-23-0285. They do have a special program offered in English, both for short sessions of a few weeks and for longer periods.

MA Degree in Screenwriting Program, Institute Medievitenskop TV, University of Bergen in Norway. A new screenwriting MA program that shows great promise because of its strong emphasis on developing a variety of approaches to the craft. I can vouch first-hand for the quality of the staff involved, having been a guest of their program in the past. Contact Dr. Alvaro Raminez at the program listed above, University of Bergen, Fossvoinokelsgt 6N, 500 Bergen, Norway. Fax: 475-558-9149. E-mail: Alvaro.Raminez@media.uib.no.

The International Academy of Broadcasting in Switzerland. An excellent one-year postgraduate program in all aspects of broadcasting on an international level. Students come from around the world, including Europe, Eastern Europe, Asia, Japan, Africa and South America. A wonderful chance to understand media on a global level. I enjoy teaching there each year for two weeks and find the students are extremely motivated and talented. Contact Dr. Aleksandar Todorovic, Dean at the school, Ave. de Florimont 11, Montreux 1, 1820, Switzerland. Fax: 4121-961-1665. E-mail: atodorovic@iab.ch.

Making Your Own Comedies

I am a great believer and supporter of independent filmmaking and television. Wherever you live, you can work with video, local access television, and even film to get your comedy made. Short comic films or videos, for instance, may well attract the attention of local television stations. And we can push for the day that the United States tries out some of the innovative ideas used in other countries. In New Zealand, for instance, one funding source offered grants of up to six hundred dollars to make films or videos of no more than two minutes, which would air nationally after midnight on television. Hey, think about it. That's a real opportunity to get your foot in the door, not to mention your jokes and gags.

Then there is always making your own feature comedy. Take Kevin Smith and *Clerks* as an example. You don't need the budget of *As Good As It Gets* to make your first feature! Despite the escalating costs of Hollywood films, the independent and even home-movie route is always there!

Get to know the film crowd in your area. There's no telling what like-spirited souls can do, especially when you provide the hilarious script that captures their imagination!

And what to do once you get a film made? You could head for either coast, but I would start with film festivals. Read up on what is out there, either in *Variety* or the yearly *International Film Guide* edited by Peter Cowie, to get a feel for which festivals appeal to you and how to go about contacting them. Festivals mean exposure, press and contacts. Thus, I recommend the festival circuit before trying to sell your film to a distributor. After all, "award-winning comedy" sounds awfully good, even if the festival is not Cannes or Toronto!

Selling Your Script in the United States

I have no new wisdom to add to what most people know. Yes, you really need an agent if you wish to get in the front or back door of most production houses, stars' offices and network boardrooms. And yes, it is very hard to get an agent's attention, let alone her or his support and thus representation of your work. But if it were impossible, then the whole industry would stagnate and eventually grind to a halt.

Start with the general recognition that *a whole lot more comedy is bought, optioned and sold than other genres,* so in a real sense you start with good news. I wrote a drama about the Bosnian war that I cared about a lot, but a very good Hollywood agent friend was quite honest in pointing out that Bosnia was not a subject Hollywood as he knows it would feel comfortable with in any shape or form. Comedy, however, is very different.

It is not within the scope of this book to give a lengthy description of how to get an agent and how to work up business connections, since so many other useful books cover this topic fully. I would particularly recommend Richard Walter's *The Whole Picture: Strategies for Screenwriting Success in the New Hollywood* (New York: Plume/Penguin, 1997). He offers very helpful suggestions and takes an encouraging attitude. As he notes: "If agents are hard to reach, if they are reluctant to consider new writers, how can one explain all of the telephone traffic, letters, faxes, E-mail and even messengers showing up in the flesh, refusing to leave until they are handed a screenplay for delivery to their bosses?" (199).

Well said. And let me close out with five suggestions of my own that I hope are of use in the totally wild world of marketing your own comic product. If you have succeeded in getting an agent, that cuts out a lot of what follows—but not all of it. Even if you have an agent, you cannot immediately buy a condominium in Hawaii. You need to stay alert and active as well. Meanwhile:

1. *Try joining one of the multitude of Internet script chat groups, both for support and for contacts.* Several of my former students have had a lot of luck and help from such groups, and I know a growing number of writers who have gotten an agent of their own through such Internet support groups.

2. *Especially for your television series comic pilot, check out the production companies that make the comedies you like and get directly in touch with them.* Going directly to a major network like ABC, NBC, Fox or CBS will not yield much success, for they deal with production companies themselves to create the "product." The trick is to get to know the production companies. They may well say they only take referred work, but some do accept spec scripts.

3. *When writing cover letters,* be brief; always write to a specific person, not "To Whom It May Concern"; do not try to be "cute" or use gimmicks like brightly colored paper or fancy print fonts; and keep the whole letter or e-mail to one page, with your script summary also being no more than a page. Include a self-addressed, stamped envelope as well.

4. *Got an actor or actress you feel would be great for the part? Why not try to contact him or her through their agent? You should be able to access such information through the Net or reference books.* This goes especially for up-and-coming stars and for those who are, shall we say, not working every day, for one reason or another. I was able to help the producers of *The Dark Side of the Sun,* which I was hired to rewrite, get Brad Pitt to be the lead, because, aside from some television work and bit parts, he had not yet had a lead role. Worth a shot, definitely! Yes, Brad has a sense of humor, and I still feel he should try his hand at more comedy!

5. *Enter screenwriting competitions.* Each year former students and writers whose scripts I've helped to evaluate have gotten the attention of agents and producers, in part because they have done well in various script competitions around the country. There are various lists of these contests, which come and go, but you should be aware of them and give them a try.

Yes, there needs to be a "comic guide to marketing your script." But until it appears, do remember, above all, to keep your sense of humor! That goes for meetings with agents, producers, actors and everyone else. Too many of them are too serious, too stressed, too distracted. A good sense of humor always gets someone's attention and hearty appreciation.

Feel free to contact me for any feedback, questions or help I may be able to pass on, including professional script evaluation and information on script seminars I run in Greece and the United States:

Andrew Horton
The Film and Video Studies Program
The University of Oklahoma
Norman, OK 73019
Phone: (405) 325-3020
Fax: (405) 325-0842
e-mail: ahorton@ou.edu

Food, Recipes
and Comic Screenwriting

Since the first custard pie was thrown in the early silent farces and Chaplin consumed his boot in *The Gold Rush,* and on through memorable scenes such as the oyster-eating scene in *Tom Jones,* all of *Who Is Killing the Great Chefs of Europe?* (1978), diner scenes in Sturges's *Sullivan's Travels,* all of *Big Night* and countless other moments, food and laughter were meant for each other.

For inspiration, we include the menu for the meal in *Big Night:*

ANTIPASTI
Eggplant salad (caponata)
Parma Ham
Focaccia
Crostini with goat cheese

LA ZUPPA
Consomme

I PRIMI
Il Rissotto (Spinach, Seafood or Quatro Formaggio)

I SECONDI
Baked Salmon
Capon Stuffed with pomegranates
Half Roasted Pig
Platter of roasted artichokes
Platter of sautéed mushrooms
Platter of sautéed string beans
Platter of roasted vegetables
Grilled zucchini
Grilled eggplant
Grilled carrots
Bowl of roasted potatoes with peppers

IL DOLCI
Fresh Fruit
Tray of Pastries
Nuts
Amaretti di Saronno Cookies
Grappa
Espresso

A Screenwriter's Recipe
for Comic Jambalaya

Now it is your turn.

Many readers of my *Writing the Character-Centered Screenplay* have written that they enjoyed the recipe for Screenwriter's Gumbo that I added at the end of that book. In the same spirit, I urge you to call up your comic and even noncomic friends and cook up the following main dish. Why not serve this first and then do a reading of your script afterwards? A hearty Greek salad goes well with this. Jambalaya is stick-to-your-bones Cajun food, and during our twenty years of living in New Orleans, my wife and I served more than our fair share of it to friends, as laughter filled the evening along with the spicy aroma. Good luck and bon appétit.

SERVES 6

INGREDIENTS

1 chicken, cut up
½ pound of hot sausage
½ cup of olive oil (This is a MUST! It will not be the same,
     believe me, if you use vegetable or corn oil!)
1 cup of diced onions
½ cup of sliced green onions
¼ cup of chopped parsley
½ cup of red or green bell pepper
¼ cup of minced garlic
3 cups of chicken stock
2 cups of long-grain rice, uncooked
salt and pepper to taste
¼ teaspoon each of cayenne pepper, thyme, oregano and basil, or
     to taste

DIRECTIONS: In a large pot (a five-quart cast-iron Dutch oven would be great!), heat the olive oil over medium high heat. Season the chicken parts with salt and pepper and the cayenne, thyme, oregano and basil. Sauté parts until golden brown. Add sausage and cook another ten to fifteen minutes. Add bell pepper, garlic and chopped onions. Sauté three to five minutes longer. Add the chicken stock and bring to a rolling boil. Reduce to a simmer. Add the rice and any more salt and pepper desired. Reduce the heat to the lowest setting and cover, cooking thirty minutes. Remove and stir in the green onions and parsley. Cover and cook another five minutes. Serve hot.

NOTE: Substitutes for chicken work well too. I've had fun with rabbit, and I'm told squirrel jambalaya is fine too, though I haven't tried it. The same recipe would hold.

BIBLIOGRAPHY

On Comedy

Adler, Jerry. "The Happiness Meter." *Newsweek,* 29 July 1996, 78.

Arieti, Silvano. *Creativity: The Magic Synthesis.* New York: Basic Books, 1976.

Bakhtin, Mikhail. *Rabelais and His World.* Translated by Helene Iswolsky. Cambridge, Mass.: MIT Press, 1968.

Barber, C. L. *Shakespeare's Festive Comedy.* Princeton, N.J.: Princeton University Press, 1959.

Bergson, Henri. 1900. *Laughter.* Translated by Ellen Raskin. In *Comedy,* edited by Wylie Sypher. New York: Doubleday, 1956.

Bermel, Albert. *Farce: From Aristophanes to Woody Allen.* New York: Simon and Schuster, 1982.

Brook, Peter. *The Shifting Point: Forty Years of Theatrical Exploration, 1946–1987.* London: Methuen, 1988.

Cook, Albert. *The Dark Voyage and the Golden Mean: A Philosophy of Comedy.* Cambridge, Mass.: Harvard University Press, 1949.

Freud, Sigmund. *Jokes and Their Relation to the Unconscious.* Translated by A. A. Brill. New York: Random House, 1938.

Gurewitch, Morton. *Comedy: The Irrational Vision.* Ithaca, N.Y.: Cornell University Press, 1975.

Horton, Andrew. "Aristophanes." In *Encyclopedia of World Drama,* 191–202. New York: McGraw Hill, 1984.

Horton, Andrew, and Michael Brashinsky. *The Zero Hour: Glasnost and Soviet Cinema in Transition.* Princeton, N.J.: Princeton University Press, 1992.

Houston, Jean. *A Mythic Life.* New York: HarperCollins, 1996.

Huizinga, Johan. *Homo Ludens: A Study of the Play Element in Culture.* Boston: Beacon Press, 1955.

Hutcheon, Linda. *A Theory of Parody.* New York: Methuen, 1985.

Jenkins, Ron. *Subversive Laughter: The Liberating Power of Comedy.* New York: The Free Press, 1994.

Kerr, Walter. *Tragedy and Comedy.* New York: Simon and Schuster, 1967.

Koestler, Arthur. *Insight and Outlook.* Lincoln: University of Nebraska Press, 1949.

Kundera, Milan. *The Unbearable Lightness of Being.* Translated by Michael Heim. New York: Harper & Row, 1985.

Levin, Harry. *Playboys & Killjoys: An Essay in the Theory of Comedy.* New York: Oxford University Press, 1987.

Levin, Harry, ed. *Veins of Humor.* Cambridge, Mass.: Harvard University Press, 1972.

Lipman, Steve. *Laughter in Hell: The Use of Humor During the Holocaust.* Reprint. Northvale, N.J.: Jason Aronson, 1991.

Paton, George, Chris Powell, and Steve Wagg, eds. *The Social Faces of Humor*. New York: Arena, 1996.

Perez, Evan. "Carjack Victim: 'I Was Playing Mother, Friend, Comic.'" *The Orlando Sentinel*, 23 August 1997, 12.

Ricks, Delthia. "Scientists Hail Laughter as Serious Medicine." *The Orlando Sentinel*, 6 November 1996, 13.

Rourke, Constance. *American Humor: A Study of the National Character*. Originally published 1931; reprint: New York: Harcourt Brace Jovanovich, 1959.

Rowe, Kathleen. *The Unruly Woman: Gender and Genre in Laughter*. Austin: The University of Texas Press, 1995.

Sypher, Wylie, ed. *Comedy*. Garden City, N.Y.: Doubleday, 1956.

Winnicott, D. W. *The Family and the Individual*. New York: Routledge, 1965.

Wittgenstein, Ludwig. *Philosophical Investigations*. Oxford: Basil Blackwell, 1968.

On Film and Television Comedy

Appelo, Tim. "10 Reasons We Already Miss Seinfeld." *TV Guide*, 17 January 1998, 34–37.

Babington, Bruce, and Peter William Evans. *Affairs to Remember: The Hollywood Comedy of the Sexes*. Manchester, England: Manchester University Press, 1989.

Baldwin, Kristin, Mike Flaherty, A. J. Jacobs, Mary Kaye Schilling, and Ken Tucker. "Thanks for Nothing: A Celebration of *Seinfeld*—America's Prime Time Comedy King." *Entertainment Weekly*, 30 May 1997, 20–47.

Bushman, David. "The Stand-up Comedian on Television." In *Stand-up Comedians on Television*, edited by Robert Morton. New York: Harry Abrams, Inc., 1996.

Cader, Michael. *Saturday Night Live: The First Twenty Years*. Boston: Houghton Mifflin, 1994.

Carter, Bill. "Seinfeld Says It's All Over, and It's No Joke for NBC." *The New York Times*, 26 December 1997, 1, A15.

Cavell, Stanley. *Pursuits of Happiness: The Hollywood Comedy of Remarriage*. Cambridge, Mass.: Harvard University Press, 1981.

Corliss, Richard. "Balloon Story." *Time*, 12 October 1996, 46.

———. "Mad about Her." *Time*, 15 December 1997, 22–28.

Durgnat, Raymond. *The Crazy Mirror: Hollywood Comedy and the American Image*. New York: Dell, 1969.

Eaton, Mick. "Television Situation Comedy." In *Popular Television and Film*, edited by Tony Bennett, Susan Boyd Bowman, Colin Mercer and Janet Woollacott, 26–52. London: The British Film Institute, 1981.

Essex, Andrew. "A 'Monty' Haul." *Entertainment Weekly*, 7 November 1997, 16.

"The 50 Funniest People Alive." *Entertainment Weekly*, 18 April 1997, 23–38.

Flaherty, Mike. "The Seinfeld Chronicles." *Entertainment Weekly*, 30 May 1997, 24–47.

Gehring, Wes D. *American Dark Comedy: Beyond Satire*. Westport, Conn.: Greenwood Press, 1996.

———. *Personality Comedians as Genre: Selected Players.* Westport, Conn.: Greenwood Press, 1997.

Gelbart, Larry. *Screwball Comedy: Defining a Film Genre.* Muncie, Ind.: Ball State University Press, 1983.

———. "Send Out the Clowns." In *Stand-up Comedians on Television,* edited by Robert Morton. New York: Harry Abrams, Inc., 1996.

Green, Bob. "Low Budget Banquet: *Big Night.*" *Honolulu Weekly,* 16 October 1996, 13.

Groening, Matt, and Ray Richmond, eds. *The Simpsons: A Complete Guide to Our Favorite Family.* New York: Harper Perennial, 1997.

Hall, Barbara. Personal interview. 13 April 1998.

Handy, Bruce. "It's All About Timing." *Time,* 12 January 1998, 77–84.

Harvey, James. *Romantic Comedy in Hollywood from Lubitsch to Sturges.* New York: Knopf, 1987.

Hills, Miriam. "Hollywood Pens Mighty in Germany." *Variety,* 24–30 November 1997, 46.

Horton, Andrew. "A Well Spent Life: Les Blank's Celebrations on Film." *Film Quarterly* 35 (Spring 1982), 25–34.

———. *The Films of George Roy Hill.* New York: Columbia University Press, 1985.

———. *Writing the Character-Centered Screenplay.* Berkeley: University of California Press, 1994.

Horton, Andrew, ed. *Comedy/Cinema/Theory.* Berkeley: University of California Press, 1991.

———. *Buster Keaton's "Sherlock Jr."* New York: Cambridge University Press, 1997.

Jenkins, Henry. *What Made Pistachio Nuts? Early Sound Comedy and the Vaudeville Aesthetic.* New York: Columbia University Press, 1992.

———. "This Fellow Keaton Seems to Be the Whole Show." In *Buster Keaton's "Sherlock Jr.,"* edited by Andrew Horton. New York: Cambridge University Press, 1997.

Katz, Susan Bullington. "A Conversation with Larry Gelbart." *Writers' Guild Digest,* December/January 1997, 50–56.

Lear, Norman. "Our Lost Passion for Something Better." *Writers' Guild Digest,* December/January 1997, 47–48.

Lehman, Peter. "Penis-Size Jokes and Their Relationship to Hollywood's Unconscious." In *Comedy/Cinema/Theory,* edited by Andrew Horton, 43–59. Berkeley: University of California Press, 1991.

Maltin, Leonard, ed. *1998 Movie & Video Guide.* New York: Plume/Penguin, 1997.

Marc, David. *Comic Visions: Television Comedy and American Culture.* Boston: Unwin Hyman, 1989.

Marshall, Garry. "10 Tips from an Old Sitcom Writer for Today's Sitcom Writers." *Writers' Guild Digest,* December/January 1997, 24–26.

Martin, Linda, and Kerry Segrave. *Women in Comedy.* Secaucus, N.J.: Citadel Press, 1986.

Mast, Gerald. *The Comic Mind: Comedy and the Movies,* 2d ed. Chicago: University of Chicago Press, 1979.

Morton, Robert, ed. *Stand-up Comedians on Television.* New York: Harry Abrams, Inc., 1996.

Neale, Steve, and Frank Krutnik. *Popular Film and Television Comedy.* New York: Routledge, 1990.

O'Donnell, Steve. "'Yeah, Right': The Wiseguys." In *Stand-up Comedians on Television,* edited by Robert Morton. New York: Harry Abrams, Inc., 1996.

Palmer, Jerry. *The Logic of the Absurd: On Film and Television Comedy.* London: The British Film Institute, 1988.

Perret, Gene. *Comedy Writing Step by Step.* Hollywood: Samuel French, 1990.

Rafferty, Terrence. "Feast and Famine: A Culinary Comedy." *The New Yorker,* 15 September 1996, 100–103.

Roman, Monica. "TV Execs: Send in the Clowns." *Variety,* 17–23 November 1997, 1, 82.

Schatz, Thomas. "The Screwball Comedy." In *Hollywood Genres: Formula Filmmaking and the Studio System.* New York: Random House, 1981.

Seidman, Steve. *Comedian Comedy: A Tradition in Hollywood Film.* Boston: G. K. Hall, 1994.

Seinfeld, Jerry. *Seinlanguage.* New York: Bantam, 1993; reissued 1998.

Siegel, Scott, and Barbara Siegel. *American Film Comedy: From Abbott and Costello to Jerry Zucker.* New York: Prentice Hall, 1994.

Sikov, Ed. *Laughing Hysterically: American Screen Comedy of the 1950's.* New York: Columbia University Press, 1994.

Spines, Christine, and Anne Thompson. "Class of '97 Sundance." *Premiere,* April 1997, 85–86, 134.

Sprecher, Jill. Personal interview. May 1997.

Thompson, Kristin, and David Bordwell. *Film History: An Introduction.* New York: McGraw Hill, 1994.

Tucker, Ken. "Television: The Best and Worst." *Entertainment Weekly,* 1997 Year-End Special, 143–46.

Wild, David. *Seinfeld: The Totally Unauthorized Tribute.* New York: New Rivers Press, 1998.

Winokur, Mark. *American Laughter: Immigrants, Ethnicity, and 1930's Hollywood Film Comedy.* New York: St. Martin's Press, 1996.

Screenplays and Works on Comedy Screenwriting

Auster, Paul. *Smoke & Blue in the Face.* New York: Miramax Books, 1995.

Coen, Ethan, and Joel Coen. *Fargo.* Boston: Faber and Faber, 1996.

David, Larry, and Jerry Seinfeld. "The Kiss Hello." Episode 100 of *Seinfeld.* Table Draft: January 5, 1995.

Muir, Frank, ed. *The Book of Comedy Sketches.* London: Elm Tree Books, 1982. (Monologues and dialogues by a variety of comics, including John Cleese, Michael Palin, and Peter Cook.)

Muscio, Giuliana. *Scrivere il film*. Rome: Dino Audino Editore, 1981.

Niccol, Andrew. *The Truman Show: The Shooting Script*. New York: New Market Press, 1998.

Saks, Sol. *Funny Business: The Craft of Comedy Writing*. 2d ed. Los Angeles: Lone Eagle Publishing Co., 1991.

Sturges, Preston. *Five Early Screenplays by Preston Sturges*. Introduction by Andrew Horton. Berkeley: University of California Press, 1998.

Sverak, Zdenek. *Kolya*. Translated from the Czech by Ewald Osers. London: Review Paperbacks, 1997.

Tucci, Stanley, and Joseph Tropiano. *Big Night*. In *Scenario* 3, no. 2 (1997), 7–47.

Vorhaus, John. *The Comic Toolbox: How to Be Funny Even if You're Not*. Los Angeles: Silman-James Press, 1994.

Wolff, Jurgen. *Successful Sitcom Writing*. 2d. ed. New York: St. Martin's Press, 1996.

Literature, Stage Comedy and Specific Studies

Aesop. *Fables of Aesop*. Translated and introduced by S. A. Handford. Originally published 1954; reprint: Harmondsworth, England: Penguin, 1982.

Beaumont, Cyril W. *The History of Harlequin*. Originally published 1926; reprint: New York: Benjamin Blom, 1967.

Berendt, John. *Midnight in the Garden of Good and Evil*. New York: Random House, 1994.

Bernays, Anne, and Pamela Painter. *What If? Writing Exercises for Fiction Writers*. New York: Harper Perennial, 1990.

Evans, B. *Shakespeare's Comedies*. New York: M. Q. Publications, 1960.

Gordon, G. *Shakespearean Comedy*. 1944.

Gordon, Mel. *Lazzi: The Comic Routines of the Commedia dell'Arte*. New York: Performing Arts Journal Publications, 1992.

Kundera, Milan. *Slowness*. Translated from the French by Linda Asher. New York: Harper Perennial, 1996.

Lea, K. M. *Italian Popular Comedy*. Two volumes. Originally published 1934; reprint: New York: Russell & Russell, 1962.

Menander. *The Dyskolos*. Translated and introduced by Carroll Moulton. New York: New American Library, 1977.

Molière. *The Miser and Other Plays*. Translated with an introduction by John Wood. Harmondsworth, Middlesex: Penguin, 1974.

Muir, Frank, ed. *The Oxford Book of Humorous Prose*. New York: Oxford University Press, 1990.

Phialas, P. G. *Shakespeare's Romantic Comedies*. Chapel Hill: University of North Carolina Press, 1966.

Plato. *Symposium*. Translated and edited by Avi Sharon. New York: Focus, 1997.

Pulcinella, the Physician by Force. In *Lazzi: The Comic Routines of the Commedia dell'Arte*, edited by Mel Gordon, 81–90. New York: Performing Arts Journal Publications, 1992.

Sanders, Norman. Introduction to William Shakespeare, *The Two Gentlemen of Verona*. London: Penguin Books, 1968.

Segal, Erich, ed. *Oxford Readings in Aristophanes*. New York: Oxford University Press, 1996.

Shakespeare, William. *A Midsummer Night's Dream*. London: Penguin Books, 1994.

Stevenson, D. L. *The Love Game Comedy*. New York: AMS Press, 1966.

Taplin, Oliver. "Fifth-Century Tragedy and Comedy." In *Oxford Readings in Aristophanes*, edited by Erich Segal, 9–28. New York: Oxford University Press, 1996.

Autobiographies

Buñuel, Luis. *My Last Sigh*. Translated by Abigail Israel. New York: Knopf, 1983.

Capra, Frank. *The Name above the Title: An Autobiography*. New York: Da Capo Press, 1971.

Chaplin, Charlie. *My Autobiography*. Originally published 1964; reprint: New York: Pocket Books, 1996.

Guinness, Alec. *My Name Escapes Me: The Diary of a Retiring Actor*. New York: Penguin Putnam Inc., 1997.

Keaton, Buster, with Charles Samuels. *My Wonderful World of Slapstick*. New York: Doubleday, 1960.

Marx, Groucho. *Groucho & Me: The Autobiography of Groucho Marx*. Originally published 1959; reprint: London: Virgin Publishing, 1995.

———. *Memoirs of a Mangy Lover*. New York: Da Capo Press, 1989.

Rico, Diana. *Kovacsland*. New York: Harcourt Brace Jovanovich, 1990.

INDEX

Designer:	Margery Cantor
Text:	10/12.5 Minion
Display:	Ellington
Compositor:	G&S Typesetters, Inc.
Printer and binder:	BookCrafters, Inc.